W9-DGT-160

THE SILENT LANGUAGE OF PSYCHOTHERAPY

Third Edition

THE SILENT LANGUAGE OF PSYCHOTHERAPY
Social Reinforcement of Unconscious Processes

Third Edition

ERNST G. BEIER and DAVID M. YOUNG

ALDINE DE GRUYTER
New York

About the Authors

Ernst G. Beier is Professor Emeritus, Department of Psychology, University of Utah. Dr. Beier is the author of many research papers on psychotherapy and clinical psychology, and is co-author of *People Reading*.

David M. Young is Professor, Department of Psychology, Indiana University-Purdue University at Fort Wayne. The author of numerous journal articles, Dr. Young is also engaged in consulting and the private practice of clinical Psychology.

Copyright © 1998 by Walter de Gruyter, Inc., New York
All rights reserved. No part of this publication may be reproduced or transmitted in any form or by any means, electronic or mechanical, including photocopying, recording, or any information storage or retrieval system, without prior permission in writing from the publisher.

ALDINE DE GRUYTER
A division of Walter de Gruyter, Inc.
200 Saw Mill River Road
Hawthorne, New York 10532

This publication is printed on acid free paper ∞

Library of Congress Cataloging-in-Publication Data

Beier, Ernst G. (Ernst Gunter), 1916–
    The silent language of psychotherapy : social reinforcement of unconscious processes / Ernst G. Beier and David M. Young. — 3rd ed.
      p. cm.
    Includes bibliographical references and index.
    ISBN 0-202-30609-7 (cloth : alk. paper). — ISBN 0-202-30610-0 (pbk. : alk paper)
    1. Psychotherapy. 2. Interpersonal communication.
    3. Reinforcement (Psychology). 4. Subconsciousness.
    5. Psychotherapy. 6. Interpersonal communication. 7. Reinforcement (Psychology) 8. Subconsciousness. I. Young, David M., 1949– .
    II. Title.
RC480.B35   1998
616.89'14—dc21
    97-48669
    CIP

DISCARDED
WIDENER UNIVERSITY
WIDENER UNIVERSITY
WOLFGRAM
LIBRARY
CHESTER, PA.

Manufactured in the United States of America

10 9 8 7 6 5 4 3 2 1

To Francis

To Mary Ellen

Contents

Preface to the Third Edition

We were told by a friendly scholar whom we respect that this book represents a most adequate integration of dynamic and behavioral theories. You may think of a blending of Freud and Skinner. Our phrase "the social reinforcement of unconscious processes"—which furnishes this book with its subtitle—labels our effort at such an integration. In the third edition this consolidation will become even more obvious with the introduction of our concept of the development of behavioral "patterns."

We also faced the challenge of integrating new knowledge and rapidly changing methods of practice into Communication Analytic Psychotherapy, our basic theoretical system. Since the release of the second edition of this text, we have found much to have changed, especially in how psychotherapeutic health care is being managed and delivered to our patients. Another area of rapid change has included advancements in biological treatment and the professional issues relating to the new medications and who may prescribe them.

There is yet another area of change since the second edition of this book appeared, which requires a preliminary disclaimer on the authors' part. It has to do with the changing gender conventions of current English rather than the language of psychotherapy. We have sought to avoid the universal pronoun "he" to denote a human subject, and equally to avoid the implication that the therapist is always a "he" and the patient a "she." Common sense and specific cases do require a singular, third-person pronoun, however, and we have also avoided throughout the "he-or-she" construction, which may be acceptable at public gatherings but reads awkwardly and loosely. If our practice should offend a reader, we apologize in advance. That was not our intent.

We have addressed these developments in our text, realizing, of course, that changes will continue to appear as the political, legal and scientific landscapes evolve.

Acknowledgments

Bev Saalfrank deserves a special thank you for her untiring assistance in preparing the manuscript. Jeri Lovell provided much energy in assembling the advances in nonverbal communication. Adam McCray patiently assisted with assembling the bibliography. Dr. John Kay has greatly contributed with his stimulating discussions of issues related to health care delivery. Dr. Pat DeLeon is thanked for generously sharing his work on prescription privileges. The comments from Professor Sherwin Kepes on some of the newer material in the text are appreciated. Our students continue to contribute by keeping us up to date and by providing feedback on the earlier approaches to the material. We would also like to thank our patients for their courage in personal exploration and for providing us with so many valuable experiences.

1

Introduction and Overview

THE THERAPEUTIC MODEL

In psychotherapy, two or more individuals affect each other through a mutual exchange of information. The contact should allow the patient to replace old behavior patterns with more appropriate ones, leading to greater satisfaction and more effective functioning.

Many theorists have attempted to explain how therapeutic changes occur. Often these investigators talk about "therapeutic gains" or "therapeutic changes" as if these occurred only in the unique setting of the therapeutic hour. But there is evidence that such changes occur in many places, and among animals as well as humans. A theory that attempts to explain therapeutic changes should be based on principles that apply not only to those changes occurring during formal treatment, but also to those observed in the educational process, in interpersonal relations, and in the social milieu, as well as in nonhuman species. It would be desirable to discover principles broad enough to provide a deeper understanding of therapeutic change in a wide variety of situations.

Reaching this goal is not extraordinarily difficult, once we search empirically. For though the theories and principles of various therapies vary enormously, the actions of most psychotherapists are remarkably similar. During an hour with a patient they do pretty much the same things and they may not follow their own theories too closely. There probably is some relevance in a comparison of psychotherapy with a concept-formation test: subjects give the correct answers but are unable to state or agree on what principles they followed in making their choices. The therapist, too, may help a patient or offer an intervention spontaneously in a session, but is often uncertain as to why and how. The effective principles in therapeutic work probably rest on processes that are much more general than those principles advanced by different schools.

Much additional confusion has resulted from the fact that change and improvement have been considered together. It is probable that more accurate explanations of psychotherapy can be advanced when the processes of behavioral change and behavioral improvement are separated. In the following, an attempt will be made to do just that. First, we shall analyze *what sort of information* effects change in a patient. Then we shall discuss the conditions under which changes are directed toward improvement.

The information exchanged during the therapeutic hour has both verbal and nonverbal content. Many therapeutic models stress vocal and non-vocal communication, from "primal screams" (Janov, 1991) to staring at video wallpaper. Yet most psychotherapists probably think of verbal communication as the essential element of the therapeutic hour, and most therapeutic models elaborate on the nature of verbal interaction. A general theory, especially if it is ambitious enough to include unconscious processes, needs to concern itself with information from both verbal and nonverbal sources.

We do know that humans can countermand conditioning efforts at will (at least sufficiently to give conflicting results) if they are aware of such efforts and if they desire to do so. Models that try to explain psychotherapeutic efforts in terms of simple operant conditioning are likely to encounter problems; they disregard subtle and covert behaviors of which a person may not be aware but that may allow a psychotherapist to identify unconscious motivations. Our model of communication analytic therapy is interested in *conscious as well as unconsciously coded* communication. Unconscious cues help the therapist know where the patient hurts and what experiences have to be provided to help to decrease suffering.

In the communication model, each message is of great importance. Some messages convey manifest meanings designed by the sender to be fully recognized by the receiver. But a message can also convey information that is not designed to be understood as easily or at all. The purpose of these components is to elicit a desired emotional reaction from the respondent. The remarkable fact is that in any given message the manifest and the covert components can represent different motivational states of the person, sometimes even mutually exclusive states. The nature of the message and how it specifically affects a given respondent is at the base of the communication analytic therapy model.

The initial psychotherapeutic goal, then, is to analyze the communication processes, look at the conscious and the unconscious expectations conveyed by each message, and discover how a given response affects the sender. The foundation of this theory requires a marriage of Skinner and Freud; an attempt to facilitate changes of unconscious motivational states. Communication analysis tells us how people maintain continuity in their conduct as well as how changes can be brought about.

TOWARD A MORE SOPHISTICATED MODEL
OF HUMAN COMMUNICATION

Skinner's model of scheduled learning has been widely used, both in rigorous research efforts as well as in somewhat hasty applications to clinical practice, which a historic review demonstrates: a schizophrenic patient who talked very little was trained to talk more by being rewarded with chewing gum for talking (Isaacs, Thomas, & Goldiamond, 1960); a decerebrate individual was trained to raise his arm when hungry (Fuller, 1949); very young children have been trained to type and to master languages (Haas, 1964); a whole industry (teaching machines) (Schramm, 1964) was developed that used programmed instruction based on Skinnerian scheduled reinforcement; and many families apply scheduled reinforcement methods for raising their children.

Reinforcement schedules have been introduced into school systems, state hospitals, and even the courts. Public criticisms of these programs claimed that they were too mechanical, that human beings should not be "conditioned" or manipulated. The criticism of many clinicians was that these direct applications of reinforcement methods indeed oversimplify human behavior and do not take into account the complexity of mediating stimuli to which humans respond. If parents reinforce a child's getting up on time with a monetary reward, the child may learn that "it pays" to get up early, that this behavior is significant to the parents, that failure to comply is likely to make the parents anxious or raise the ante, and that violating the contract gives the child the delicious feeling of being a person in his or her own right!

Operant conditioning probably works well with fairly simple behaviors. If a child is knocking his* head against a wall until it is bloody, aversive conditioning such as administering light shock might be indicated. In more complex behavior, there are always surprises. A poor reader was given M&M candies for each line read correctly, and the reading improved rapidly. After a few hours, the child threw the accumulated M&Ms into the wastepaper basket. She said she hated them. She said that she was always called stupid when she was helped with her reading, and that she liked the idea that her therapist didn't!

People attach personal meaning to certain acts or objects that they perceive as either reward or punishment. These "attachments" are not necessarily conscious. Human needs are complex, and we must respect the fact that there is much we do not know about another person.

When we think of reinforcement systems that are a reasonably good analog for a therapeutic model, we think beyond the elements of simple

---

* Please see the disclaimer in the preface with regard to our use of gender-specific pronouns in the book.

Skinnerian conditioning. It is true that classic work on nonverbal operant conditioning shows that individuals properly reinforced with "Mm, hmm" (Greenspoon, 1976) will produce more of the reinforced words (such as nouns); and that the length of time of the therapist's comments predicts the average length of time of the patient's response (Matarazzo, Wiens, Saslow, Bernadene, & Weitman, 1965). But the operant aspects are at best limited: "Mm, hmms" as reinforcers of nouns do not merely increase their frequency. When we look into the substantive meaning of these "Mm, hmms," or head nodding, we realize that probably these responses say, "Keep talking," and are also likely to tell the patient that the therapist is attentive, is listening and caring, and respects the patient for "working through" the problem.

These latter meanings are not overtly communicated. They are directed at an unconscious system of the patient and are thought to create an emotional climate of uncertainty that is a challenge but not a threat to the patient. The motivation to change is likely enhanced by these communications.

UNCONSCIOUS MOTIVATION IN THE COMMUNICATION PROCESS

Theorists who believe that people go into therapy to get away from their displeasure have an easy task of accounting for the patient's motivation for seeking help. But the "displeasures" about which patients so often complain seem to be as rewarding as they are punishing to the patients, though the rewarding function may be unconscious. (To the person who has a problem, the thought that it is rewarding is, in fact, unthinkable.) If the patient's problem occurs with high frequency, and if the patient has not learned to avoid the problem, even though he has had a chance to do so, and if the behavior fits clearly into the psychological economy of the patient, then in many ways it can be understood as the patient's unconscious search for meaning and an expression of individuality. This explanation is similar to Freud's formulation of the "pleasure in the symptom."

A brief example may clarify this confusion of rewards and punishments. A suicidal man who has learned that threatening others with his own suffering is a useful behavior said in his second interview, "I was not happy here last week. You didn't talk enough. You didn't talk about my deeper problems. I felt quite without hope when I left here." The therapist responded, "Why don't you tell me about your mother? Why don't you tell me about your dreams?"

What are the subtle meanings in this exchange? One hypothesis about the patient would be that with his message he wants to have an impact on the therapist. He is setting him up to feel guilty for having failed him. This is a form of emotional blackmail. In the past, this man has probably been successful in this subtle blackmail behavior—setting up others to do his bidding by threatening hopelessness. Note that the therapist responds by talking about "deep things" (dreams or mother), and with this response, subtle as it is, the therapist actually helps train this man to use his eminently successful blackmail behavior again. Had the therapist responded here with a simple "Mm, hmm," notifying the patient that he was listening, he would not have reinforced the response expectation of the patient. We observe that the therapist gave a reinforcing response without awareness of its meaning, and we assume that most people in whom the patient wants to create a guilt trip would do likewise. The therapist failed to help the patient to experience uncertainty about his blackmail behavior because he was caught in the social role that the patient had imposed upon him.

The patient, too, does not know what he is trying to achieve with this message. If asked, he would say that he was complaining about the therapist's effectiveness. He would hardly be aware that he was trying to blackmail the respondent, using his own unhappiness as a lever. In fact, he would probably deny that he tried to imbue the therapist with guilt, even though he had repeated this type of message again and again.

Once we assume that our interpretation is correct, we can make some statement about the unconscious motivation of this man. He has mastered a very special skill, namely, setting up an emotional climate in the other person that significantly limits the responses this person is likely to give. Every message has an expected response from the respondent, and some messages give more freedom to the respondent than other messages would. Whenever the patient is able to send messages in such a way that he will obtain the expected responses, he is, in fact, reinforcing his present adjustment. Reinforcement principles and unconscious motivation are closely related in the maintenance of problem behavior, and the understanding of both qualities is necessary to help the patient change.

A large number of unconscious systems probably operate within us. While driving a car, a person also may eat a sandwich, look at a map, and drum the fingers of one hand on the steering wheel. All these systems operate without much thought—unless a pedestrian suddenly runs across the street. At this time, the driver may drop his sandwich, forget the map, stop drumming his fingers, and give full attention to avoiding the hazard. The various systems are operating reasonably independently; the driver does not have to think how to lift his free hand, to eat his sandwich, or to figure out how to bring his map into his visual field. Yet at the critical moment, the conduct of the driver changes rapidly. He now overrules the various systems and tries to avoid the accident. Hilgard (1986) thought that this sudden change in the motivational state is due to the predominance of the "executive ego." He demonstrated that under hypnosis a person can in fact simultaneously do two diverse, separate, intelligent tasks, such as writing one story with the left hand and another story with the right hand. He also studied persons with dissociative identity disorder. He found that Personality A of a given person may be accessible to Personality B of the same person, but this may not be true in the reverse, or both may be accessible to each other. In other words, the multiple motivational states may be independent of each other or they may be partially independent. In all such cases, one can assume that the "executive ego" determines which motivational state is dominant.

While such extreme cases as dissociative identity disorder are the exception, the principle of various motivational states operating within an individual is probably true for all of us. The conduct of a person is determined by many factors, such as physiological and genetic makeup, early learning, traumatic experiences, stress-avoidance mechanisms, and the rules learned to cope with the environment. Unconscious motivations resulting from these inputs may not share the same goal, and there will surely be some that result in discordant actions. Each motivation will seek its own satisfaction, even though the person may not understand what is happening. Based on the above-mentioned input, an infant establishes manifest as well as hidden rules, and the latter ones in particular get embedded in the various unconscious systems that determine behavior and communication patterns. "Silent rules" directly affect conduct, often to the bewilderment of the person who is not aware of the hidden motivating forces that are originating the behavior. Such rules can make persons flirt with great and dangerous events, even though consciously they are trying desperately to avoid them. They can serve to isolate a person who feels lonely and who longs for company, or make persons unfit for love relationships when they perceive themselves as seeking love.

To help a person therapeutically, one has to understand the silent rules with which the person operates. Very often these silent rules can be decoded from the discordance found within a single message. A mother says, "I just hate my boy. I know he is only ten and he can't help it, but he is so much like his father. I sometimes think of putting my cigarettes out on his body, thought I hope nobody will ever do that to me." For better or worse, these are the feelings the therapist has to decode by asking, "What is the mother expecting from me with her message?" Analyzing his own feelings of pity, fear, and disgust, the therapist notes that this mother's threat that she may lose control of her aggressive impulses restricted his responses. This analysis gives the therapist some information about the mother's silent rules. A plausible one is, "People pay attention to me when I threaten harm. They may think ill of me, but it's better than not thinking of me at all."

With most patients, the procedures and communications that obey the silent rules are often repeated endlessly. The possible unconscious motivation to seek disdain and punishment from the respondent in order to achieve some "sense of being a person" is one that may illustrate that apparent displeasure is not always to be avoided. We should especially note that the messages are designed to have a significant and specific impact on others, and analyzing this impact can be most informative. That people can seek out punishment or even death can be understood if one assumes people prefer suffering to total uncertainty, indifference, or randomness.

Such an assumption is necessary to avoid simplistic theoretical formulations by which the patients are reinforced with conventional rewards. Human processes are too complex for such simple solutions. For example, a young man who attempts suicide may suggest as his reason that his parents overloaded him with demands, but we would not be amiss to assume that he probably got some gratification from thinking about his parent's guilt. Suicidal behavior is also a complex communication—a cry for help—that is the basic assumption around which suicide-prevention centers have been organized.

After examining what his social response to the mother who threatens to put her cigarettes out on her son might be, the therapist can formulate a response that is likely to create uncertainty rather than to reinforce her behavior. This response is apt to be other than a social response, and we have labeled it an "asocial" response. Whether the paradigm the therapist analyzed is accurate or correct is really not the question. What matters is his *not reinforcing* her behavior with an expected, social response.

THERAPEUTIC GAINS

Here we shall present a statement about how communication analytic psychotherapy differs from other schools with respect to providing change in patients. Historically oriented schools claim that therapeutic gain comes from reexperiencing one's traumatic history with a happy ending. The insight school attempts to produce an awareness of inner dynamics, and the relationship schools attempt to recreate a sense of human closeness through love, warmth, and understanding. Most of these schools posit that insight is needed for change, that true acceptance by the therapist is the working ingredient, or that lifting of unwholesome repression and working through of resistance by way of transference are critical elements. Behavioral therapies posit that reward and/or punishment will provide for change. All these theories assume that the experiment from the therapeutic hour will carry over into patients' lives, and that they have contributed a clearer understanding of the therapeutic process even though it is probably the therapist's temperament that largely determines his or her conduct rather than any theoretical framework.

A communications model of psychotherapy is probably the only model that provides us with a general understanding of the therapeutic process. All models are based on information exchange and the question of impact and change. Our most general formulation is that therapeutic intervention provides the patient with a new experience that does not follow the old silent rules. Therapeutic interventions give patients a sense of uncertainty, and if this uncertainty occurs in a caring, nonthreatening setting, it results in a creative search for new solutions or, more precisely, in the discovery of new rules. By shedding the old rules, the patient finds new choices that seem to have been unavailable before.

To seek out new choices is both a painful and a hopeful endeavor. It is painful because the patient has to leave familiar solutions and the cover of familiar rules behind and has to accept a degree of uncertainty. It is hopeful because, message by message, the therapist encourages a searching attitude as he conveys a sense of concern to the patient and provides a situation that is relatively nonjudgmental. The whole process occurs in various small steps, and it is the extinction of expected social responses, combined with the therapist's attitude of caring, that turn the patient's experience of uncertainty into a beneficial one. The therapist's concern communicates an existential meaning to the patient. "Another person is with me, attentive and without an intent to hurt me. My self-image, my skills, my sense of being are all in a state of uncertainty now, as none of the responses I am receiving are the social ones that I ordinarily obtain. However, because I feel that the therapist is with me, I can now look toward reordering my guidelines." The therapist's insistence that the patient's behavior is not to be judged implies an equally important meaning to the patient. "I myself am accountable for the consequences of my behavior. Blaming myself or others for my suffering is an ineffective relief system. Rather than blaming myself, I must try to think constructively what to do about the act in the first place."

The therapeutic experience, to be successful, must arouse beneficial uncertainty in the patient. The pain of uncertainty must be relieved by concern and respect—respect not for the patient's present choices, but respect for the patient as a person struggling for meaning and self-esteem. The messages of the therapist are in a true sense persuasive. They are designed to help patients experience the impact of their behaviors on others and on themselves, which in turn provides new choices for the patient. This experience can be provided only in very small steps, message by message. Advice fails because it covers too large a territory and the patient is not given responsibility for decision-making. Therapy can succeed because it can provide an existential experience small enough to be accepted, yet intense enough to help patients experience just what they are doing to themselves and to others. The patient says, "You surely have been a godsend." The therapist answers, "Tell me more about these feelings." With this rather simple response, the therapist passes a small amount of responsibility to the patient by throwing the ball back into the patient's corner. "It is you who has these feelings. You must explore the impact you want." We should note that the therapist gives an "unexpected response." The patient praising the therapist may expect the therapist's thanks. Instead the therapist remains the listener, and both shifts responsibility to the patient and advances the therapy another small step, eliciting a sense of uncertainty in the patient, who expects a response to his flattery. In a small way, the therapist helps the patient extinguish the flattery–social response paradigm and explore new options of interaction.

All these formulations do sound very much like the formulations of several other schools, and that is the way it should be. There is, however, one major point of departure. Unconscious processes and conditioning are integrated, and each message is seen as essential to therapeutic gain. This paradigm, based on the analysis of the communication process, makes therapy a comprehensible learning process and permits a more precise evaluation of each response.

ETHICAL CONSIDERATIONS

For a great many years, psychotherapists professed that they only played the "midwife," as Socrates put it so curtly, that the therapist was largely a facilitator to help the patient make more adequate choices. The ethical questions raised by this model dealt largely with confidentiality and invasion of privacy such as is involved in sexual or commercial exploitation. Most therapists today recognize that they do communicate some of their own values to the patient. Often they do so without specific intent, by showing interest in certain topics, nodding their heads at certain times, or introducing certain concepts that give direction. With such communication, they are no longer mere midwives; they help to parent the baby. The ethical question becomes even more significant when contractual agreements setting forth therapeutic goals are involved, as we are never certain when a patient's consent is enough justification for a contract. If a young boy wants to be "conditioned" never to love again after an unhappy love affair, would it be ethically sound to do so? Should a liberally or conservatively thinking therapist warn patients of possible political biases during therapy?

Do we invade a person's privacy even by encouraging exploration? The mental-health profession is thought by some to represent a danger to a free society, as it "condemns" people to a maladjusted state. This has been claimed for political purposes in some quarters. But such claims are based on a total (and often vicious) misunderstanding of the goals, methods, and purposes of these professional activities. We must try to spell out and specifically limit the conditions under which the therapist is justified for an "invasion of privacy of the individual," be it in psychodiagnosis or treatment processes. In addition, we may want to think about the problem of informed consent not only in extreme cases like the above, but in regard to questions concerning the duration, the evaluation, and the possible effects and side effects of treatment.

Another ethical problem is long-range. We are working on the under-standing of human nature and on processes of intervention that would help patients change their conduct. As we are increasingly successful and are able to accomplish such changes more rapidly, we shall change not only our patients' conduct but also the very nature of society. Patients want to change quickly to be happy and live a fulfilling life, but what would society look like if we really were able to accomplish major changes quickly and for large numbers of people? Imagine a society where significant changes of conduct could be brought about overnight. We not only would have a very unstable society, but also would be subject to early manipulation by those who hunger for power. The searching for better and more effective interventions to change conduct also imposes an awesome responsibility for accounting for possible consequences.

2

The Anatomy of a Message
Structure and Motivation

THE SIMPLE MESSAGE

We can distinguish two types of messages involved in interpersonal communication: the simple message and the complex message. The latter can be broken down into the persuasive message and the evoking message. This classification system is designed to help us understand the communication process in the therapeutic hour. In the case of the simple message the sender is operating with full awareness of what he is doing. The message itself is overt and has *not* been coded to create an emotional climate within the respondent favorable to the sender's intent. In the simple message, then, the sender is aware, the message is clear and not subtly constraining, and the respondent is consciously able to choose his response to the message (see Table 2.1).

Examples of the simple message can be found in almost any aspect of daily living. When the cashier in the cafeteria says in a matter-of-fact tone, "That'll be $3.98," the customer is overtly requested to pay, without emotional strings or any additional meanings. If our cashier adds the right contextual or nonverbal cues to the statement (such as speaking quickly and snapping fingers rapidly), the manifest content of the message is covertly changed and our responses may be constricted by the additional meaning. A simple message might be presented at the dinner table in a restaurant when the guest says to his companion: "Please pass the salt," providing, of course, it is not said with a slur and a frown directed toward the waiter, implying that the flavor of the food is inadequate. Any simple message, however, is easily transformed into the type of message that leaves the respondent emotionally constricted. Thus it is not only the manifest content of a message that makes it a simple one: it is the covert contextual and nonverbal cues that are *not* added. When our cashier adds the right contextual or nonverbal cues to the statement, the manifest content of the message is covertly colored and our responses may be constricted. (We may quickly produce money without adding up our total and leave without counting our change!) Any communi-

Table 2.1 The Simple Message

Sender	Message	Respondent
Conscious (but not covertly coding)	Overt	Response choice made on basis of of awareness, not emotional climate

cation, no matter how transparent it seems, can easily be shifted to contain covert elements found in persuasive or evoking messages. In fact, one of the great problems in human communication is that people send complex and emotionally constricting messages and mislabel them as "statements of fact." "Someone did not lock the front door last night" is a statement made by father, who labeled it a statement of fact or merely an observation, but it was perceived by his son as a punitive complex message silently accusing him as the culprit.

COMPLEX MESSAGE

The Persuasive Message

The sender of a persuasive message subtly adds a covert manipulation or meaning to the manifest content of the communication—and does so with full awareness of what he is doing (see Table 2.2). The function of this type of message is to create an emotional climate in the respondent that favors the sender's intent. To achieve the sender's purpose, it is important that the respondent remain unaware of the sender's intent and the covert cues the sender is using to achieve this goal. The respondent must be made to feel and, consequently, to think, as guided by the sender.

The persuasive message can readily be illustrated with examples from retail sales. A supermarket manager wants to sell more high-profit goods. He finds that consumers are likely to select items placed at eye level and thus changes his displays, placing high-markup brands where they are most easily viewed—and selected. Of course, this manipulation works only as long as it remains hidden. Supermarket managers intent on selling slow-moving

Table 2.2 The Persuasive Message

Sender	Message	Respondent
Conscious coding, sender is aware of climate, goal	Covert contextual and nonverbal cues	Choice made on basis of emotional climate, not awareness

goods often "toss" these items in jumbled fashion into a shopping basket and label it with a hand-lettered sign proclaiming SALE. The item, of course, may remain marked at the standard price. Consumers are receiving the carefully planned, covert message that there is a sale, yet it is the consumer and not the bargain that is being had.

Although we may not be in business and do not consider ourselves "con artists," we use this type of message frequently in daily exchange. It is surprisingly effective. A man sends flowers to his beloved, a student gives the proverbial apple to the teacher—these are behaviors designed with awareness to gain the ends of the sender by creating favorable response climates in the respondent.

The goal of a sender in issuing a persuasive message is to constrict the emotional climate of the intended respondent. The respondent, in turn, is likely to give the response desired by the sender without becoming aware of either the sender's method or purpose. The simplest explanation is that the respondent is persuaded to (1) choose a response pattern congruent with the sender's wishes, and (2) remain "in the dark" as to the sender's goal. The effective persuader does not let the respondent use his intellect, so choices remain constricted.

Persuasive messages are also generally used as a testing device. A sender may consciously use this style of coding information to see how a receiver might react to his attempts at obtaining a desired response. A woman on a first date with a new acquaintance might be surprised to find her new friend opening the car door for her. She might use this information to find out how "old-fashioned" the fellow is in other situations, and she might even be concerned what sort of role he would assign to a wife.

The persuasive message is a somewhat subtle but frequently used tool in the teaching of values, especially during early childhood. When the toddler engaged in sexual self-touching is distracted by a parent, a consciously intended subtle message is transmitted. The child will experience the effect of this type of communication in the form of feelings about sex and his body. Yet the child will not be able to clearly articulate this feeling, nor will the child be able to intellectually know why he feels this way. Repeated persuasive communications will teach an individual to hold specific values or attitudes without being able to discover the sources. This reflection on values could be an operational definition of Freud's concept of introspection.

The persuasive message is also relied on during the therapeutic hour. In order to provide new emotional experiences for the client, the therapist is consciously involved in coding messages designed to create new feelings in the client. Even the simplest utterances, such as, "Mm, hmm," and "Go on," act as powerful tools in giving important if subtle information to the client. The therapist is subtly saying: "Yes, I am listening, tell me more about this, it is important in understanding your problem!" The therapist is giving information that, to some extent is controlling the behavior of the client. Psychotherapy can be seen as an act of persuasion. (See Chapter 17, "The Ethical Problems of Control of Behavior".)

THE EVOKING MESSAGE

The evoking message is a persuasive message with a very important twist. In the evoking message, the sender has a need to keep his true goal or intent hidden from the conscious self (see Table 2.3). That is, in the evoking message the sender is not conscious of the wish to persuade, while in the case of the persuasive message, the sender is aware of what he wants and knows how to get it. Another unique aspect of the evoking message is the frequent consequence of feelings of surprise or pain in the sender. Because the sender is unaware of how his messages are coded, he is prevented from fully realizing the impact they may have on respondents. The sender of evoking messages simply cannot account for the responses he is receiving.

As an illustration of the evoking message, we can consider the individual who experiences the pain of loneliness. Despite protestations such as, "I hate being lonely" and "Don't you think I want to have friends?" careful analysis of the lonely person's communication style reveals a variety of subtle maneuvers destined to keep others at a distance. The message "stay away" can be transmitted using a number of styles and behaviors: avoiding eye contact, angering others with snappy critical responses, and maintaining sad facial expressions are just a few of the many cues that could be used without awareness by a sender of such an evoking message. Nonverbal communication, including paralinguistic (vocal) cues, appears to contribute much to creating the emotional climate of the evoking message. Nonverbal communication, including paralinguistic (vocal) cues, appears to contribute much to creating the emotional climate of the evoking message. We have known for some time that what we don't say carries more meaning than our content. Mehrabian and Ferris (1967) demonstrated that in the communication of attitudes, only 5% of the information received was a function of the "overt" verbal content being expressed. Paralinguistic cues (38%) and facial

Table 2.3   The Evoking Message

Sender	Message	Respondent
Unconscious coding with *need* of *sender* to be unaware of goal	*Covert* contextual and nonverbal cues	Choice made on basis of emotional climate, not awareness

expression (55%) accounted for the remaining variance. (See Harper, Wiens, and Matarazzo, 1978, for a thorough review.)

An important feature of the evoking message is that when "undesired" consequences occur, the sender views himself as a victim of either circumstances or the misbehavior of others. The sender is free from responsibility for the outcome of his behavior because he is unaware of the information that has been delivered. These "problem messages" actually provide satisfaction as well as unhappiness for the sender. Satisfaction results in that three important unconscious needs of the sender are met: (1) freedom from responsibility, (2) predictability of response, and (3) receipt of a partially acceptable or compromise response. We believe that the evoking message is the type of communication that helps maintain the client's hurt as well as his state of adjustment. In fact, the experienced pain is often used by the sender to convey to himself and others that he is not responsible for being the author of the response.

The idea that the evoking message results in a partially satisfying response from others opposes the notion that patients engage in problem behavior because they suffer from a lack of knowledge or skill or simply from an inability to cope under too much pressure. We argue that the evoking message provides the patient with hidden satisfaction and overt disappointment as a means of dealing with two conflicting motives: (1) the need for personal integrity and (2) the need to adjust to social demands. These two motivations are combined in the adaptive compromise (Mahl, 1987), which represents the client's symptom and is maintained by the use of the evoking messages. This is the client's way of eating his cake and having it too.

The motivational conflict of a depressed patient who complains about his wife's anger and sexual rejection would illustrate how the evoking message provides for an adaptive compromise. The "isolated" husband has been covertly encouraging attacks and rejection with his downtrodden victim style: yet he may easily deny, because of his suffering, that he holds a wish for such treatment. The husband may have the personal need to test love or want the marriage to end, but maintains what *he* feels is the appropriate social attitude of not walking out. The pain of his symptom and the depression itself provide a solution to this impasse. The solution via the symptom is twofold: first, the pain allows the husband to hide from himself and others the manipulation of the marital relationship; second, it denies the motive of divorce.

We offer another example of how evoking messages balance the budget of the individual's psychological economy—exchanging symptoms for partial goal attainment without the cost of responsibility. Let us more fully consider our original example of the lonely person. A young woman at a university counseling center complains of loneliness and lack of friendships.

We discover, however, that this woman seems to take any and all opportunities to alienate others by displaying an angry demeanor, a superior tone
of voice, and withdrawal behavior. She is not aware of her evoking messages
even though she maintains with these behaviors the very situation that is
hurting her. To fully decode this evoking message, we must explore two
questions: (1) Why is rejection at least partially satisfying to the client? (2)
Why must she keep this need a secret from herself and others? Further
inquiry revealed that this woman was under considerable parental pressure.
The parents, old-fashioned as they were, felt that engineering studies were
not suitable "woman's" work and that instead, she should go out and "find a
husband."

Here the client's overt expression of frustration with being lonely and her
"trying" to find companions represent her partial bowing to social pressure.
Her personal needs, for integrity (I am interested in my studies, and I am not
interested in finding a husband at this time), are partially satisfied when she
invites social injustices (rejections), because these injustices permit her to
feel that she is trying to make acquaintances, but that it is a hopeless cause.
The client is able to compromise two conflicting motivations, albeit covertly,
and pays a price of being rejected for her adaptive compromise.

Although the evoking message is the communication of interest in the
therapeutic hour, by no means are we suggesting that only clients, or people
in emotional pain, use them. The kind of evoking messages a person sends
probably contributes to his consistency of perception and a predictable
reaction to that person from the *Umwelt*. When communicating with some
people we use cues to elicit a feeling of being cared for; with others we elicit
fights; and with others, with different cues, we may elicit sympathy or sadness. To the extent that there is a consensus with regard to the interpretation
of the cues with which we express a given mood, we speak of these cues as
"conventional" or "redundant." Much of our silent mood language has to be
based on conventional cues, otherwise no one would understand such expressions. Yet, there is a gray area: we can use subtle cues also to hide
meaning, namely, in a way that they affect a person without his awareness.
Such information can also be sent without the sender's awareness, and a
sender can elicit painful responses from others and create a world of problems, without recognition that he is responsible for eliciting these responses.
These cues are more ambiguous and less redundant; we call them idiosyncratic cues.

Reading the emotional climates created by a given individual often provides an understanding of his psychological dynamics. Consider the dentist
who gives anxious patients the message that he is unconcerned about their
pain by subtly communicating that they are "cowards." The dentist is not
aware of the negative impact of this message (his idiosyncratic cues) and is
surprised when the practice does not flourish. Message by message, perhaps

with the *conscious* intent of helping them, by challenging them to overcome their cowardice (his conventional cues) he creates an emotional climate in which patients are ashamed of their feelings, with the effect that the dentist is experienced as unpleasant. Observing that he does not learn from the feedback of rejecting patients, we must dismiss the hypothesis that the dentist is socially naive and speculate that this dentist has a conflict about being in the profession.

Another example is the middle-level manager in the business world who evokes resentment and frustration from his employees by means of a subtle style that includes debating *every* minor point of decision and evaluating *every* possible alternative outcome. The manager is deeply hurt that his employees do not respond to him as ultimately fair, careful, and caring. Instead, the employees learn to avoid the manager, to view him as an obstacle, not a helper, and they harbor resentment toward this wheel-spinning style of leadership. Message by message, with the conscious intent of being helpful and fair, the manager covertly undermines the efforts of subordinates. We may speculate that the manager very much needs to be in control but is uncomfortable with the direct expression of power. By remaining unaware of the conflict, he can cushion the reaction from subordinates with, "But I was only trying to be fair!" It was not difficult for the therapist to understand how this manager got into trouble with subordinates. The intent obviously was to be helpful and fair, but covertly the manager undermined this goal. We speculated that the manager had a great need to be in control of all of the contact maintained with others.

It should be cautioned that not all responses coming from the environment are elicited, and we should not fall into the trap of always blaming the "victim" as presented by the "just world hypothesis" (Lerner, 1980). However, a good deal of the interpersonal universe is managed in a fairly consistent manner—even if there is dissatisfaction with this universe.

REASON AND EMOTION

The manifest cues of the message contain information the sender consciously wants to impart and for which he assumes responsibility. "Give me this book" manifestly means that the sender wants the respondent to act in a certain way and that he is willing to be held accountable for his expressed wish. With the covert component, on the other hand, the sender may convey information for which he does not want to be held accountable. Though this effort is not always successful, the covert cues of a message are coded to leave the respondent without recognition of the covert message but still subject to an emotional impact. For example, a young man with multiple body piercings and homemade tatoos says to a stranded motorist. "Can I give you a hand with your car?" The overt cues of the message are clear; the conventional meaning of the statement is one of solicitude. But the boy's unkempt appearance and possibly his intonation keep the motorist in doubt; the emotional impact may be "danger," and so he responds, "No thanks." The answer may perhaps be quite against his immediate interests and given with only the general rationale, "I wonder what this boy really wants from me."

When one considers the sender of the message, the wild-looking young man, it appears that there is some dissonance between the overt and covert cues he conveys to the motorist. Disregarding whether the boy is in fact honest or dishonest, it can be inferred that he wants to be recognized for offering help (overt) and most likely does not wish to be recognized as a doubtful or criminal character. Even if he had dishonorable intentions, it would not be plausible to suppose that he wants to alert the motorist to that fact. Assuming for the moment that the boy has repeatedly had the experience of creating doubts in respondents and having his friendly gestures of help rejected it is likely that he has some conflict about his identity. He maintains behaviors that permit him to hold on to the opinion that he is a helpful person, but that the world is hostile and rejects even his worthwhile efforts.

One could speculate that the boy's psychological economy requires the maintenance of his discordant message: he elicits and obtains the type of response that he has found to be an acceptable compromise between various needs. The conflict seems to be his need to see himself as simultaneously helpful (overt) and threatening (covert); it is expressed in such a manner that the response (rejection) is typically elicited and serves to reinforce not only his use of such a message, but also his feeling that he lives in a world filled with injustice. After all, his good efforts are not recognized or rewarded. It is quite possible that this sense of living in an unjust world also gives this boy an alibi, a sense of freedom to engage in retaliatory acts. With the discordant message he can maintain his psychological adjustment.

To generalize, through the covert component of his message a person may code his information in a way that impedes another person's recognition of certain of his needs. Yet, though he does not want to be recognized or held accountable for expressing these needs, he does want to have an emotional impact on other people, an impact that elicits a specific constricted response from them.

A person may want to impede recognition of certain of his needs because he wants to avoid having a respondent bring judgmental processes to bear on the message. The person who is trying to avoid being fully understood in what he says is possibly afraid that if he were understood he would obtain responses that do not fit his self-image, responses with which he feels he cannot cope.

On the other hand, to use a message for emotional impact allows a person to obtain a response that is at least partially determined by the emotional climate he has created, and with which he can cope precisely because he has succeeded in impeding recognition of some of his wishes. There seems to be an inverse relationship between "recognition" and "emotional impact." Information that creates an emotional impact seems to constrict recognition in the respondent. This suggests that the stronger the emotions in which a person becomes engaged, the less active are his cognitive processes. A respondent facing direct aggression such as a fist in his face is likely to react to the source of the aggression and then fight back, talk, run, or however else he typically meets aggression. It is unlikely, however, that he has the time or the inclination to try to understand and recognize the full context and meaning of the aggressive act. (Soldiers learn to yell during an attack to get into an aggressive mood and to reduce their feelings and thoughts about danger.)

The emotional impact of a strong gesture also is likely to deprive the respondent of the use of cognitive processes: the emotion is experienced at the cost of one's judgmental processes. The loss of adequate judgment becomes even more obvious in a case of covert aggression, in which the respondent has no awareness that he has been attacked. He cannot find the object and so merely feels discomfort. Since he cannot identify the source of his discomfort, he is thus constricted in evaluating the situation. The use of covert cues has created an emotional impact that affects and controls the respondent's behavior precisely because his recognition, his discriminative cognitive process, and his judgmental powers are constricted.

We may say that, for purposes of communication, the modes "to know" and "to feel" are separate and, to some extent, mutually exclusive states. These two modes need not necessarily be mutually exclusive, but one can be used to subdue the other. It is our belief that a persuasive message that uses covert cues to create an emotional impact in a given respondent is probably more effective in reaching this goal than a message that tries to persuade by the power of reason. The use of emotions constricts the choices. The use of reason, however, gives the individual freedom to make his own choice, and so is not likely to have an equal degree of persuasive power.

A number of field researchers would support this conjecture. Social scientists (Watson, 1947) placed a group of "Jewish-looking" persons in such a manner that they blocked the sidewalk. Pedestrians who had to detour into the street to pass by made various comments about the Jews. The social scientists, camouflaged as pedestrians, engaged these people in conversation using the rational and irrational methods of approach. To give an example of the rational approach, people who made a negative comment were asked, "How do you know they are Jews?" or told, "You should not call all Jews names when you find some annoying." One of the emotional comments was, "This is a very un-American thing to say." The report stated that the emotional-impact statements created more uncertainty in the respondents than statements from any other category. It appears that emotional-impact statements constrict the respondent's response activity and are persuasive, while rational-impact statements are more easily disregarded.

A message designed to have an emotional impact must be based on redundancies, i.e., cues that have been overlearned by the respondent. These cues must convey emotional meaning without benefit of thought. The words or gestures used for such a purpose must, in addition, be transmitted in the right setting and with some concern for timing.

To call a person "a Communist" at a Communist gathering is ordinarily not threatening and may even have a favorable meaning (e.g., "comrade"). However, this can be threatening when it is done in a different setting, such as at a meeting of the House Un-American Activities Committee. A redundant, conventional cue designed to create an emotional experience in the respondent must be overlearned before it is effective. It will often include several different sources of information in its coding: words, adjuvant cues (tone of voice, choice of words, sequence of thoughts, pauses, timing), and setting cues. The stickup man, in order to arouse the desired response in the bank teller, may need a determined voice, the supporting gesture of a threatening pistol, and the ability to convey the information that he is serious about his task. (If his idiosyncratic cues showed that he were fainthearted he would not succeed!) A father, in order to impress others with his authority, may raise his voice and, as Machotka and Spiegel (1974) pointed out, may also raise his head!

These subtle cues are important elements of the message, often determining the nature of the response in a more significant way than the manifest component of the message. By shifting the emphasis from one component to the other, a person can choose to what extent he wants to constrict the response activity of the respondent or to what extent he wants to allow judgmental processes to enter in the choice of a response. The above distinctions are made to remind us of the great lability in human communication and the large number of possible connotations a person can code into a message.

MOTIVATION AND EMOTIONS

We have explored how evoking messages work and what they may accomplish for the sender. It is appropriate now to more fully discuss the origins of basic styles of evoking messages. We posit that early in development, children learn basic principles or rules (Bruner, 1987) motivated by their own need for mastery or basic competence, not merely by a stimulus-response pattern. Accepting this principle permits us to account for the important role that beliefs, attitudes, and values play in so much of our behavior. Just as children seem to possess an innate capacity or readiness to learn the grammatical rules of a particular culture or household, they also seem prepared to learn the rules for and the limits of emotional expression. There are probably several different key rules operating in every household, and some of these rules may be focused on specific children or other family members. Just as the complex rules of transformational grammar are not overtly taught, we maintain that the complex rules of emotional problem solving are also transmitted through covert means.

As an example of how such early rule learning may set the stage for future evocative styles of communication, let us consider a family in which parents are uncomfortable with the direct expression of tender feelings or affection. Family members might develop a number of compromise solutions to meet this need: perhaps encouraging an argument and then secretly cherishing the making-up process. In this case, the child learns the rule that direct expression of intimacy is unacceptable; closeness is tolerated only if preceded by an appropriate amount of pain or conflict. Carried into adult life, this rule may serve as the basis for an evocative style of stormy intimacies, where closeness may be had only through conflict. With this style, the individual is free from having his affectionate feelings rejected. Even if there is an eventual major rejection, the user of this style is free from acknowledging it as such; after all, "We just never got along anyway." Because he is operating without awareness, the user of the stormy intimacy principle is fully free from accepting responsibility for the outcome. Of additional interest in this example is that the events produced by evocative styles further serve to strengthen the original rule that was learned. When the user of stormy intimacy is ultimately rejected (and he often is), the original lesson— it is dangerous or unacceptable to freely get close—is upheld: it is made to be true.

We assume that everyone learns such rules in order to maintain a consistent level of adjustment in the face of inevitable environmental or intrapsychic threat (Beier, 1989). An effect of working under overlearned covert rules is that responsibility for negative events is assigned either to an external source or to a relatively stable personal characteristic out of one's control: "I am as I am." While this type of blaming may provide some temporary relief for an old motivational conflict, the "blamer" is often doomed to encounter the problems again and again, as he is free from having to make changes in habitual patterns of thought and behavior. Community surveys (e.g., Zautra, Young, & Guenther, 1981) have consistently found blame attributions to be positively correlated with psychological measures of maladjustment. Murray (1980) found a decrease in blaming attributions in successful psychotherapy.

We need to restate that not all rules learned in early experiences eventually cause significant problems. Neither is all blaming a process that fully limits growth or change. The emotional rules and blame styles become problematic when they are so rigidly adhered to that little or no probability remains for exploring alternative behavior styles.

We have been looking at the message in terms of its consequences on the respondent and the motivating forces of the sender. We have distinguished between the manifest or overt component and the hidden or covert component of the message. With varying emphasis on these components, the sender can determine (consciously or unconsciously) the type of restriction he wishes to impose on the choices of the receiver of the message. With the persuasive message, the restriction by covert coding is conscious. In the evoking message, the motivation and manipulation occur without the sender's awareness. We believe that the evoking message is the vehicle, that individuals maintain maladjustment as well as consistency of style.

The learning of emotional rules has been discussed as contributing to the development of evocative styles of communicating. We hope that our analysis of the message will aid in the understanding of the origin and maintenance of psychological discomfort as well as the psychotherapeutic process.

3

Developing Patterns
Choosing Responses to the Environment

The powerful use of subtle cues by adults can be more readily understood when we explore how these skills are acquired. How does the child master covert communication as both an encoder and a decoder? The work of Gewirtz (1991) demonstrated the effect that varieties of "feedback" from three-month-old infants had on mother's facial and vocal behavior: children shape parents. Thus, it appears that parents respond characteristically to the subtle behavior of their children (and vice versa) early in infancy, developing what may be called synchrony patterns of communication (Donovan, Leavitt, & Balling, 1978). Anecdotal testimony even points to the possible influence of maternal emotional states on fetal behavior.

It is certainly not clear when the infant actually organizes his needs and behaviors sufficiently so that needs are inferred on an accurate and consistent basis. Yet it is generally accepted that the developing child continually learns to replace highly personalized behaviors with actions that have greater interpersonal significance. Early in infancy, a baby learns to intensify its efforts to gain mother's attention, especially when mother is slow or does not respond to the baby's attempts for eye contact or cooing (Brazelton, 1990). Securely attached infants demonstrate an "interactional synchrony" with their mothers while insecure infants appear out of synch with mother (Isabella & Belsky, 1991). Secure babies and their mothers also tend to match emotional states (Stern, 1985). Thus, the process of differentiation of needs and specializing communication develops. Feeding no longer satisfies the baby when he is cold; rocking no longer serves to pacify hunger; the child must invent methods of coding information that result in predictable and satisfying outcomes. As the child develops differentiated needs, it becomes necessary for the child to send an ever-increasing amount of information or cues to his environment. As the child's interpersonal world expands, his cues must become less idiosyncratic: the search for language begins.

In addition to learning how to get a message across in a generally understandable way, the young child learns very early that some of his nonverbal messages result in satisfying or desired outcomes more often than others. The child is learning about degrees of probability of obtaining a given response. We believe that at this early stage "styles" or "patterns" of communication are nurtured. The child who repeatedly finds love coming his way after complaining about pain can easily learn to employ this complaining style when seeking such a reward, and may even learn to point at certain body locations to show where it supposedly hurts. This complaining about pain may not always fetch a reward and indeed may yield an unwanted consequence (the child may actually feel the imagined pain), yet if this pattern continues to get favorable results often enough, the child will experience it as a predictable pattern. The chances are that with sufficient repetitions it may eventually become one of the patterns used in adult life as well. It is interesting to note that the child is probably more in touch with an understanding of the subtle cues he is sending than the adult. The child appears to be aware of the cues that have an impact on his parent. The adult uses the patterns of behavior he has learned in his youth automatically, i.e., without awareness of history or its communicative impact. In fact, should someone suggest to the adult that he carelessly broke his leg because he wanted to obtain love from another person, he would most likely deny this and call it ridiculous.

The pattern that has been meaningful in childhood represents the unfinished business of the child seeking love, and while the pattern may be seen as a mere habit, we believe that there is gratification derived from engaging in this habit: the forlorn hope to find the missed love. We use the term "delicious satisfaction" for adults' motivation to use the "infantile patterns," as they do so compulsively and frequently. Obviously the child, before commanding language, has to rely on his ability to send and to understand communications based on subtle cues. Before he can understand the meaning of words, he interprets his parents' subtle communications, such cues as the tone of voice, loudness, the facial expression of the speaker, the particular sequence at which the communication took place (as, for instance, "Johnny was yelling his head off when his parents yelled at him"), the proximity of the person, and possibly the odor of the person. However, the child is not a mere recipient of subtle and not so subtle communications. He increasingly learns to assess which of his own behaviors will provide the parent with information to respond in a desirable or undesirable way. We believe that even the infant makes decisions: either to comply to demands made on him, or to express whatever he has on his mind. We call these two response modes reflective of the child's "need for compliance" on one hand and his "sense of integrity" on the other. This battle starts indeed in very early childhood and lasts a lifetime. At this early time the child will form his ideas about the world he lives in, and not surprisingly, these ideas will pervade throughout his life. For example, his early experience may expose him to extrarigid demands of compliance, where he does not feel at all "understood." Under such conditions the child may very well learn that in order to feel like a person, he needs to defeat those who force him to comply. He will learn to fight and hate authority, and do so perhaps throughout life. Under these circumstances he may feel that his sense of integrity can only be safeguarded by fighting the authors of compliance. In the extreme case, we have the formula for the criminal, who needs to commit his criminal acts (under whatever pretenses) in order to experience an identity and to feel like a person. This goes along with the observation that many criminals report that they do not know why they committed the criminal act. The behavior is most noticeable in the young who are committed to gang warfare. Even the sign or signal of the opposing gang is perceived as an affront to one's integrity. Violence against perceived authority has become the condition of experiencing a sense of integrity.

Subtle cues are present in all communications. Think of a simple one: Mother tells daughter, "The lights were on all night." Daughter correctly reads the subtle cues and says, "It wasn't me!" A more complicated pattern of subtle cues can be present in a family setting: Husband comes home and yells at his son, asking him why he has not done his homework. Wife is nearby and interrupts the yelling. She tells her husband that the boy has indeed completed his homework. The husband interrupts her to tell her that the boy obviously did not do it well enough. The wife says that the boy has always had above-average grades, and the husband should shut up. The husband now gets really angry and tells her that instead of protecting the boy, the wife should join her husband telling the boy that he should do better. He yells at her that she is either too dumb to know, or never knew, that one does not get ahead in the world by just getting by, one has to do one's best at all times. At that point, she grabs her young son and runs up the stairs to escape the argument, threatening to call the police in response to her husband's verbal abuse unless he moves out. He responds that he will do so with pleasure. Later, they both calm down and when the husband asks for his supper, she tells him that he has insulted her and that she is not going to prepare supper for him unless he apologizes. He goes down on his knees in a mocking manner and asks for her forgiveness.

This would be just a brief family fight with a semihappy ending, if not for the fact that this scenario is repeated about three times a week. It is not always the homework and the cliché about "doing one's best," but the pattern stays pretty much the same. The father makes a negative comment about the son and the mother responds in a heated way, there is name-calling and threats are made to break up the family, then a calmer air prevails, and finally comes the mocking apology. This example shows that this pattern, nonsensical as it appears, has deep roots in both partners' history. Husband and wife experience some "delicious gratification" engaging in it: for both of them it relates to the experiences of early childhood. We know the clinical history for both; the husband reported that he had had heavy run-ins with his own father and had a very seductive mother who was deeply involved with him. His father used to berate him frequently in front of his mother and criticized him for every error he committed. His father frequently punished him, and he eventually came to identify punishment as love. As an adult, he acted out the essence of this early experience in the pattern he adopted, practically aping his father as some sons are apt to do. He berated his son and "forced" the mother to take his side. Even the funny mocking gesture rang familiar; his own father had made light of his mother's seductive behavior, telling her that she simply looked funny when she put her arm around her son.

The wife responded very well to the husband's pattern: she defended her son lovingly and threatened to leave her husband, indicating for the moment that her love for her son was greater than her love for her husband. Then after the mocking apology the family stayed together. The clinical history of the wife shows early patterns of behavior that may explain why she, too, continued these theatrical exchanges. She thought of her mother as an inadequate person because she did not assert her rights with her husband, but had secret affairs, thereby taking love away from him. Taking her son's side was a symbolic act: taking love away from a mean husband. The fact that she would eventually forgive him was based on the idea that he had accepted her ultimatum. Patterns give continuity to a person's life. In this family the two patterns of the couple were symbiotic, which permitted them to get along with each other. We do not claim that the delicious satisfaction of engaging in childhood patterns is the only motivational factor. For example, one factor present in many family fights is boredom. People who live together can experience a deeper sense of boredom than people living by themselves. An argument is a simple way of getting a "rise" and feeling a little more alive. In some families an intense fight a day keeps the family together.

Patterns are triggered by certain subtle cues, often deeply hidden. Most of the time we do not know what it is that makes us do things that we may regret later. Even in the choice of our friends, and certainly in the choice of a life companion, we are acting on cues of which we are not aware.

A fellow is at a party and says to one of the women, "Your hair is all messed up." On closer inspection, this "kidding" remark is very meaningful indeed, because it can produce important subtle information. The woman may disregard him, implying that she does not wish to open contact. She may run to the bathroom to straighten out her hair, implying that she is overly sensitive. She may tell the fellow that his hair is messed up as well, implying that she can take care of herself. The fellow can now make a further choice to continue his contact, depending on whether he likes the "attitude" he has helped to produce. We will feel attracted to someone who responds to us in a way we desire, and the desired way always relies heavily on subtle cues.

The family fight we reported on was a complex example of a symbiotic pattern, but patterns can also be very brief. A man hits a woman. He says he does not really want to hit her and he knows that she may be leaving him if he continues to hit her. His patterns are set off by a specific trigger, perhaps by her telling him about problems with the children or by his thought that he needs some excitement. The trigger is very powerful, the patterns are well established. The episode is very brief. We should note that the fellow, even if he wanted to, can hardly stop hitting her while he is in the very process of doing it. There is a good chance that he could stop it, once he discovers the trigger that precedes his violent act. This would give him some time to change his mood if that is what he wanted to do. In fact, with some under-standing and some good will on her part, his wife could help him to inter-vene. Should she notice the trigger, and if she has an agreement with him, she could make a bland remark such as "Oh" which may be enough of a cue for him to stop his "impulse" in its tracks. The secret here is the discovery of hidden subtle cues that comprise the trigger.

Another example of a simple pattern is the alcoholic woman who marries one alcoholic husband after another, each of them worse than the one before. She uses "love" as her guideline, which works for many people but misguides others, as the nature of love is probably determined in the first six years of life and may not be designed for a happy life as an adult. (When we told her that perhaps she should marry someone she did not love so deeply she thought we were crazy. She actually followed the advice and years later reported that she was still married to a good man.) Sometimes the subtle cues, which represent a pattern, do not need a trigger, such as the young woman who sported an unbelievable hateful facial expression. She was totally unaware of it, but we had enough evidence that in fact her facial expression was perceived by others as very angry. She did complain that she could not make any friends and we were not surprised.

Some patterns produce severe physical harm to either the sender or the recipient (such as hitting someone or getting into fights), some result in financial devastation (such as the con man's work), and some are designed to frighten, to intimidate, or inflict insult. These behavior patterns are fre-quently repeated and the key to understanding a pattern is that the person does not think of his behavior as a pattern, but labels it as unique, or denies any motivation for it whatsoever. When he suffers from the responses (such as losing his job after insulting his boss) he will deny that he had any desire to insult his boss. He will not understand what might have motivated him to do that and he can honestly deny that he had had such intentions. The reason for the blindness is that his motivation to act out his patterns is not easily detectable, but is determined by the memory storage of the past, which is not accessible to the person. It is the search for the "deliciousness," the continuity with the past, which is motivating him. The reasoning here is that we ordinarily learn from a behavior that results in punishment (such as losing one's job) but that when a pattern is involved we do not learn. We repeat the behavior regardless of the consequences.

Not all patterns have a negative outcome. Different homes and different genetics produce different memories in children. Some patterns produce indifferent responses, others positive ones. Some people are typically "ingratiating," others are seen as "open," others as "friendly" or "understanding" or "kindhearted." They act out their pattern as frequently as the people who have developed negative patterns. However, with positive patterns you obviously get very little negative feedback, though sometimes somebody may ask these people, "Why are you always so nice to everyone?" With positive patterns it is not difficult to explain why they are maintained; they obviously are rewarding. However, we believe that even with these patterns there is a sense of "deliciousness," because these patterns, too, represent the person's connection to his past!

We always give important information through the use of subtle cues, but often we are not even aware that we are sending them. We send out these cues both when we are talking and when we are silent. The way a therapist sits in his chair gives significant information to his client. Whether the therapist is talking or not, leaning forward, or closing his eyes is carefully noted by the patient. Think of a person who lounges in his chair with his feet on his desk. There is nothing inherently wrong with this position but it gives rather specific information to the person coming to talk. The "message," here unspoken, certainly may tell the client something about the therapist.

Most people are aware of what they are saying to another person, but they are often dismally uninformed regarding the additional information they are giving. They may feel that they make themselves perfectly clear (for example, asking an obese person, "Have you read the article on losing weight?") but their subtle cue information may add the meaning that it is "about time" to do something about it. The receiver may be deeply offended, but the sender may claim that he just wanted to alert the receiver to some reading material. Subtle cues are frequently used intentionally as a way of avoiding responsibility for some meaning of the message. When a tobacco company's advertising portrays young, happy, active smokers in various athletic contexts, it still can deny that the intent is to lure the young into becoming addicted to the habit. Con men use subtle cues all the time when they try to gain the confidence of innocent persons in order to take advantage of them.

Patterns may or may not be accessible to the person's awareness. The girl with the tense, angry face did not know that she conveyed certain information with this pattern. On the other hand, the husband and wife probably knew that they were going into the same old game all too often. In a certain way they knew what they were doing but they did not know why they were playing it out. The husband thought that he was an involved, but strict father and the wife thought that she had to protect her son from unjust criticism. With this sort of understanding they did not see any great reason to stop their behavior. However both stated that they hated the run-ins, particularly as they repeated them so frequently. Awareness of the pattern may be present, but the meaning and motivation of this behavior is hidden.

When a person repeats an activity often enough for the observer to say that he appears to be intending to do what he is doing, but when this same person is not aware of such an intent, the process is generally called "unconscious motivation." This is a difficult and disputed concept but we believe that it is a necessary one to understand human behavior. Examine the case of a person who is extremely jealous and is in his fifth marriage. When the wife he is now married to comes home five minutes late from shopping he swears at her and accuses her of sleeping with other men and tells her that she cannot leave the house again unless he is with her. Occasionally, this pattern also includes physical abuse. When questioned, he claimed that he loves his wife very much. Ordinarily after a few of these episodes, the wife calls the police and tells him that either he has to move out or she will move out herself. Under these circumstances every one of his four wives had left him.

This case reminds us of a relevant folk saying: If a person calls you an ass, you should ignore it. If two people call you an ass, you have the right to be very angry. If three people call you an ass you should buy a saddle.

When the man was asked why all five wives had left him, he told us that he had not expected such treatment from them. All he wanted was for a wife to be loyal to him. He did not connect his need for controlling the women, the swearing, and the beatings he gave them as relevant to his loss. He claimed that he loved them very much and each loss hurt him deeply. The man's conscious "intent" was to make sure that his wives would be loyal to him. This argument is not very convincing. Unless he is intellectually retarded, he should have learned that his way of ascertaining the wife's loyalty did not work very well. To find a more fitting "intent," one could reason that this man wanted to be married but also wanted to secure his freedom and independence. He obviously was ambivalent about being married. He should have bought a saddle. To us it appears reasonable to assume that this man repeated a pattern; he was guided by a definition of marriage that he had learned very early in life. We know that almost everyone has a pattern attached to the word "marriage." We know that when a male and a female live together happily it does not predict that they will be happy in their marriage. It is more likely that the early experience with their own family determines what new rules and regulations they would want to impose on their married relationship. The general emotional atmosphere within their family or origin and childhood competition with mother, father, or siblings probably play a large role in a person's definition of marriage.

We discussed some of these cases in detail because we firmly believe that many of the problems we encounter as therapists have a common characteristic. This characteristic is based on the nature of subtle cues. People intend to communicate with each other and they know quite well what they want to communicate and what sort of impact they want to have on another person. For example, they want to tell someone to shut up in order to quiet them. But all too frequently they do not take into consideration that with their message they also communicate an entirely different meaning than they had intended. During a music performance a man told a couple sitting several rows behind him "Shut up" in a very loud voice. He was surprised when a good number of others who attended the concert pointed at him and told him to shut up himself.

People who have psychological problems often fail to understand the common impact of their message. They are so preoccupied with the meaning that they want to convey that they fail to read, understand, or care to learn what their message actually conveys to another person. When a person does not get the response he expects, he is in a position to learn something about the nature of his own message from the response that he does obtain. We believe that many patients with psychological problems fail to understand the true impact of some of their important messages.

The confusion arises precisely because conscious and unconscious motivations may be at loggerheads. The unconscious motivation, dating back to early childhood, formulates a different response than the conscious intent. A suitor wants to tell his sweetheart that he loves her, but when he says, "I love you," he typically does not look into her eyes. By avoiding eye contact, he modifies the message he wants to give. The woman does not respond by declaring her love for him. Unfortunately the suitor has not committed a simple error. He wants to say the he loves her but the unconscious motivation not to commit himself is expressed in the lack of eye contact. Here, some stored experiences come to haunt the lover, as he cannot understand why his sweetheart turns away from him.

When we speak of stored experiences as the source of patterns, we firmly believe that the memories of these experiences might not be available to consciousness. Sometimes, under the right conditions, they can be restored to consciousness through hypnosis, although the memories may not always be factual. At times we have noticed that these memories appear spontaneously during the therapeutic hour.

One other avenue to get at stored memories is dreams. An interesting theory regarding dreams claims that dreams, through REM sleep, function to assess the importance of present observations and experiences by comparing them with stored memories of the past. Obviously we cannot store every single observation we make, for example, the color of all the books we see. Storage has to be selective. The theory is that during REM sleep we discover which of our present-day observations have relevance to observations stored at an earlier time. Winson (1985), who did the research, claims that for the most part "selected observations" that have connections with past storage are actually stored. (The exceptions are traumas that lead to posttraumatic stress disorders.) In other words, Winson believes that REM sleep helps us to determine what we need to remember of the day's information and that dreams help us to integrate this information.

So far Winson's proposition would not differ significantly from that of Freud, except Freud would say that the "present" and the "latent" events determine the individual's unconscious behavior. Winson believes that this storage system is just a storage system, as a cigar is just a cigar. Winson supports his proposition with the observation that dreams apparently serve a general useful function, since all mammals but one have REM sleep. Additionally, Winson notes that the exception (the Echidna, a spiny ant eater from Australia), which does not have dreams, has a prefrontal cortex larger than any other animal by body weight. Winson reasons that this enlarged cortex probably serves both to evaluate as well as to store information necessary for functioning.

Dreams, if they indeed serve the function of selecting which of the day's observations and experiences are meaningful and relating them to one's past, can be an important source of information about patterns. And indeed they are. We mention this because triggers that release a pattern sometimes appear to be part of the dream. A patient who was in the habit of beating his wife, but desired to give up this behavior, dreamed that he saw a woman looking at him on an elevator longer than she should have. He reported that this "look" was teasing and seductive. After this look the elevator crashed. As it turned out, it was a seductive look on his wife's part that was the trigger to get him into his rage. He had not been aware of it and would not have been able to report it, but now that he knew, he said that he was able to "put on the brakes" whenever he experienced the "look." In fact, he had not beaten his wife ever since he discovered the trigger.

With the present interest in Brief Therapy we may suggest that Pattern Analysis is probably a very effective way to obtain some results in a reasonably short time. We want to mention that we do not believe that Pattern Analysis can replace the therapeutic interview. Pattern Analysis consists of some fairly simple steps: (1) discovery of a major pattern of disturbance for a given person, (2) search for and discovery of the trigger, (3) helping the person recognize the trigger in order to counteract its effect by bringing it to consciousness, and (4) possibly enlisting others to help interrupt the pattern. The statement of the problem and the discovery of the pattern would not be difficult for the experienced therapist. Triggers, on the other hand, need more attention.

There are three roads leading to the discovery of the trigger that permits the undesirable patterns to commence. Dreams are one way to get this information. Another one is a very careful exploration of the thoughts and behaviors preceding the onset of the pattern.

A third road to discovering the trigger is through the analysis of the consequences of a given pattern, that is, carefully analyzing the behavior after the pattern has occurred. The contribution of existential theory to therapy is to gain some notion about a person's motivation from the outcome of the given behavior. The man mentioned above would typically, after the beating, become very remorseful and would start wooing his wife, begging her to make love. After they had made love he would promise her jewelry provided she told him that he is the best lover ever. His act of hitting, his sexuality, and his need to be the chosen lover would supply important information to the therapist. They would also provide him with at least a hypothesis regarding the trigger: it would be reasonable to suggest that he hit her because some signal made him feel inferior as a man.

Triggers can be very obvious although they can also be elusive. A trigger for a given pattern is often specifically related to the pattern, such as the "seductive look" we discussed earlier. The therapist should be able to discover the trigger in a reasonably short time and might even hypothesize as to the nature of the trigger. There is nothing lost in trying out a number of hypotheses (probing) and the therapist will find out soon enough whether his interventions are successful. Most patients are as eager as the therapist to discover just what the trigger might be. In our experience, many patients will do all they can to get to the bottom of it.

Once the brief therapeutic work is successful in discovering the trigger and the therapist brings this subtle information to the person's awareness, the frequency of the pattern usage is often significantly reduced.

Freud stated that no one willingly gives up libidinal pleasure. As with all patients, there can be resistance to giving up the deliciousness of continuation with the past. In our experience, however, the pleasure in the act of discovery and the success in getting rid of undesirable responses outweigh the resistance.

Sometimes after what triggers a certain pattern in a given person has been discovered, a husband, wife, or even a friend can be of help in alerting the perpetrator when the trigger becomes noticeable. As stated earlier, a simple neutral word such as "Oh" may be the type of signal that prevents the pattern. This simple device has probably saved a good many relationships.

Again, this is merely seen as a contribution to Brief Therapy, and much work has to be done in this area. We do not claim in any way that Brief

Therapy can help a person remodel his life; it will merely help a person overcome a particular problem.

There often is a question with regard to subtle cues: How do people identify a partner who would play their games? How is it that the alcoholic woman, who had been beaten by three drunk husbands, would end up with another? How is it that the boy who had been significantly hurt as a child by a mean mother would marry a woman who, in many essential elements, resembles that mother?

We believe that it is all due to the nature of love. The child's experiences linger on into adulthood and influence his definition of love. We believe that choices in love are probably learned in the first six years of life. Husbands are said to recreate the image of their mothers in their wives, and wives the image of their fathers. Sometimes it is not the direct image but a modified one or even an anti-image of mother or father, as with the man whose mother was extremely religious who married a prostitute and encouraged her to continue in her trade.

Interestingly, these love choices are not as clear when there is a live-in relationship. Statistics show that people who marry, without previously having lived together, have a slight advantage in staying together. To us this means that it is the image of "marriage" rather than of the "relationship" that prompts an individual to introduce or emphasize his patterns of love. We reason that in a live-in relationship people get to know each other, but in a marriage they are more likely to follow the guidelines laid down by earliest experiences, and they use their knowledge of each other to introduce new demands.

4

Information-Gathering Process in Psychotherapy

WHERE DOES THE PATIENT HURT?

In communication analytic therapy, the objective is to open new choices to the patient, a goal held by most other theories as well, since psychological survival is most likely related to the number of choices perceived to be available to a person. To accomplish this task of helping a person broaden the perceived choices, the therapist has to discover where the patient "hurts": where he feels that his choices have become limited.

This searching is not as easily accomplished as it may appear. There are two obstacles: first, to discover where the patient hurts, and second, to have the patient consider choices that he does not even know about or that he had previously decided not to consider at all.

Many difficulties impede an accurate understanding of where the patient hurts. Most patients simply do not know, as they engage in patterns of behavior that they are not aware of. They may come to the hour with an idea, a story, or a description of some symptoms. Some patients come armed with psychological jargon to describe their hurts in precise detail. However, the overt content of such descriptions gives the therapist very little information. It merely tells him where the patient thinks he hurts or where the patient wishes to believe the hurt is, and often he describes his current behavior which he feels describes his hurt most adequately. The patient may complain of depression, of a loss of motivation, that nothing seems worthwhile anymore. But it is not his depression that is his "hurt." A depression may have a genetic origin, or be based on a toxic condition. It may be a side effect of medication, or even attributable to certain chemicals that the brain itself manufactures. We have an additional explanation about the onset of depression. We believe that, provided a patient has the genetic "channel" to experience depression, it will set in when the individual feels himself to be in a critical situation that produces heavy stress. Should his channel be alcoholism, he will drink; should it be schizophrenia, he will have an episode. In that sense, depression and the other channels are the mind's way of "healing" when stress has become unbearable. Once depressed, the individual feels (correctly) that he is now incapable of dealing with his stress. This, in a peculiar way, gives him some sense of relief. The relief comes because the patient no longer has to cope.

We are not saying that the patient is hopelessly caught in his depression, but that he has given up dealing with the cause of it. There are good medications that reduce the effect of depression. If he has an opportunity to seek out psychotherapy as well, along with the proper drugs, he might be in a position to work through his predepression state of stress. While depression hurts, to become well he has to deal with the stress that has triggered it. If the pain is too intense, it becomes almost too difficult to attend to or cope with the stress. As stated, we assume that the genetic predisposition of a given patient includes "channels" that are activated when significant stress occurs. These channels may include "conversion reaction," "schizophrenia," "alcoholism," "depression," and even "suicidal impulses."

Interestingly enough, the genetic channels available to a given person have their own meaning to self and others. Depressive behavior may communicate to self a feeling of helplessness and to others a call for help. Alcoholism may communicate to self the sense of being out of control and not being responsible for one's behavior, and perhaps to others a more willful act, perhaps that the drunkard is weak and unwilling to abstain, that he is an irresponsible person.

The patient very well may tell the therapist that he is coming to seek therapy to get relief from depression: his perception is that depression is his "sickness." This perception is greatly enhanced by the common perceptions that a given drug will "cure" the depression. We do believe that some drugs indeed alleviate depression; however, with regard to depression, the NIMH research has shown that drugs plus psychotherapy are in fact most effective when combined. The reason is that, while the proper drug may alleviate the symptoms, the underlying stress is not dealt with by any of the drugs. Consequently, the patient who does not have the opportunity to work through the stress state will likely stay on the drug for a lifetime, or will revert into depression when the drug is no longer taken.

Our proposition is that stress is the underlying cause of the manifest behavior (i.e., depression). The therapist needs to discover what the patient's existential experience of stress was before the onset of any of the manifestations. This investigation will reveal the nature of the stress and the feeling of helplessness that accompanied it. Such an analysis will not only help the therapist to understand the true nature of the patient's hurt, but will permit the patient to make choices that previously have been avoided. We know that depression and most of the other "manifestations" available to humans are painful, but we also know that stress can be deadly.

We are also subscribing to a second proposition: Stress does not simply appear from nowhere. Stress is at least to some extent generated by the individual. It is probably correct to state that the patient does not know just how he is "generating" stress. We do not doubt that many stressful situations are a matter of fate: the loss of a loved one, an accident, financial distress, to mention only a few. But beyond these obvious causes of stress, people also seem to seek out stress—or daring as it is called—more benignly: some people seem to do that almost every time they talk. Their "communication system" involves frequent threats, challenges, and cries for help. It also includes very subtle covert information, of which the sender is unaware, and triggers responses in his environment that can be a great burden. This chapter will go into much greater detail into this problem of just how the patient is producing stress for himself and just what the therapist needs to do when he is trying to help him. When looking for the patient's way of dealing with stress, the therapist can often learn about significant problems of the patient by being sensitive to all aspects of the patient's communication. For example, while a patient will tell the therapist about his pain, he will also communicate other more subtle information, some of which he may not know he is giving away.

The statements the patient makes to tell the therapist of his pain we call his "overt" communication. The other information that is included is more subtle, and has to do with covert cues, which are invariably part of all communication. This information we shall call "covert." It comes across, for example, in the tone of voice, in the way words are emphasized, in pauses, in body and hand movements, and in eye contact. People can of course control their covert information as well as their overt information. We only need to think of con men, who use covert information to trick their victims. Patients are ordinarily not trying to trick the therapist, and they convey their covert information most frequently without being aware of it. In fact, we believe that patients, because they are not aware, often use covert information to maintain and trigger the problems that cause them stress. Covert information is the most critical information the psychotherapist can get, as it gives him a direct road to the patient's unconscious manipulative behavior, which is typically related to his problem.

When we say that the patient appears to perpetuate his problems with his covert communications, we need to add that he accomplishes this by what we call the engagement process. We can always engage another person with our communications, that is, we can evoke an emotional reaction. When a person pulls a gun and points it at you, he is engaging you emotionally. When a person yells for help, he is engaging you emotionally. However, there are two levels of engagement processes that pertain to the therapeutic hour. One is overt: the patient may want to arouse your sympathy and efforts to provide help by telling you of his suffering. This overt engagement process is, to a great extent, motivated behavior. The patient knows (in most cases) what he is doing. But there is also another engagement process, which is very different. The major difference with the second, covert engagement process is that the patient does not know that he is triggering the other person for an emotional reaction, one that in a peculiar way serves his purpose. He does not know that he is doing it and would deny it when alerted. Very frequently this covert triggering causes the patient a great deal of displeasure—the patient would not understand why he should cause pain for himself.

The patient, without awareness, uses his covert information to activate his patterns (which, as we noted earlier, gives the patient a sense of "deliciousness": a connection with his childhood). He does take the pain, which he also triggers into the bargain, and since he does not have any awareness of the covert cues he is sending out, he does not know how to help himself, how to get away from unhappy consequences.

Here is where the therapist comes in. He has to pay attention to the very covert cues with which the patient perpetuates his problems. This does not take extraordinary skills but rather requires the therapist to be in touch with his own feelings. In the therapeutic hour the patient will inevitably use these covert triggering cues, and the therapist will need to learn to read his own feelings.

The patient, a young woman, let the therapist know that he is her dream man. He is so handsome and bright and modest, that she could easily fall in love with him. She wonders whether he has some time this evening to go out with her.

This woman's complaint was that she turns off the men she meets. The therapist has to understand the woman's engagement processes. Overtly she has said very flattering things, which she surely interprets as being nice and suggestive, but the way she said them and the occasion she chose to say them were anything but suggestive! In fact, she probably could have predicted that her therapist would be obliged to reject her.

The covert cues, both from the setting and the way she talked, aroused in the therapist a feeling that she was teasing and demanding. Obviously, in the therapeutic hour he has to reject her one way or another. At the same time he wants to help her and should not respond in terms of the discomfort and anger he feels. He wants to tell her to get lost, but controls this impulse. Instead, from his emotional experience with her, he learns the way this patient turns men off. He realizes that the patient gave him, unwittingly, an example of why men did not want to go out with her. She engaged him emotionally in a negative fashion probably without awareness. Had it been for real, she surely would have gotten another rejection from her therapist!

The therapist has learned that he must disengage from the impact of the covert message (that in spite of her inviting words, her invitation comes through as both threatening and demanding). He has learned much about how she perpetuates her problem just by inspecting his feelings elicited by her message. He has learned that in order to help her he has to disengage from the emotional demand of her message. He responds with a fully disengaged statement, "I know that you would be very surprised if I said yes." Should she continue with, "Why don't you say yes?" he would have to respond, "I want to explore with you why you get so many rejections." Had he stayed engaged, he might have responded to her in anger, "Get lost." This would not have helped her; he would be just another man rejecting her.

Disengagement is an essential element of communication analytic therapy, and the therapist's understanding of what the patient is demanding is one of the keys in the discovery of the patient's hurt. As stated, the patient is not aware of the demands that are the hidden part of her message (that is why this woman was always surprised when she got a rejection). Disengagement gives the therapist firsthand information regarding the procedures the patient is using with other people to maintain the present state of adjustment.

A patient suffering from depression interrupts himself to say that he feels that nothing can come of this talking to the therapist. While making this statement he shakes his head slowly. During the hour he no longer makes this brief negative statement but every few minutes shakes his head slowly and silently says "no good." This aside surely impacts the therapist significantly, not only because it seems to be an expression designed to minimize the value of the hour, but it allows the therapist to make the hypothesis that the patient has the habit of "putting down" his respondent. This type of message is probably unconsciously motivated, a pattern that the patient learned early in life. By either distrusting the person he is with or letting it be known that he is gravely dissatisfied, the patient possibly attempted to engage the therapist with the feeling that this was a hopeless situation. The therapist learns from this how desperately the patient is clinging onto his depression. The therapist might advance the hypothesis that the patient gets some gratification from telling people to leave him alone, and that this attitude possibly has some bearing on the original sense of stress he has experienced.

To summarize, in the model presented here, the therapist—from the information gained from his emotional response to the patient's statements—can learn (or at least hypothesize) where the patient hurts and even what likely stress the patient experienced prior to the onset of the present complaint. The inferences regarding the patient's hurt will become more accurate as they are based on more information, but useful inferences can be made even from a few repeated patient messages. A good therapist will make inferences from minimal information but will revise them as more data becomes available.

THE THERAPIST AS AN INSTRUMENT

The patient who has a feeling of vulnerability will try to protect himself. He will try to place the "receiver" of his message into an emotional position that reduces his sense of vulnerability. For example, a young woman was sent to therapy by her parents after she had attempted suicide. During the first hour she stated that she was deeply afraid of being asked by her boyfriend for a sexual encounter. She did not want to lose her boyfriend, nor did she want to lose her virginity. She felt that she had to hide her motivations of avoidance, and did not want to be seen as running away from the question. She described the particular evening, when they both were alone at her parents' home. What she did could be best described in our terms: she *engaged* her boyfriend in an emotion that accomplished the compromise of neither losing him nor giving in to him. In this particular case she sprained her ankle. The therapist learned that she had had several other psychosomatic occurrences earlier in life, which resolved problems for her. An attempted suicide had also occurred when she felt she had to give an extreme demonstration of avoidance to resolve another serious problem.

The patient's investment in pain had solved her emotional problems on several other occasions as well. When the therapist discussed the suicide attempts with her, she stated that she would have gone through with it just to let people know that they were to blame for the stress under which they had put her. Her pattern of expressing her anger by hurting herself was demonstrated in the therapeutic hour as well. After an especially stressful hour in which she felt rejected because she had asked the therapist to hold hands with her and he had refused, she got up from her chair and literally fell on the therapist, apparently accidentally. When she had come close to him the therapist held out his hands to protect himself, and the young woman supported herself for a moment by holding her own hands against his. This "accident" required such a remarkable sense of prediction and skill that shortly after the encounter, when she apologized for stumbling, both of them started to laugh, recognizing that the stumble was not all that accidental. Laughing, the therapist remarked, "That's what you wanted in the first place,"and to his knowledge, this was the last "somatic" message she sent out.

The therapist will obtain evidence for his interpretation of the meaning of the covert components of the patient's message from three sources: (1) the overall frequency of occurrence, (2) the degree that the covert component differs significantly from the overt component of the message, and (3) their repetition on a variety of occasions. Based on this understanding, the therapist will develop a psychotherapeutic strategy of disengagement that is designed to arouse uncertainty in the patient regarding the use of discordant messages.

To summarize, the therapist's skill is to properly read both the overt and the covert meaning of the patient's message. The patient's statements and the subtle covert meaning have both an intellectual and an emotional component, which are designed to have an impact on the respondent. The therapist will identify the impact the patient's message has on him and will formulate a hypothesis as to "where the patient hurts."

Even the experienced therapist will often become socially engaged and respond to the patient's subtle demands without awareness: a process that Freud labeled "countertransference." In fact, the therapist, technically speaking, cannot disengage unless he is first engaged by the patient's covert actions. The therapist's skill consists in the ability to free himself from countertransference in order to be able to disengage from the emotional components of the patient's message. This disengagement permits him to recognize the patient's unconscious motivation. The therapist will listen to the patient's cues as an information-gatherer, rather than as a partner in an emotional experience.

Two factors often interfere with the therapist's ability to read the sender's message properly. First, the therapist has his own patterns of behavior, which will alert him to some information but avoid other. (That is why it is very useful for the therapist to have undergone his own therapeutic experience.) The patient will be striving to be successful in engaging the therapist, and undoubtedly will discover the therapist's "weaknesses." We only need to think of the cases where the patient is able to go along with or encourage seduction. The patient will know intuitively that he cannot create feelings, but can only elicit those of which the therapist is capable. To involve another person requires sending messages that are meaningful to him. Second, the patient's responses may be determined by extratherapeutic stimuli such as a knock on the door, a telephone call, or the therapist's momentary absent-mindedness (the patient senses the therapist's preoccupation with feelings that are not related to the patient).

The therapeutic information obtained by the therapist can be only as precise as the instrument receiving it. Using his own emotional responsiveness as a barometer for accuracy, the therapist must know how to "read" himself, to understand his own contributions to his interpretations. When a therapist feels threatened by a statement made by the patient, he may know that his first impulse is to respond with a defensive statement. But a therapist, preoccupied with this feeling of threat and his automatic ways of dealing with it, is in no position to analyze the meaning of the patient's messages accurately. Under these circumstances he cannot act therapeutically. Only if the therapist is able to truly disengage from the emotional climate of the patient's message can he recognize just what the patient had in mind for him. When a therapist, after withdrawing from the emotional climate the patient has imposed, can give a disengaged therapeutic response, such a response will be extremely meaningful to the patient, as it will produce uncertainty, which is a precursor of change.

Understandably, certain messages (such as displaying a weapon, or even a suicide attempt in the office) are so powerful that the therapist is likely to become engaged and react emotionally. In such cases, obviously, there is no time available to help the patient other than by responding to the act itself. But we must keep in mind that all patients have learned to be masters in manipulating others with their communicative skills. The range of their skill may be limited, but the skills are formidable. After all, patients have been practicing their skills for a lifetime, simply because they were important to them for survival. However, the patient is a master without acknowledging his skills.

Since neither he himself nor the addressed person is fully aware of the manipulation, there is very little the patient can do to change his patterns. The therapeutic hour is suitable for understanding what goes on between the two participants, but the very fact that the information is covert and subtle is the reason that it takes many contacts to resolve the problem. This difficulty in discovering the meaning of the covert component of the message is probably one of the reasons that patients sometimes wonder whether anything is really happening in their work with the therapist. To paraphrase Reik (1948), the therapist has three ears: one to understand the manifest meaning, one to sense the covert meaning, and one to recognize the motivation behind the total message.

TO DEDUCE MOTIVATION FROM A MESSAGE

Why are therapeutic responses thought to be unique? Why should a few critical responses generalize to behavior, even though patients and therapists frequently have only 1 hour of weekly contact versus 167 hours of no contact? Why a patient should generalize from the therapeutic experience is not easily explained. Our best guess is that the therapeutic hour is unlike any other contact with people: the patient is motivated to reduce a pain, but the pain comes from actions and thought processes that he does not fully understand. He goes to the therapist to seek relief from the stress and anxiety—and the consequences—caused by these thought processes. He finds in the therapist a person who really listens, who tries to discover a solution to a problem that he, the patient does not really understand. The patient finds himself in a unique situation, where he is not criticized, not blamed, and not given a schedule of advice that he is supposed to follow. The therapist encourages him to talk about all aspects of the problem and helps him to discover his own solutions. He presents the patient with an emotional climate that permits him to feel safe. It is this atmosphere of acceptance that permits the patient to let his guard down and that permits him to accept a sense of uncertainty, which is of course the basic condition for change. The therapist's responses, particularly when the therapist is properly disengaged, are not following the patient's expectations, but instead they provoke thought. These same responses would be perceived as a threat under most other circumstances, but because of the sense of acceptance the patient tolerates them. He feels safe and permits himself to experience uncertainty in this condition. He inspects his customary action more freely than he ever has before. He even decides that certain disturbing behaviors can be left behind and he can explore replacement with behaviors that would not lead him to stress. In the therapeutic hour the patient can accept uncertainty because he is listened to and not talked to. It is in the therapeutic hour that the patient can explore the truth about himself.

We would think that the reason that the therapeutic hour, even though of short duration, has a great effect on the patient's behavior is that the patient wants to know a truth about himself that he feels he cannot face alone.

The nature of the interactive process permits us to gain an understanding of one of the peculiarities of communication: How can a person act without "really knowing" why he is acting? And how can a person communicate without really knowing that he does so? But that is the nature of communication, because we do not really know what we communicate with our covert, hidden communications and neither do we realize that we communicate at all, as we are often enough totally unaware of our hidden messages! The discordant message is one where the covert element of the message does not match the overt element. The discordance is the result of the conflict between the need to live by certain standards and the need to express one's own sense of integrity. In the process of coding the discordant message, the person will typically only be aware of the overt message he is given (unless he desires to manipulate others with full awareness). It is the ignorance of the covert meaning of a message that gets people into trouble.

While a patient obviously suffers from the use of his discordant messages from time to time, we should note that most people may not suffer from affecting others in a way they consciously do not desire. We may experience some surprises, simply because we do not account for our message being different from what we had intended. The reason we all need to use discordant messages is that such messages represent an adaptive compromise between what we want from another person and what we also desire but are not really ready to put into words.

For the patient, the discordant message is a more urgent proposition. He has been hurt in earlier experience and he is involved in a battle for mastery over a situation that has caused great anxiety in the past. Discordant messages permit the patient to stack the cards to fight on a familiar battleground without having to face the painful problems with awareness. The patient uses great skill to be "misunderstood." In a way he wants to have his cake and eat it too. He wants to introduce the painful problem, but does not want to take responsibility for it.

Only when the patient chooses to go into therapy and reveal some of the pain and how it is collected is the therapist likely to recognize the meaning of the problem the patient is concealing. The therapist has the motivation to help the patient take responsibility not only for the overt, acceptable components of his messages, but also for the covert, "unacceptable" components. Only when the "hidden" needs become visible can the patient resolve his problem.

We supervised a beginning therapist who reported that he could no longer work with one patient because "this guy" made him "too angry." The young therapist was not impulse-ridden or generally unable to control anger. We had reason to believe that his strong feelings were a response to the emotional climate set for him by the patient. On the basis of this hypothesis, we guessed that the patient's procedure to maintain his own psychological economy was to elicit anger and rejection from his respondents, the very feelings he had so successfully elicited in the therapist. The patient was making a bid to reinforce his present state of adjustment by reaffirming that he was living in "an angry world" that rejected him. The therapist has to learn to recognize the cues the patient uses to elicit the emotional climate (here anger and rejection). Were the therapist to be caught in the social role and become angry (as our inexperienced therapist did), the therapeutic hour would not differ from the patient's experiences in everyday life. The patient would have continued in his belief that this is an angry world and that the therapeutic world is no exception. He would have learned that seeking therapeutic help is useless. Disengaging from social responses is often difficult because the social responses pack a great deal of power. It is like a patron at the movies yelling "Fire!" The covert coding of a message relies on very well-established expected responses. The therapist's responses are unique precisely because of this disengagement from the social demands of the message.

INFORMATION THROUGH SCANNING

How does the patient code his discordant message? Anyone who wants to communicate effectively must "tune in" to his respondent, varying his message after assessing the reactions to each previous message and sensing how a particular word and the accompaniment covert loadings affect the respondent. As people send out a variety of messages, they learn when the respondent feels bored (does not listen), attentive, or threatened, how he can be pleased, and to what extent his message has the desired effect. This process, cueing in on the respondent, is what we have called *scanning.* The process of resistance in the therapeutic hour, as outlined by Freud, is based on the use of information gained by the patient's scanning of the therapist. In Freudian terms, the patient scans the therapist carefully and uses the information gained to throw him "off base" at critical times, to protect and maintain the patient's own libidinal position, and in this manner resist the therapist's impact on him. The therapist scans the patient as well for maximum impact. With most people, including patients, scanning appears to be largely an unconscious process of sensing another individual's emotional attitudes. The well-trained therapist however, will be aware when he is scanning his patients, as the information he gains is the key to a successful therapeutic effort. For all we know, the ability to "tune in" to or to listen and understand the emotions of another person may be based on a genetic capability. Certainly, the specific information is learned in early childhood. A young child is often upset when the mother is nervous, but feels at ease when she is composed. The child does not analyze the stimuli, but reacts to them nevertheless. Communication at this age seems to take place on the basis of prehension rather than comprehension (Sullivan, 1953). From the information gained by scanning, a husband can learn to press his wife's love or hate "buttons." The art of triggering often develops without awareness, though it can be learned and practiced willfully. Scanning is a skill that is not peculiar to humans. Animals obviously "scan" the attitudes of other approaching living beings. Horses seem to be able to sense the attitudes of a person and respond to the inexperienced rider by bucking, grabbing the bit, or running off. A dog will bark at some approaching strangers, but not at others. Most animals seem to scan for emotional attitudes such as danger or safety. Among humans, the process of scanning becomes most obvious when we think of the encounter with a stranger. A person does not know whether the stranger is friendly or unfriendly and a first impression is formed on the basis of subtle, undifferentiated cues. Hamlet's demand of the ghost, "Whither wilt thou lead me? Speak! I'll go no further," and his request for the ghost to tell him if he is "a spirit of Hell or a goblin damned," are typical of first encounters, including therapeutic interviews. The patient often judges the therapist, scanning his attitudes and value systems without much awareness, but arriving easily at a summary judgment such as "I like him," or "He does not understand me." The patient's strategy of responses throughout therapy is based on information gained through continuous scanning. He will be affected by the cues he obtains from scanning, even though he cannot recognize or label them. On the basis of these cues, the patient will decide whether to flee or hold back, whether to try to impress, exaggerate his problems, or understate them. The patient obtains much of his understanding of the therapist's messages through such a scanning process. In turn, many of his own responses are sent without awareness and represent his style—his typical approach to a stranger. With the information he gained through scanning, his approach is custom-made to fit in with the therapist's characteristics. The patient wants to be as safe as he possibly can be giving intimate personal information to another person. Surely, a therapist's overt statement, "Anything you say will be safe with me," alone would not carry much weight.

The patient will agree, pacify, seduce, even upset and immobilize the therapist—whatever he has learned to do to prompt the therapist to behave in ways that will give him useful information for scanning him. The patient has practiced a lifetime to achieve his skills and he will be most skilled when he is having severe problems. Severe problems make a person more vulnerable than insignificant problems, hence there is a greater need to protect oneself from danger. His purpose is to engage the therapist on his terms, on his battlefield, so to speak, in an area where he has the most skill. We should remember that the patient is motivated not only to solve problems, but also to protect his investment in them.

A patient typically first scans the therapist for any predictable reactions. There may be physical responses such as eye contact, head movement, use of hands, a smile, or a smirk; or they may be mental, such as a peculiar word use, brief lectures, or pauses in speaking. The therapist simultaneously scans the patient's style of approach to a stranger, which differs from person to person and in a concentrated way reveals significant information. Typically, the patient will be careful to discover whether he has encountered a disciplinarian, a kind-hearted person, a bright person, or one who at least seems to understand him. At the same time he will try to find out where the therapist is vulnerable, where he can be hurt, flattered, stopped, encouraged, and even to what extent he can be fooled.

Some scanning processes have been investigated. Scanning appears to lean heavily on information gained from the observation of posture, facial expression, gesture, way of speaking, choice of words, the appearance of the office, the knickknacks, the noise level, the appearance of other persons, etc. The therapist's clothing plays a role, as well as his way of sitting, the arrangement of things on his desk, when he nods his head and how deeply (Greenspoon, 1962), whether he encourages the patient to produce certain types of disclosures while discouraging others. Some of this type of research based on retrospective reports of patients supports the notion that the patient can, if asked, recall some of the therapist's covert cues.

Patients often use scanning in a more desperate way because of their vulnerability. Responses have to be controlled rigidly and narrowly, as they could trigger any of their symptoms. For this reason patients generally attempt to elicit the very narrow range of responses, those they most comfortably can deal with. One of our patients demonstrated this very clearly: he was bulky and very strong and was given to "trigger" others into fights with him, which he knew he could win. Of course, he tried this with the therapist. In a surprise move he went to the bookcase and threw a number of books to the floor, yelling that they were "no good." Then he turned around and asked the therapist directly, raising his fists, "You want to do anything about it?" The therapist, taken aback, had not expected this dramatic but revealing behavior. He did not lose his cool: "Do you really want to fight a weakling like me?" This puzzled the man and both started laughing. The patient was satisfied as he had an answer to his scanning behavior. He knew that the therapist understood him, and accepted him as a powerful person.

Most patients are extremely sensitive and easily perceive weaknesses in others. People who deal with them are often afraid of their sharp observational powers. Many hospital patients are very much aware of their fellow patients' difficulties and use them to their own advantage, taking food, getting help in cleaning up, etc. This contradicts the general perception that patients are weak and incapable. This misleading diagnosis is attributable to the fact that patients are evaluated by conventional standards rather than by their own idiosyncratic skills. For example, while some patients appear to be unable to get along well with others, they actually get along only too well by eliciting, within a limited repertoire, responses that fit into their psychological economy.

EVIDENCE USED FOR A FORMULATION OF A THERAPEUTIC HYPOTHESIS

Generally people understand the responses of others as best they can, even though there is a minimal amount of verification, lest communication be slowed to a standstill. The meanings conveyed are composed of the verbal meaning of the words, as well as their covert supplements. A "Good morning" is not easily verified for its underlying meaning: it can be hostile, friendly, distant and perfunctory, or even loving. In most everyday conversations, people have learned to accept the face value of the statement, but they are also cognizant of the attached covert meaning, at least to some extent. In many verbal exchanges, the underlying covert meaning has also become a convention. When a teacher says "YOU" to a student, the content lets the student know that the teacher means him, but by the tone of voice, he can tell whether he is in trouble, is being reprimanded, or is perhaps being praised. People simply use the conventions of language to gain some general understanding of what they say, and the covert cues can be part of the convention. When a guest asks the waiter to bring him a glass of water, the waiter knows exactly what the guest means, even though he may also have understood that the guest is impatient (having asked for water three times before), is embarrassed to ask, or tries to be extra friendly. He is not likely to inquire what the request really means. In the absence of a verifiable understanding of the idiosyncratic meaning of a message, the conventional meaning is all that is available, and in many exchanges this is adequate.

In the therapeutic process it is precisely the alertness for the idiosyncratic meaning imbedded in the patient's message that challenges the special skill of the therapist. He will try to discover whether his understanding of the underlying meanings of a message is accurate. He certainly cannot ask the patient directly for commenting on the covert meaning of the message, but the therapist can use certain devices to obtain a reasonable degree of certainty for his interpretation.

We repeat that the single most important condition for the therapist is to disengage from the emotional demands of the patient's message. He knows that he will be set up for certain emotional responses, and when they occur he will have to recognize the emotion he feels in response to the patient's statement. Let us assume that he feels annoyed by one of his patient's comments. He then may ask himself, "What are the cues the patient used to annoy me?" Differentiating the cues, he may discover that the patient suddenly changed the topic from the one that the two had been discussing and that the therapist felt had benefited the patient. He will note that a change in topic under these circumstances may be a way of "avoidance" of a demanding topic and he will try to verify whether this behavior recurs in future exchanges.

The therapist will be the sounding board, the instrument. The therapist will know of his own contribution to being annoyed. He knows that under certain circumstances he will be annoyed, even though it would not be because of the patient's covert cues. For example, the patient talks about hitting a woman. The therapist always feels annoyed when he hears talk like this, but he also knows that this is his own contribution, and that the patient needs to talk about this problem. Consequently he will not be listing this annoyance as one of the patient's manipulations. Once the therapist has identified the patient's cues that have an emotional impact on him—and of course, he has disregarded those "impacts" that came from his own contributions—he will observe the frequency with which the patient is trying to engage him with such cues. Under certain circumstances the patient may strongly criticize the therapist, and here the therapist may be in a dilemma: Is this criticism one of the modes of behavior that causes him, the therapist, to be annoyed, or is the sensitivity to criticism "his" hangup? The answer comes from the frequency of occurrence. How often does the patient blame others? When there is a high frequency it will tell the therapist that criticism is a way the patient gets himself into trouble. This type of an analysis also permits the therapist to measure his own effectiveness in reducing the patient's preferred covert behavior. Another benefit of this careful listening is that the patient's responses to the therapist's interventions help the therapist to discover the underlying meaning of the patient's messages. Typically the therapist will not ask for a verbal verification of a feeling he has discovered but rather will respond to the covert cues of the patient by letting the patient experience the fact that these cues are no longer covert! "You tell me that your former therapist was better than anyone you met since; she obviously was very competent indeed." With this disengaged intervention, the therapist lets the patient know that the comment has not annoyed him, that he is disengaged but understands that the patient tried to involve him emotionally by "putting him down." That is to say that he, the therapist, wants the patient to know that he has recognized the covert hostility. The therapist will use this information to pay specific attention to the patient's use of emotional words, gestures, facial expressions, and body movements.

Letting the patient know that his covert cues are no longer hidden permits or better encourages the patient to deal with the previously hidden aspects of his communication. When the patient is ready, permitting himself to experience uncertainty, the recognition that he does not need to hide will lead to new behaviors.

In order to accomplish the gathering of information, the therapist has to be a genuinely concerned person. In order for the patient to accept the difficulty of giving up his most prized skills (the manipulation of others through covert cues) the patient has to permit uncertainty, which can only occur when the therapist is perceived as a caring person. While the frequency with which an emotion is being elicited by the patient is one of the basic tools for verifying the meaning of unconscious motivation and while careful listening and intervention-probing is a further tool for the purpose, a third piece of evidence should be considered to verify the therapist's interpretation of the hidden meaning. This verification needs to establish that the patient is reluctant to learn even though he experiences pain from his problems. Most individuals will learn to avoid choices that produce pain. In contrast, the patient will not be able to learn from exposure to pain, as he will deny having contributed to being exposed to it. We assume that a patient's behavior is based on having learned a pattern in earlier life and that this pattern will often be activated by the patient without awareness when there are opportunities. Not aware or admitting that he helped to cause the pain, the patient is not in a position to learn from the outcome. The therapist will notice that when the patient is able to avoid behaviors that previously caused pain he is on his way to recovery.

The therapist will have to make judgments regarding his understanding of the patient's hurt. He will first make a hypothetical judgment, as he has only a few responses and minimal information. Eventually, he will have to support some of his propositions and will have to discard others. Thinking about the three aids to making a learned judgment will be of some help in making the most learned judgment. The therapist cannot wait for certainty before responding to the patient. He obviously has to respond in terms of even his earliest hypothesis perhaps made on inadequate information. He should always be aware that his understanding of the patient is "hypothetical," and a certain amount of doubt as to whether he is correct is healthy.

To summarize, the therapist is the instrument in the therapeutic hour. The therapist has to analyze the sense of hurt (the silent rules) that the patient uses to get himself into trouble. The therapist will do so by being a caring person, by listening carefully to the patient's attempts to "engage" him with emotional demands, and by disengaging from these demands appropriately. When the therapist is able to disengage, his responses will serve to help the patient to accept a state of "uncertainty" because his private coding no longer works and he is understood where he previously felt he had to hide. In this state of uncertainty, the patient will learn from the events that pain him and will begin to avoid setting them up. In the broadest sense, psychotherapy is a way of helping a patient to learn again in the areas of life that he had excluded from such learning. The lifelong effort to hide his motivations will no longer be necessary.

CHAPTER

5

The Use of Conventions

Convention refers to social practices that have been established by general consent and sanction. Certain communications almost automatically elicit rather specific responses, and we call those highly related stimuli-response patterns conventions. In terms of communication theory, conventional practices may be seen as behavior to which responses can be predicted with high probability.

A person can use conventions to constrict another's response activity, and one can often count on conventions to elicit a predictable response. Conventions also can be used by a sender to hide certain meanings of a message; the person who receives an expected, conventional response has completed the communication exchange and is not likely to think of the sender's hidden motives. There are, of course, exceptions: the husband who brings his wife flowers may get a proper "thank you," but also may raise her suspicions about why she got the present.

CONVENTIONS AS A HIDING PLACE

A person can, with or without awareness, hide behind well-established conventions. The conventional "good morning" implies a wholesome wish for another person; a friendly mind-set is established, and the sender "sets up" the respondent with a conventional symbol that is, of course, immediately understood and does not require much thought to decode. In some cases though, the greeting may also include other meanings. A gruffly spoken "good morning" does not send a friendly message at all. It may communicate that the sender doesn't feel well or doesn't mean well. Similarly, a quiet and flatly detached (minus eye contact) "Hello John, how are you?" also covertly sends the message "I couldn't care less about the receiver." In this way a convention can be used to hide the wolf in sheep's clothing, to send discordant information. The sheep's clothing helps the sender to reduce the chance of an inquiry and to deny responsibility for the covert part of the message. The ambiguity of this message permits the sender—even when taken to task—to escape with the retort, "I didn't mean it that way. I don't know what you are talking about."

A person can also hide behind a convention without awareness. Here the individual is not aware of the adjuvant intonations; they have become his "style," and this person would be surprised to learn that discordant information has been sent. The senders of unconsciously coded ambiguous information very often are unable to communicate their underlying feelings directly. Were these people able to express the negative feeling directly, they would not need to go through the complex process of ambiguous codings. By cloaking their negative meanings with expressions that carry conventional meaning, they can express themselves without having to face the consequences.

This process undoubtedly takes place in many subtle ways in the interaction between most people. Using certain conventions or standard patterns, an individual first creates a mind-set in the respondent that limits his response activity, and then introduces stimuli (without the receiver's awareness) that represent the sender's hidden purposes and desires. Advertising people, people involved in political campaigns, religious speakers, and educators have all used this process, embedding hidden meanings within conventions in order to promote specific emotional attitudes in the respondent (Packard, 1980).

Interestingly, these hidden cues will often create very strong, lasting attitudes that become quite inaccessible to reason. The person who is made to feel strongly about something through the use of subtle cues is unlikely to become confused by facts. Typically, the victim of a con man who has established himself as a "friend" will not believe the assertion that the man is a con artist, even after the victim acknowledges the loss. Capitalizing on this, many con artists return to the scene of the crime to revictimize their "marks," who still wish to maintain the earlier emotional climate achieved in the relationship with the con artist.

The part of the message that contains the conventional meaning, of course, must be overt at all times. Otherwise, it would not be understood by the respondent. A speaker may hold out his hand for greater emphasis; people will know that such a gesture means that the speaker wants to emphasize a given point rather than receive a gift. The beggar, on the other hand, holds out a hand in a similarly conventional gesture, but the same gesture conveys an altogether different meaning.

Obviously, the same behavior can be interpreted differently in different contexts. Therefore, the conventional, formal meaning of a message cannot be fully understood out of context. The conventional meaning, however, is usually understood by both sender and respondent because they both have learned to interpret the context in which the message occurs. A child learns to raise a fist to communicate anger. Typically, this behavior is correctly understood by others and therefore can be used as a convention. A child would be deeply disappointed if the raising of the fist produced a burst of laughter.

BLIND SPOTS IN THE USE OF CONVENTIONS

In trying to understand maladjustment, it is important to discover how the patient hides meanings with conventions. For conventions not only convey immediate meaning to others, but often also convince the sender that he means the obvious, even though powerful adjuvant cues do not support this claim. A husband tells his wife, "Drive safely," just when she has had a "close shave." To the husband, "Drive safely" means that he wants his wife to be on the alert. His wife, however, experiences the words as an insult—a jab about the incident—and begins to nag about his insulting manner. The husband now feels unfairly attacked. "I didn't mean anything!" he says. Yet his wife interpreted the contextual cues (recent accident) along with the overt message and felt criticized.

Often without awareness, patients use conventions to promote an emotional climate they desire but for which they do not wish to be held responsible. In the case above, the husband engaged his wife in an emotional climate of criticism through the hidden meaning of the message, using the setting as a cue. The husband probably, stylistically and without awareness, wanted to put his wife down and also wanted to feel free to deny this intent. His message skillfully attempted both tasks.

Here is another example: A woman behaved in a manner that made the men she met think she was both charming and shy, yet her unconscious goal was to shock. Her style permitted her to attract males who wished to meet charming but shy females, perhaps with the expectation that they themselves could be assertive with her. On one occasion, this young woman had attracted a returned missionary of a very strict religious sect, and when they got to talking she suddenly said, "Gee, it's fun getting laid." The statement predictably shocked the young man. Unaware of her pleasure in shocking men, she did not recognize that with her style she attracted men with whom she could play her shocking games. She said that she felt this missionary was a little too "thick" and that she wanted "to loosen him up a bit." The missionary reacted as expected: he ran from her. If we want to understand the woman's underlying meaning in using these sequentially discordant cues, we have to look at the consequences of her action. The existential underlying meaning of her behavior is her love test: "Will I be loved in spite of the hurdle I throw in the way?" She obviously was more interested in testing men than in establishing a relationship with them. Yet she did not have to take responsibility for the failed relationships: she could feel that she wanted to help the men become a little more liberated, and that they were dumb enough to reject her offer. By proclaiming him too narrow-minded, the woman could add the missionary to her collection of men who had rejected her.

The base of such discordance is found in conflicting motivations. The secret love test was administered because the woman wanted to experience (1) that she was attractive and open-minded (after all, she offered intimacy) and (2) that she was rejected, or at least that her offer was rejected. Since the rejection of her offer was elicited covertly, one may speculate that this woman was motivated not only to attract but also to repulse. Such love tests are not infrequent and take many different forms. In this particular case, the young woman labeled her slang as a "challenge." She was not aware of the underlying meaning and would likely behave again in a similar manner.

The wish to misunderstand one's own basic motivations is frequently found in people with problems. Such individuals often experience responses that they term undesirable—often rejection or hostility—yet they do not learn from the responses. They typically mislabel the meaning of their own messages and appear to be blind to their true impact. They do not want to face their hidden motivation. They are, in fact, perpetuating their particular psychological state with this discordance and, in the process, report that they cannot understand why the world treats them the way it does.

While many patients are not aware of the misuse of their messages, others are fully aware. These people know that they do not get the response they desire, but they feel that there is nothing they can do about it. To stay with one of our examples, a person might communicate a gruff "Good morning" to her secretary. In this case, she knows that she *sounds* gruff, but does not know why she would want to *be* gruff. When challenged, she simply states, "It's just my style." She does not learn from the bewildered response she obtains, for she feels that she cannot make a change. Even when she is not gruff with the secretary, her attempts at gentleness sound hollow and cold. She reports, "I'm just not that way."

Our best explanation as to why people who know their shortcomings may be unwilling to give them up is that even when there is awareness, changes are not made because the cross-motivations demand responses that partially fulfill both motives expressed in the discordant message. The response, although puzzling to the sender, fulfills some unconscious wish. The young woman we described earlier may receive gratification from setting men up to shock them. Even were she to recognize her scenario, it is likely she would still seek the responses required by her discordant motivations, because insight is not enough to provoke change. She has actually to experience uncertainty to explore her motivational discordance. The middle-level manager who treats her secretary gruffly is conscious of her conflicting needs to be seen as socially appropriate (conventional meaning) and to experience herself as tough and insensitive to criticism. She is afraid of experiencing and expressing tenderness and permitting others to view her tender side as well. This manager probably developed this pattern out of early experience. She may have been punished for displaying caring in an overt way. Warmth met with ridicule or indifference is replaced by a veneer of toughness. Responding with a lack of genuine warmth or involvement prevents injury. Hiding behind convention insulates further. So the delicious sense of satisfaction results from this compromise—and keeps the pattern in motion.

The above analysis should give the therapist useful cues about how to discover the rules the patient has learned. In this process, the therapist must observe the patient's behavior sequences with great care and empathy. These patterns or silent rules are very stable, as if written in granite; they are an individual's personal commandments. The therapist must attempt to discover not only what the rules are, but also what psychological advantage accrues to the person who maintains them.

UNUSUAL CONVENTIONS

Sometimes when an individual attempts simultaneously to express and to hide strong feelings, the discordance does not work properly; the feelings are so powerful that they are recognized even when hidden under the safest conventions. Unable to hide, the sender uses personalized and idiosyncratic language that permits the expression of feelings and greatly minimizes the danger of being understood. An illustration of such a case might be an individual's belief that he is being tracked by aliens and the patient's statement that he is being followed by a UFO. The patient's fear of having his feelings identified has become so severe that he does not wish to let the others know what is bothering him. Nevertheless, this message communicates that *something* is bothering him. He does not communicate in ordinary, conventional terms but still uses a standard convention, at least a symbolic one—the kind of language used in some modern poetry, which may have an emotional impact on us without our having a thorough understanding of its literary meaning.

The patient's unusual statement about being followed by a UFO probably evokes in the respondent a picture of danger as well as a recognition of the inappropriateness of the statement. Through much practice, the patient knows that the UFO talk elicits a shock reaction. It is quite possible that the patient has found a sense of existence, a desirable compromise in promoting these feelings of danger and unreality in the respondent. (Many mental patients have unbelievable skill in promoting feelings of anger, mirth, jealousy, strangeness, or even bewilderment. These patients are also usually adept at finding respondents who are predisposed to have strong feelings in the patient's area of skills.) The mental patient, through the unusual use of conventions, is typically very successful in reaching personal goals. Such patients are, after all, well practiced in their one area of competency. We observed a case where a patient restricted the response activity of another person by babbling nonsense syllables. He clearly was hiding some vulnerable wish (perhaps to be an infant), and yet he could achieve the impact, showing his sense of helplessness, on the respondent. We propose that the sender is motivated, albeit unconsciously, to create these feelings in the respondent. The patient who elicits an emotional state in the respondent very likely experiences this as success, and the response thus serves to reinforce the patient's state of adjustment.

The interpretation that this behavior is unconsciously motivated is based on the observation that the manipulation is likely to be repeated again and again, that the patient does not learn from responses perceived as painful, and that the response often seems to fit into the patient's overall psychological economy.

CONVENTIONS IN THERAPY

The increasingly closer contact between people in modern civilization, which brings so many previously isolated subcultures into contact with one another, also creates a need for each individual to have a greatly expanded knowledge of conventions. The child has the ever-growing task of mastering the conventions of the age: knowing what these conventions mean is a precondition to growing up successfully in society, for without this knowledge one cannot successfully predict, control, or even respond to the behavior of others.

The use and misuse of conventions is in fact one of the keys to understanding others, as well as to recognizing psychological deficits. The maladjusted person who has developed blind spots for conventional information or who uses conventions to express private, unusual, unconventional meanings is necessarily socially deprived, even though this person may be successful in achieving a response that fits into his private psychological economy. Such a person is surely unable to communicate efficiently with others. One might say that through messages this person reinforces the maladjustment, continually proving to the self that he can remain safe and yet obtain some gratification from engaging others. Such a person is an idiosyncratic communicator.

To understand the concerns used by a particular patient, the therapist uses himself as an instrument. When receiving information, the therapist can grasp the meaning of the person's use of conventions by speculating about what sort of response the information demands. The information "I am terribly depressed" will ordinarily constrict the respondent (therapist) and arouse sympathy, concern, or even anger. The experienced therapist, however will not stay with these emotions for long, but will wonder why it is important for the patient to arouse such emotions. The therapist will look at both the procedures the patient uses to achieve the impact and the motivations behind these procedures. The experienced therapist will be able to disengage from the emotional climate created for him, and will be in a position to give other than reinforcing responses to the patient.

6

Interventions in Psychotherapy

When the therapist has formulated hypotheses to answer the question, Where does the patient hurt? he is in a position to formulate tentative therapeutic objectives specific to this patient. These objectives should then determine the nature and focus of interventions in working with the patient's areas of vulnerability.

Many systems of psychotherapy have developed objectives at the extremes of both generality and specificity. Schools of therapy with very general objectives describe goals for the patient with such terms as "maturity," "adjustment," "well-being," and "reaching potential." These general objectives are useful and universally desirable, yet they do not give the therapist much guidance. With such general goals, much of the therapeutic hour may be "free-floating." Good reasons for such a "nondirective" approach are often advanced: it will give the patient the chance to express thoughts and ideas that were not rehearsed and will permit the patient to take the initiative in looking at problems and alternative solutions.

At the other extreme are those schools of therapy that maintain that certain targeted goals (behaviors) must be isolated and rigorously practiced, improved, or erased to the exclusion of other exploration. These types of therapy may be seen as proceeding down a relatively narrow pathway. When we speak of maintaining a specific therapeutic objective, we do not want to squelch the searching attitude of the patient. On the contrary, we want to follow up on major themes that the patient has introduced. Thus, the therapeutic objective should not be seen as discouraging a searching attitude on the part of the patient, but rather as a way of helping the patient find new answers for often-hidden dilemmas.

We should note that the therapist may not be readily able to formulate specific objectives for the patient simply because the subtle dynamics of the patient's communication have not yet been decoded (see Chapter 4). Therapists have learned to deal with this uncertainty, primarily by encouraging the patient to provide more information, especially when patients are sending out strong emotional signals. A simple but useful device to achieve this end is to assume a listening attitude and to give short responses that communicate to the patient that the therapist is interested and wants to know more. This type of "delay" response provides the therapist both with more information and with more time to formulate a meaningful hypothesis about the patient's vulnerability, a safe "perch" from which to assess the emotional pulls of the patient's interaction style. Thus, delay responses such as "Mm, hmm," "Go on," and "Tell me more about . . ." are more than listening devices. They are the prototype of asocial (emotionally disengaged) responses, which fail to reinforce the patient's expectation or hidden wish. An example might be:

> *Patient:*   I hate you.
> *Therapist:*   Go on.

When delay is used, the patient's subtle expectations are blocked, and he will experience uncertainty about them and may begin to explore alternative routes to meeting needs. Delay responses also provide the therapist with time to obtain a deeper understanding of where the patient "hurts" and to formulate more strategic responses. In the above exchange, the patient may have had one of many covert wishes in mind—to scan the therapist to determine if an angry statement would prompt rejection, fear, comparison, or any of a host of secretly desired reactions. Instead, the patient was faced with a caring sort of uncertainty while the therapist had time to search for the meaning of the exchange.

Therapeutic objectives have two goals in communication analysis:

1. Through exploration of the communication process, the patient will experience how he creates a share of the problem.
2. The therapist's responses will provide the patient with the experience that his covert messages (which are the means by which problems are created) are no longer responded to in the customary manner. This experience, in turn, is thought to lead to exploratory behavior.

How a therapeutic formulation for a proper intervention is made can be aided with some case material.

A young woman came to the sixth hour with the statement, "You did it! You made me accept this job [top management instead of administrative assistant], and I feel totally inadequate. I constantly make a fool of myself. You are incompetent not to know what I can and cannot do. How dare you set yourself up as a therapist when you don't know what you are doing?"

The therapist was reasonably certain that he had not given any such advice. While listening to the patient, he experienced a wish to defend himself, but checked this wish and responded with delay statements like "Mm, hmm, tell me more about it." This statement immediately provided the patient with the knowledge that the therapist would not accept responsibility for her change of job, but more than that, she obtained the information that her communication did not arouse defensive behavior or guilt in the respondent. The therapist then formulated the hypothesis, on the basis of this and other similar behavior, that the patient's "hurt" led her to arouse guilt in an authority figure to justify her advancement. She apparently was incapable of accepting responsibility for striving to get ahead, and needed to blame someone else.

Why was this idea of getting ahead so dangerous to her? The therapist answered tentatively that staying in an inferior position was perhaps desirable for this woman. A number of statements made by the patient came to his mind: "Mother always wants me to be in there slugging. . . . I am their [parents'] only hope; they want me to support them. Girls who are too far ahead in the game never find a husband."

He then formulated the hypothesis that this woman had "libidinized" her inferior position, that it was to her a way of arousing guilt in the parents whom she believed to have pushed her too hard.

Although the available data fit the hypothesis, the therapist needs to constantly test the theory at hand. Here, the therapist may have erred in his selection of events, and this hypothesis may have been wrong. Correcting a hypothesis with new evidence is a constant procedure. However, this hypothesis did give the therapist an operating base. He had experienced and understood the patient's attempts to arouse guilt in him, had not responded in a conventional customary manner (feeling defensive), and instead had shifted the responsibility for accepting the job back to the patient for further exploration.

Given a hypothesis, the therapist could formulate the therapeutic objectives: (1) to have the patient learn by experience what her messages meant to another person (to learn how she perpetuated her problem), and (2) to help with the discovery of other more adequate ways of maintaining her integrity with her mother or other authority figures.

Having identified a therapeutic objective, the therapist will work toward it by developing a sensitivity to the behavior he has identified. Here, for example, he became sensitive to patient messages designed to evoke guilt in him; and message by message, he responded to the patient's subtle manipulation, providing her with the experience that this behavior no longer created the desired emotional climate. His responses were designed to guide her into a feeling of uncertainty about her message. His aim was for her to open up the closed question and inspect whether her guilt-arousal mechanism was the most adequate behavior to achieve her goal of integrity.

The patient had just blamed the therapist for advising her to take the better job. He responded with:

Therapist: I am a quack, an ignoramus. How could I have advised you toward such a miserable goal?

The therapist at this point was using a paradigmatic approach (Nelson, 1962), which is intended to "join the patient's resistance" rather than fight it, and force the patient to use her ego strength rather than her defenses. This response, sailing with the wind, as it were, shifted the responsibility back to the patient, who could not longer use a "hostile" environment as an alibi. With this response, the therapist created some uncertainty within her as to the righteousness of her case. Even though he believed he was not to blame, the therapist did not defend himself.

Patient: You are such a quack. I don't think I should come to see you again.

The patient had not given up her guilt-arousal scheme and was still determined to win her point. Or perhaps she was really testing the therapist with this message, to ascertain if he was truly disengaged.

Therapist: To seek help from an ignorant man like myself, this is crazy.

The therapist exaggerated the guilt-arousal mechanism in the best paradigmatic tradition, at the same time telling the patient that her guilt-arousal had not created the emotional climate she desired. But it also told the patient the therapist was not angry—that he would stay with her despite her punishing tests.

Patient: Well, I guess I could have said no to the boss, but you must never do that to me again.

The patient then acted from the experience of realizing that the job change was, after all, her responsibility, and added the last sentence as a face-saving device.

Therapist: But you are stuck with being a manager rather than an administrative assistant. You are in there slugging now, as your mother wants you to be.

The therapist wanted to tie in the fear of advancement with the fear of being ruled by Mother. On the surface, this sounds like a comment directed toward a greater insight. In this particular context it was, however, a truly disengaging statement. The therapist provided the patient with the experience that the guilt-arousal behavior was unnecessary: the real problem had not been solved but was still around.

Patient: Maybe Mother was right after all.

This statement was probably said in irony, a ploy to test the therapist's interest in this subject. The statement also implied that on this playful level the patient was considering a new exploration: how to deal with Mother.

The formulation of therapeutic objectives was based on information available to the therapist. He accumulated information from various sources: the content of the message, its covert component, and his own response to it. Certainly, he could have erred. A therapist's most convincing quality is to be aware of this fact.

BEING AND THINKING

We speak specifically of the patient's "experiencing" rather than "having" insight because the two therapeutic objectives can be most successfully realized if the patient is alerted to his own, immediate behavior both when it occurs (is caught in the act of behaving, as it were) rather than when it is discussed in the abstract. This immediacy is essential because the patient is more likely to recode when his expectations are unfulfilled and he is in a state of uncertainty. One can compare this process to the learning of a new service in tennis. The player will become uncertain if one points out how to hold the racket; provided there is motivation, the player can better learn to restyle when the faults are pointed out on the spot.

The analogy is only a crude approximation to what happens in the therapy hour, and the key phrase "provided there is motivation" suggests the greatest difficulty in therapy. We know that the patient is often as much motivated to maintain the "libidinal" position as to get well. That is precisely the reason why the first therapeutic objective—alerting the patient to the fact that he perpetuates the problem through communication—is not sufficient in and of itself.

The patient says, "Yes, I see now how I always arouse the anger of my wife by telling her the very things I know will make her mad, but I can't help myself." Translated into psychological language, the patient says, "Part of me needs to create the anger in her." An understanding of how the patient does so is clearly not enough. Patients often find such "understandings" to be comfortable hiding spots, and bask in their newfound static position without submitting to the risks of sampling alternative behavior patterns. The patient must be brought to *experience* that the anger he arouses in his wife, contrary to his beliefs, gives him some gratification and perhaps some sense of freedom. Only when he *experiences* that, ever so subtly, he is seeking to anger her, can he learn that his behavior is not simply "part of me" but has purpose.

In other words, the patient does not learn insightful phrases, but accepts responsibility for covert communications made unknowingly, because they have been recognized by the therapist. The therapist, not the patient, has the insight! The patient, not the therapist, takes responsibility.

Thereafter, the patient experiences that the old subtle communications no longer hide intent, and needs to recode. Besides being alerted to just how he is coding anger, the patient is also alerted to the fact that personal behavior (such as angering a spouse) has meaning within his psychological economy.

Once a patient learns to take responsibility for being the agent who *wants* to anger his wife, a host of new questions, all previously off-bounds, is open to him, and he can now explore for himself whether more adequate ways exist for dealing with the problems he had previously treated automatically, without success. Every patient must experience uncertainty before undertaking this new exploration.

We realize that this formulation sounds almost like Ellis's Rational Emotive Therapy (1964), or other current cognitive-behavioral approaches, but there is a difference. Ellis argues the patient into behaving rationally, while we propose to provide the patient with responses that give the experience of beneficial uncertainty about previous expectations. We propose that with the proper, disengaged response by a therapist, the patient is placed in a position to make more adequate choices. The therapist is not representing rational behavior to the patient, but rather a unique relationship that permits the patient to accept a transitory state of uncertainty without having to provide a defense. The uniqueness probably comes from the "representative" nature of the relationship, the unreality of it, and its temporary sanctuary from the world of judgments.

DISENGAGEMENT AND BENEFICIAL UNCERTAINTY

The therapeutic hour gives the patient an unusual opportunity to explore. The tennis player experiments with new technique in practice, not during a critical match. People apparently cannot look at their behavior objectively when they feel defensive, threatened, or judged.

The therapist, trained to listen without making evaluative decisions, needs to show acceptance, understanding, and caring even though there may be a general therapeutic objective such as broadening the patient's choices. In our analysis of the communication process it became clear that the permissive atmosphere that the therapist must create to allow the patient new explorations is a necessary but not sufficient condition for therapeutic change. The purpose of this permissive condition is to give the patient freedom to inspect his previously automatic behavior, to open new questions and choices, and to try out new behaviors. For a patient to explore life in this manner, he first must become uncertain of previous behavior. This experience of uncertainty is a luxury that most people cannot afford to tolerate in ordinary living, unless in very specific areas, which are labeled "challenges."

A sense of uncertainty in areas not labeled challenge is experienced by individuals who permit their vulnerability to be exposed. If a man feels vulnerable because he questions his masculine adequacy, for example, he will generally hide this vulnerability from recognition by others, and often even from himself. When he leads others to think that he is uncertain, he risks being hurt. So he avoids expressing feelings of uncertainty—or when he does so, he more often than not misleads the respondent in order to defend himself.

However, there are various methods of leading a person toward accepting uncertainty in order to influence behavior. We are very familiar with advertisements that use such methods of arousing uncertainty as the warning that we may have a mouth odor or that we need life insurance because we may collapse any day now. The psychology graduate student who uses a "psychological line" with her boyfriend is a familiar example of the use of uncertainty-arousal in everyday living. So is the demagogue reaching for votes.

Although the purpose of therapeutic uncertainty is to open options, the arousal of uncertainty by breaking down defenses can also close off avenues. The movie gambit of a husband who drives his wife insane by making everything she does seem wrong, until she stops doing things and retreats into a world of her own, is probably exaggerated, but it serves as an illustration of how uncertainty-arousal without safety can produce constricted responses rather than exploratory behaviors. Uncertainty aroused in a hostile atmosphere, such as when schoolchildren use ridicule, is likely to produce anything but exploratory behavior in the victim. And creating merely a permissive atmosphere is not enough, for the patient may enjoy this uniquely safe experience without making new exploratory efforts. The patient must have the rug pulled out from underneath, but also must have a safe place to land.

What makes a safe landing spot? Or, to put the question another way, what makes the experience of uncertainty beneficial and growth-producing? A first introduction to this asocial form of treatment may lead the reader to see therapy as primarily punishing to the client, especially, as in our text, if key interventions are isolated to illustrate the input of uncertainty on the patient. We would like to stress the importance of creating a warm, caring climate of exploration in the hour. And we should note that the effective therapist often responds to patient in a socially engaged manner—but is aware of this response. We can hardly imagine a therapist who is fully disengaged at all times with a patient; no patient would remain in the consulting room for very long!

Within the experience of a caring and permissive atmosphere, the patient has to be challenged to experience and tolerate uncertainty, but as such a challenge does occur within the framework of a permissive atmosphere, the sense of uncertainty experienced by the patient is likely to be beneficial— one that leads to an exploration rather than a defense. While on first inspection this challenge—to experience and tolerate uncertainty in a beneficial emotional climate—may sound somewhat contradictory, the behaviors involved are not. The permissive climate is created by the therapist's responses, which do not question the patient's right to think or feel in any way he wants. Listening, following the patient production with care, giving responses which communicate to the patient that he is understood and not judged—all these responses give the patient experience with a therapist who has genuine concern and who shows that the patient is of some importance to another person, and with a climate in which the patient may test his fears and hopes.

However, some behaviors of the therapist also contain a very real challenge to the patient because of the asocial character of the responses used. The "Mm, hmm" response given when the patient speaks of suicide, for example, is essentially an asocial one, as it does not follow the general social convention of either reprimand or sympathy. The therapist's challenge consists in making the patient—within the permissive atmosphere— uncertain of the expectations that are associated with *the patient's* messages. The asocial responses of the therapist necessarily create uncertainty in the patient, who can no longer properly predict the outcome of behavior in this setting. The uncertainty that the patient gradually learns to tolerate becomes the very basis for new hopes about life.

PREFACE TO BEING ASOCIAL: KNOWING ONE'S SOCIAL OUTPUT

Before the therapist can freely use the tactic of altering his style of communication in response to a client's evocative message, the therapist should have a working knowledge of his standard impact on others. If the effective therapist needs to recalibrate the emotional climate for a particular client, that therapist should know at what levels the thermostat is set to begin with. If, for example, it would be wise to provide a new experience of warmth to a client who subtly pushes others (and the therapist) away, the therapist should have some idea of his baseline level of output in this area. A "cooler" therapist, in this instance, may have to take extra measures in gauging a response. Conversely, when a patient is making attempts to please the therapist with dutiful reports of change, acknowledging the therapist's expertise, the "warmer" therapist may have to "turn down" ordinary responses in order not to accept the patient's accomplishments as his own. Response styles vary with therapists as with clients, and a predisposition toward certain feelings (e.g., seriousness, humor) need not be a handicap. Indeed, such predisposing styles may serve the therapist well, if they are accompanied by awareness on the part of the therapist of the general impact of the style. Of course, it is helpful if the therapist is able to vary his style of communicating as the clinical situation dictates.

The therapist is handicapped only if unaware of his characteristic social output. Therapists, of course, are not immune from the same sort of motivated hiding in which their patients indulge. Thus, it is most important that therapists maintain a supervisory or consulting relationship in order to monitor the stylistic features that are out of the range of their own radar screens.

GENERAL AND SPECIFIC DISENGAGEMENT RESPONSES

There are two categories of asocial responses—general and specific—that serve the therapist in disengaging from the expectations of the patient. The first category contains the generically evolved responses that are often given in the absence of real understanding of what the patient is saying. The "Mm, hmm," or "Go on" type of response is frequently used when the therapist is still unable to respond more specifically. With this response, the patient is told that the therapist is listening but that the relationship is an asocial one: none of the socially expected responses is given.

The second category of asocial responses is not as general in its aim. These responses aim at specific disengagements and are in the nature of counterpersuasive responses. The labels *interpretation, reflection,* and *probing* have been given to responses that guide the patient through a state of uncertainty to act out specific behaviors. These responses are counterpersuasive inasmuch as they make the therapist's value system understandable to the patient. The therapist translates the patient's message into a new, dynamic language, not only teaching the patient to think in a new language, but also freeing him from the ordinary consequence of his own language. Korzybski (1958) recognized this process and emphasized the aspect of reteaching language, making the error, perhaps, of thinking that this new language should be "more precise." It seems more likely that the new language the patient learns simply serves to break up earlier associations and suggest new ones. These responses of the therapist are grounded in comprehensive theories that prescribe rather definite consequences through new semantic ordering. By teaching the patient a new language, the therapist becomes both the persuader and the one who arouses beneficial uncertainty. The exchange below illustrates specific disengagement responses and both their asocial character and their persuasiveness.

A female patient says, "Mother told me I couldn't go out with the boy." The therapist gives an interpretation: "Mother's love for you makes her very protective."

This interpretation may or may not be the best one but it is first of all asocial, for it does not follow the social expectation of the message, does not say, "Go anyway, and be a person in your own right," or "Mother probably has your welfare in mind." The therapist trains the woman to think, "Whenever mother interferes with your choice to go out with a boy, she is old-fashioned and shows a bit of constricting love." Of course, this represents the therapist's language and way of looking at things, and the belief that learning new language will help the patient discontinue her usual associations and eventually aid her in exploring alternative relationships with her mother.

A "reflection of feeling" is also an asocial, counterpersuasive response. Another therapist may respond differently to our female patient's statement, "Mom told me I could not go out with the boy."

Therapist 2: You feel angry at your Mom for this interference.

This type of reflection is again asocial. It is persuasive inasmuch as it trains the patient to think of her own emotional response rather than of her mother's actions. Again, this asocial, persuasive response is thought to be helpful for the patient because she learns a new language and, with it, new ways of looking at things.

Although such responses are effective, often the therapist is not really aware that he is, in fact, persuading the patient. It is likely that the therapist would be more effective if the communicative meaning of his action were fully recognized.

Probing, too, can be counterpersuasive. A third therapist might respond in yet a different way to the same statement.

Therapist 3: "Did your father mind as well?"

As previously, the asocial nature is clear, though the question appears to minimize the impact of the asocial character of the response. (Questions are conventionally allowed to interrupt the social expectation of the message.) The statement is clearly counterpersuasive because it teaches the patient that she should be concerned with the family triangle as an interrelated part of her father's actions.

It has been shown here that responses can serve specific and useful therapeutic objectives. The therapist should not suffer the delusion of being merely a midwife; the therapist is also the child's parent. He should plan responses to arouse beneficial uncertainty in the patient, and use them to reach a given therapeutic objective. Responses are the therapist's tool.

ENGAGING TO DISENGAGE

Before pursuing other, more specific methods of disengagement, we should note that disengaging from a patient's emotional pull involves more of the therapist's repertoire than simply providing verbal surprises. The goals of disengagement include providing the client with a new emotional climate in response to covert bids for the predictable. Thus, all of the therapist's mannerisms, paralinguistic cues, response latencies, etc., are of major importance. The therapist must present a complete and emotionally congruent message in order to provide the client with the new emotional experience. This is to say that the effective therapist must be a master actor.

If a client's behavior is powerful enough to frighten the therapist, perhaps with threats of suicide, and the therapist is barely able to manage the most basic delay response, the patient will surely be able to read this "whistling in the dark" for what it is. The therapist is emotionally handcuffed, and the patient has achieved another success with the preferred covert style. Similarly, we may consider the patient who consistently and covertly uses a "take care of me" style to evoke protective warmth from the therapist. If the therapist disengages in content only, the patient has learned nothing new on the experiential level. The patient may learn that the therapist has discovered the pattern but is unable to stop repeating it.

What frees the therapist from the patient's manipulation is not an academy award–winning performance, but the ability to experience deeply *and* to recognize how one is feeling and how one is made to feel. Thus, it is important that the therapist actually becomes emotionally engaged by the patient's actions.

Many of our beginning practicum students equate disengagement with maintaining emotional coolness, toughness, being critical of the patient, or with the wearing of a poker face. They believe they are not doing therapy in the Communication Analytic Therapy model if they become engaged. Nothing could be further from our goal. Therapists must be sensitive instruments and permit themselves to be moved in order to gauge the nature and depth of the patient's problem. Only then can adjustments in response style be made.

THE PARADIGMATIC RESPONSE

One class of response, developed by Nelson (1962), is labeled the paradigmatic response. The emotional character of a paradigmatic response is that it "travels with resistance" rather than analysis. When a patient brings to the hour disguised information that serves to maintain a libidinal position or, in simpler terms, to prevent exploration of new alternatives, many therapists feel that this shows the patient's wish to resist change. They therefore seek to make the patient aware of this resistance, with the expectation that the patient needs to know where he is resisting in order to "work through" it. In the paradigmatic response, the therapist desires to help the patient to overcome resistance not by description, but by confrontation through the patient's own resources. To accomplish this feat, the paradigmatic therapist will exaggerate or dramatize the patient's way of behaving and thereby take the "wind out of the sails" of this behavior, with the hope that the respondent can behave more genuinely. A patient may complain to a therapist, "You only see me for the money anyway." The therapist may smile and respond paradigmatically, "Why would anyone want to see a fellow like you for anything but money?"

This response is counterpersuasive. It calls the patient's bluff. But it also brings his worst fears about himself into the open, and in that way trains him to face, not camouflage, those real fears. With this response the patient is taken aback and made to feel uncertain. When said within a positive emotional climate, it is likely to arouse a beneficial uncertainty.

The paradigmatic response often used throughout a whole hour is a dramatic form of disengagement accomplished by role-playing a social engagement. It is played with the strongly implied suggestion to the patient, "Must you really use your social skills in this manner? Is it really necessary to engage me in this way? You can face these fearful thoughts without the anticipated danger coming true."

There are, of course, dangers in the use of the paradigmatic response, and they lie in failing to properly estimate the comfort of the emotional climate. If the patient feels that the therapist is not playing a role paradigmatically, but in fact means what is said, the response can bring a severe threat into the hour. However, even when the patient misunderstands the meaning of a paradigmatic response and sees it as the therapist's real feeling, the experienced therapist will be able to deal with such distortion. A patient who complains that most men eventually "come on" to her says to her therapist "I like you so much, I even dream of you." The therapist responds paradigmatically, "You want me to lie with you on the couch?" This response was designed to recognize the mildly implied sexual wish in the message, with the therapeutic objective of giving the patient the experience that her own subtly suggestive sexual communication may have something to do with the complaint that men only respond to her sexually. The response verbalizes that which was supposed to remain hidden. This dangerous exchange can be successfully accomplished only by the therapist who is actually free from "countertransference," i.e., from desire for the patient. Only the disengaged therapist can continue:

> *Patient:* Yes, why don't you come?
> *Therapist:* Tell me what we would do if I were to come.
> *Patient:* Hell, you weren't born yesterday.
> *Therapist:* What would you want me to do?
> *Patient:* Embrace me, care for me—but you're just hedging. Why don't you come?
> *Therapist:* You are challenging me to come?
> *Patient:* I sure am.
> *Therapist:* What would you do if I really were to come over?
> *Patient:* Yell.
> *Therapist:* Because you really were only teasing. You would have again had the experience that a man was only interested in you physically.

This daring exchange gives the patient an immediate experience of her share in the problem of which she complains. The response also contains the suggestion, "Must you really deny responsibility for your sexual wishes?"

The paradigmatic response stresses the ability of the therapist to maintain his role. The patient may not always give up the social expectation of the messages, as she did when she responded, "Yell." The therapist must know when to clarify the meaning and withdraw from the role he has been playing. The therapeutic impact of a well-handled paradigmatic exchange, however, is rewarding, as Nelson's monograph points out.

The paradigmatic response fits well into our theoretical basis of behavior. It is asocial by being too loudly social in its nature. It is so social, indeed, that it forces the patient to deal with his own social behavior as if it were projected into a convex mirror. This view forces the patient to explore new alternatives in behavior.

DEMONSTRATING THE IMPACT

Felder (Ellis, Felder, & Rogers, 1963) demonstrated another technique that could be called paradigmatic, but that concerned a different aspect of the message: when the patient extended unaware expectations to the therapist, the therapist played the role by verbalizing these expectations aloud. For example, when a patient touched the therapist's foot with her own, then quickly moved it away with "Sorry," the therapist sensed that the touching was not accidental. "I liked it when you touched my foot," was the therapist's response. The therapist thus tried to verbalize her unaware expectation in the message, believing that she wanted the therapist to be pleased. In our terms, the therapist attempted to alert the patient to the consequences of her covert coding of information, and to give her the experience that these feelings do not have to stay hidden—that even though they were recognized, no harm actually had occurred.

In addition to being an excellent teaching device for patients, verbalizing or demonstrating the impact of the patient's behavior on the therapist may function as a consistently available disengagement device, especially when the therapist is probing in murky waters. While still struggling to complete a formulation of the problem, the therapist is able to maintain an effectively disengaged vantage point from which to continue information-gathering.

This acting-out process may also offer the patient a degree of flexibility in examining his own behavior. It is as if *both* members of the dyad are able, at times, to step across the consulting room and replay the interaction. Indeed, using a videotape machine may help achieve this goal. Rather than having the impact of "I've got you now," the instant replay provides enough distance so that the patient is able to join forces with the therapist in providing a play-by-play commentary. Of course, the engaged therapist may use videotape to "catch" the patient, but doing so may only serve to further resistance.

An example of how videotape feedback may be used in gaining beneficial distance involves a family session in which a distraught mother was threatening to abandon her children because of their lack of cooperation around the house:

> *Patient:*   (screeching) I've had it with you three. I'm going to the nearest adoption agency and dump you. Now do you care? Now do you know how I feel? Why don't you say something?
> *Children:* (silent, with bowed heads)

Playback with commentary followed. During playback, all family members were smiling. The urgent climate had changed.

> *Therapist:* That was quite a performance.
> *Patient:*   (smiling in amazement) My God, do I really look like that?
> *Therapist:* You held the stage and quieted your audience. Is that what you wanted to do?
> *Patient:*   (laughing) I think I'm overreacting! How could anyone take me seriously?

The feedback here provided the patient and her family with a safe amount of distance from the engaged interaction, allowing them to gain perspective. If the therapist had merely pointed out how the mother succeeded in pushing the children away, only further defensive statements might have been elicited from the mother—e.g., "I've had it!"

RATIONAL EMOTIVE THERAPY

Even Ellis (1977, 1994) and other cognitive-behavioral therapists can be said to use paradigmatic responses, though they often give a different explanation for them. If a patient were to say, "I cannot marry this boy. It would hurt mother," Ellis perhaps would respond, "Why not hurt her? She is the tyrant who hurts you by having trained you not to hurt her—the worst kind of tyranny, because you cannot even fight her outright." This response also exaggerates the social expectations of the message. "It would hurt mother" is a nice, considerate statement that demands social endorsement. Ellis does not give endorsement, but instead attacks the convention. He admits that his responses are persuasive, though he believes they are persuasive insofar as they help people engage in clear, rational thinking. Ellis's responses probably work because they interrupt the patient's social expectation in a beneficial climate.

The paradigmatic response is a way of playing at social involvement: even though the exaggeration makes it asocial in nature, it sounds like a social response. Some therapists feel uneasy about it. It seems to bring a half-honest, manipulative note into the therapeutic relationship. The serious, searching therapist and the therapist ready to use a smile or a game are both deeply concerned with effecting a beneficial change in their patients. They play the role most comfortable for them, and it would be difficult to state that one method is superior to the other.

COGNITIVE-BEHAVIORAL THERAPY

The almost universal appeal and acceptance of cognitive-behavioral therapy appears to stem from the very "straightforward and practical approach; bad thinking and interpreting lead to psychological difficulties" (Gorman, 1996, p. 51). The application of this therapy extends to the idea that when we teach patients better thinking habits they experience relief from their symptoms. Similar to the approach taken by Ellis and others in the rational-emotive school, the cognitive-behavioral therapist seeks to discover and then confront the error-filled or negatively biased patterns of thought held by the patient. Aaron Beck (1987) used the term "schemas" to describe cognitive patterns with stable characteristics through which the patient interprets experience. He reported depressive schemas as rigid or occurring in the extreme, without shades of gray. Cognitive-behavioral therapists following

Beck's paradigm differ from Ellis's followers in that they actively seek to confront evidence for faulty thinking and generalization while Rational Emotive Therapy practitioners focus more on patients' emotional overreaction to evidence. Consider as an example the depressive parent of a child who gets caught with drugs at school and berates himself for being a bad parent. Ellis might attempt to get the patient to accept that he couldn't be a perfect parent at all times. In other words, he attacks the impact of the conclusion. Beck would take the more empirical approach and search out and confront evidence regarding the idea that this father was (or was not) an inadequate parent. Beck's process would eventually move to the point of working with the father on the idea of being perfect in every facet of parenting as a means of feeling well adjusted. The cognitive-behavioral model helps provide the patient with a new or asocial experience in that the therapist and the patient work together to interrupt the fixed action pattern of the patient interpreting his behavior within the context of a fixed, possibly negative schema. Even if the empirical focus of cognitive-behavioral therapy uncovers behaviors that might need to be worked on by the patient, they are viewed within a manageable context, and not simply as proof supporting a negative schema. From a communication analysis point of view, we remind those therapists using cognitive-behavioral techniques to question the patient's need to interpret (or misinterpret) data into schemas that continue to provide negative experience. Even though such schemas are negative and painful, some benefit from maintaining the problem may still be involved.

HYPNOSIS

Hypnosis in the psychotherapeutic hour has been used most often to (1) recover particular memories that are difficult to locate, (2) assist in symptom removal, and (3) help a patient relax.

We should be aware that there is no physiological indicator, independent of testimonials and judgment, to show that a hypnotic trance really is present in a given person. We should also be aware that the literature on hypnosis is controversial in many of its findings. The reports of lasting changes in personality characteristics, state of adjustment, state of concentration, effectiveness of learning, etc., can be seriously questioned in the light of numerous contradictory findings.

Using hypnosis to discover early memories is a doubtful enterprise. In his early investigations of hypnosis as used during World War II, Orne (1961) pointed out that an informant under hypnosis will produce information but, unfortunately, not reliable information. Consequently, it is very doubtful that the early memories produced under hypnosis result, in fact, from anything more than the subject's wish to please the therapist. Ongoing controversies such those surrounding hypnotically retrieved "repressed" memories of trauma remind us how unclear the information retrieved during hypnosis may be.

Although both hypnosis and waking-state devices can be used to induce relaxation, hypnosis is probably inefficient in symptom removal. There are, however, some ways in which hypnosis can be used to *initiate* symptom removal. Some particular disorders (such as stuttering) can often be temporarily affected by a suggestion not to stutter while under hypnosis (Kroger, 1976). A person thus may learn that he has the ability not to stutter. This experience produces a sense of "uncertainty," which may result in a wish to discover why he would "want" to stutter. Such a temporary demonstration then motivates the patient to search for alternatives. Occasionally, of course, a symptom can be directly removed by hypnotic suggestion. That should not surprise us too much, as some individuals can even be talked out of their symptoms (such as smoking) at least temporarily or can abandon certain behaviors like smoking or engaging in risky sexual practices simply after reading specific reports.

Nevertheless, from a communications point of view, hypnosis is quite useful. Conventionally, it stands for a shift of responsibility from the subject to the hypnotist, a shift readily believed in by both the public and many practitioners. There is a widespread belief that a hypnotic subject in a trance cannot control himself. While this may not be true, we have here a medium of communication that, conventionally speaking, does leave the patient free from responsibility for thoughts and behaviors. A medium for shifting responsibility to the therapist is an exceedingly useful tool for intervention in therapy—especially when the patient needs to hide, is afraid of responsibility, or seeks a sanctuary.

Hypnosis may be particularly useful in cases where somatic symptoms are found. A patient's symptom can be viewed as a communication to the effect that he does not wish to be held responsible for behavior. In hypnotic treatment, what the patient says is not important, but it may be necessary for the patient to discover whether talking itself is dangerous. This discovery seems to be useful in hypnotherapy: during a hypnotic trance, the patient can discover which messages can be expressed without fear of retaliation.

Another use of hypnosis in psychotherapy has been hypnotic role-playing. Here, hypnosis is used in order to obtain a characteristic shift of responsibility. The therapist suggests that patients live through the most-feared episodes of their lives. A newlywed man afraid of sexual relations with his wife might be told, under hypnosis, to imagine that he was approaching his wife, had made a pass at her, etc.; a patient afraid of talking back to her boss would role-play being assertive under the command of the therapist. This method makes use of the "shift syndrome." The therapist openly accepts responsibility for bringing the patient face to face with fears in order to provide him with "cognitive rehearsal" to explore himself in relation to the feared acts.

ROLE-PLAYING

Ever since Moreno (1972) popularized it in the form of psychodrama, role-playing has been a frequently utilized intervention in psychotherapy. Called by a variety of names—such as behavior rehearsal or social skill training—in role-playing, as in hypnosis, the overriding principle is that an individual is only playacting, that is, that he is not fully responsible for the behavior. Role-playing presents a trial situation in which to discover one's freedom of action.

However, even role-playing can be a severe threat to some individuals, and they may refuse to act out certain modes of behavior even though there can be no retaliation. A young man once was supposed to say to his father, played by another patient, the harmless-sounding phrase, "Thanks, Dad," but could not bring himself to do it. Of course, whether the "Thanks, Dad" was eventually said is not important; the young man experienced his difficulty in the open, and this was enough to arouse uncertainty.

Role-playing has had many uses. A hospital patient–government group once decided to role-play a different woman's symptom at each of their meetings. The woman wailed loudly every few minutes, so the other patients decided to break into a loud wailing chorus whenever she wailed. The woman continued to wail during the hour. Later, when she heard a playback of the behavior, she said, "No wonder they threw me out of my house." She attempted never to wail again. This is not to say that all these episodes turned out beneficially or that they offer examples of successful one-trial learning. But some of these efforts did work, and we attribute their success to the forceful asocial response in a beneficial setting. Failures are possibly due to the patient's inability to perceive the benefits of the setting. In some cases, the patient perceived the imitation of the symptom as an affront, and it is quite possible that the group intent in such cases was not just beneficial: they must also have wished to punish the patient.

At the Utah State Hospital, another role-playing device was an agreement among patients to compete for a prize to be awarded to the one who could prove he had suffered most. This cruel-sounding device was suggested by a patient. The structure of this competition set a new counterpersuasive convention for suffering as something "put on," something under one's control, and something slightly ridiculous. The patients' performances seemed to help the patients take their own suffering less seriously. This asocial competition in a beneficial setting (without malice) was a powerful tool to force patients to become slightly uncertain about their previously automatic self-indulgence in suffering.

The role-playing device has also been used in our work with groups of delinquents, where some of the children took the role of teachers or parents—not so much to learn directly how adults see the situation, but (using our term) to produce pseudosocial responses in a beneficial situation. Conversely, an individual patient may role-play himself or herself in an idealized situation, and in this process learn about his own resistance.

As a tool, role-playing has some very real advantages in providing a patient with a sanctuary. However, in suggesting this method the therapist is also suggesting that, in his opinion, such an artificial climate is needed, that the patient is not yet able to assume responsibility. As the therapist's evaluation of the patient is of great importance to the patient, this method must be, at best, used only as a temporary tool because of its covert message. In the final analysis, the therapist who wants to help the patient must communicate that he holds the patient responsible.

7

Labeling the Therapist's Activity

Based on hundreds of recordings and transcripts of therapeutic hours, an attempt was made to find classes of responses that could easily be distinguished by their impact on the respondent. This attempt to categorize by impact is consistent with the hypothesis that communication is designed to elicit emotions, thoughts, and actions in a respondent. In previous chapters attention was paid to the meaning of the patient's messages, and especially to the differentiation between the messages and manifest and covert cues. We made that distinction in order to show that the patient symbolically represents a problem in many covert messages, that the patient "acts out" maladaptive behavior with discordance in the therapeutic hour. Therapeutic gain was directly linked to what can be called a "sophisticated reinforcement" model: while the patient tries to engage the therapist with such messages, the therapist seeks to break up the redundant message-response association of the patient by using asocial responses. To do so effectively, the therapist not only must carefully analyze the patient's communication, but also must be aware of his own behavior and the information it conveys to the patient. A truly disengaged response by the therapist provides the patient with the experience of challenge and hope. New choices will have to be made.

The very fact that a statement to which a response is expected has been made conveys covert information that goes far beyond the manifest content of the statement. A therapist's statement, such as "Tell me more about your childhood," gives certain covert information to the patient regarding its content. It may tell one patient that the therapist is a person in authority and that the patient is dependent; it may tell another patient that the therapist is bored and wants to fill a silence.

Customarily, psychotherapeutic responses are classified by the intent of the therapist. "Reflection of feeling," "probing," and "interpretation" are all labels describing what the therapist desires to do. In the following sections we categorize the therapist's responses in terms of the impact they are likely to have on the patient rather than on the impact the therapist wishes. This shift of emphasis permits us to look at the covert information the therapist conveys and how it affects the patient. It calls to our attention the reinforcement values of the more subtle behaviors of the therapist, a group of behaviors that are all too often overlooked.

THE THERAPIST'S ACTIVITY PRIOR TO THERAPY

Therapists who want to be certain that they are treating a psychological rather than a physical deficit may refer some patients to a physician for medical examination, often including a neurological examination, before they proceed with treatment. The expectancy created by this recommendation prior to the therapeutic contact is important to the treatment process, because the patient learns from the start that the therapist does not deal directly with physical illness. The therapist's recommendation may allow the patient to avoid treatment: "Then I was really sick!" The therapist should be aware of helping to elicit such responses in the patient.

In most referrals from a court or a school office, much covert information is transmitted prior to the first hour. A student may be suspended from school until the therapist "clears" him. The therapist who ignores the covert cues created by such conditions may overlook critical information needed to properly code the meaning of the patient's statements.

Prior psychological testing also creates preconditions and expectations. Some therapists seek diagnostic information because they feel it will help them understand the patient. Others avoid it because they feel it biases their views or places them in a position where they may be expected to render expert decisions rather than helping the patient to "help himself." Prior diagnostic information is probably helpful in many ways, particularly when the therapist is alert to the covert meaning of the testing experience. For example, the use of prior testing may promote increased fear of a therapist "who knows more about me than I want her to know." The therapist who is on the alert for such information can use it for therapeutic advantage.

The physical setting of the therapist's office also may be significant: it may create feelings and expectancies that can be anticipated. A therapist who practices at home with noisy children next door or in a university office with students or colleagues periodically disregarding the DO NOT DISTURB sign may do well to consider what feelings this setting generates in the patient. Any other peculiarity of the physical setting—the size of the office, the distance from town, or the adequacy of seating facilities—must be considered as eliciting some response in the patient.

THE THERAPIST'S ACTIVITY IN THE THERAPEUTIC HOUR

Requests for Descriptive Information

In the early hours of therapy, some therapists attempt to obtain a description of the patient's problems, a detailed personal history, and some memories of important childhood events. The quest for descriptive information also occurs in later hours. Questions such as "What is your brother's name?" "What, precisely, did you do yesterday after you went to bed?" and "Would you elaborate on what the boss said to you?" represent demands for descriptive or elaborative information. In this type of exchange, the patient is given certain covert cues. The very fact that such questions are asked means that the therapist applies some significance to the answer. The therapist determines the direction of the discussion and implies that the answer will advance therapy. The therapist who asks such questions assumes a directive role.

The question itself is hardly ever as important as the covert information that accompanies it. For example, should a request for elaborative or descriptive information typically come during the pause that follows a discussion of embarrassing problems, the patient is cued to expect the therapist to take the reins at such moments. With this type of intervention the therapist tells the patient that the therapist can be manipulated into changing the direction of the discourse.

Some questions are more leading than others. A patient may say, "I was afraid when I saw all of these people coming toward me." The therapist responds, "Do you recall whether these people were predominantly males?" This question not only elicits specific information, but also hints as to what the therapist sees as significant. The question suggests yes or no answers: it is a question that permits the patient minimum participation in the discourse, giving the therapist responsibility for the exchange. The covert information teaches the patient that the therapist has taken the lead and has specific goals and objectives in mind. This, of course, is not necessarily a wrong plan of action for the therapist, provided that he admits to having elicited certain feelings in the patient and to having persuaded the patient to talk about a restricted set of topics.

There are also the unfortunate times when the therapist covertly shows the patient how inattentive he has been. A patient talks about Freud, and the absentminded therapist asks, "Who is Freud?"

Is the therapeutic process advanced by the use of elaborative or descriptive information obtained through questioning? All therapists need some manifest information to understand the covert cues the patient is giving. But some therapists constantly ask questions, whereas others do so only occasionally, and still others do so only during the first few hours. Some schools

of psychotherapy have outlawed questions altogether, just because the covert information transmitted through the questioning process gives the therapist a directive role inconsistent with their theories. We believe that, if
understanding the covert cues of the patient is the goal, there is certainly a
place for ascertaining the manifest meaning of the messages, with the provi-
sion that the therapist be aware that any question can produce more information than meets the ear.

Requests for Dynamic Information

Sometimes the therapist encourages the patient to give information that
illuminates the thought processes underlying certain activities and suggests
the meanings of covert cues. The techniques for gaining such information
include encouraging free association, dream narratives, and elaborations:
the continuity of thought processes and feelings can be analyzed from this
raw material. It represents information the patient cannot easily give in any
other way. The therapist knows that information the patient can give only
covertly is likely to lie in areas where the patient feels vulnerable. This is
valuable information pertaining to the automatic behavior that promotes the
patient's problems. Dynamic information thus can be an important source of
knowledge about the operations the patient goes through to perpetuate
problems.

In communication analytic therapy, the information is analyzed for its
sequences of emotional meanings. A patient who recounts a dream with
emotional sequences—a reckless, violent truck driver, a beautiful woman in
bed, a hallway that goes on and on—and who tells of waking up in terror
uses certain emotional conventions that present us with a significant silent
rule by which the patient lives. A fear of violence interferes with his love
feelings, and the patient sees no end to the problem (perhaps this last is a
special bid for the therapist's help). The silent rule here tells the patient not
to invest in a love relationship. This type of interpretation is based directly
on the communication of the feeling sequences, rather than on psychoanalytic theory that would deal with this dream in terms of the dream
work—the transition from latent to manifest dream content.

We should note that a request for dynamic information also gives covert
information to the patient, information that is strikingly different from that
involved in the request for elaborative information. With the request for
dynamic information the therapist asks the patient to depend on an authority
figure and to divulge significant information that only the patient possesses
but that can be meaningful to and decoded by only the therapist. In this
exchange the therapist becomes truly indispensable. A request for dynamic
information transmits such covert meaning easily, and the therapist must be
on the alert for the feelings generated by it.

By glancing through records one also discovers that a request for dynamic information often becomes a vehicle for the therapist to communicate to the patient that both of them are now engaged in "detective work." Sometimes the two can even conspire to discover a particularly interesting dynamic, as if they were putting a puzzle together. The therapist may say, "Go ahead. you are on the right track." This type of comment promotes the idea that both are looking for something rather specific, and that the patient will be rewarded for helping in the discovery. The patient may now seek to please the therapist, and much of the true meaning of the covert information can thereby be lost.

But silence, too, transmits covert cues. The therapist's prolonged silence can be perceived by a patient as a competitive bid: who will take the initiative and restart first? Interruptions or "Mm, hmms" often are interpreted by patients as an invitation to elaborate and give novel and more dynamic information. Again, to understand the succeeding productions of the patient, the therapist must recognize that such covert orders have been given.

In client-centered therapy, the "Mm, hmm" reflections are intended to be nondirective leads. We are quite certain that this theoretical intent is likely not fulfilled. In fact the covert information conveyed seems to be contrarily directive. We know from research conducted by Matarazzo, Wiens, Greenspoon, and others that our "Mm, hmms" and even the nodding of the head can encourage certain directions in conversation. The argument is frequently made that any request for dynamic information is leading and interferes with the patient's own productions and thereby offends integrity. Patients, they argue, thus receive the information that their own work is not good enough, that they cannot be trusted to handle their problems by themselves, and that they need to depend on a therapist. Such requests are seen as establishing an unwholesome dependency by reinforcing the idea that the therapist is in authority and determines the course of events. This argument is based on the recognition that simply asking this sort of question subtly conveys the above information.

It is probably correct to assume that, were we intending only to minimize an authority relationship, this type of inquiry would indeed be out of place. The fact is, however, that the therapist assumes authority merely by becoming a resource for help, even though he may not want to directly suggest a solution to patients' problems. The therapist's job is to obtain as much knowledge as possible about the patient's behavior and the discordance the patient suffers. Such knowledge about the covert component of the patient's message is often impossible to acquire without the therapist's asking dynamic questions. Naturally, the therapist has to be aware that the questioning elicits certain emotions and certain responses in the patient, and must be careful as in all other inquiries not to assign these emotions entirely to the patient's stylistic behavior.

Client-centered therapists used to see themselves as entering into a warm, understanding relationship with patients, a relationship involving none or at least few of the therapists' own values. Our thesis is that the therapist is more human and therefore more fallible than this, that the therapist cannot keep his personality out of the treatment hours, and that the patient will skillfully involve and engage the therapist. The therapist's strength is not in remaining uninvolved, but in being able to disengage from involvement in a beneficial manner.

Delay

Typical delay responses are "Mm, hmm," "I heard you," and "Tell me more about it." "I don't understand it yet; elaborate," "Go on," and silence are simply reflections of feeling. Gestures, sounds, and breaking the rhythm of an exchange all can serve to tell the patient of an expectation to go on or to elaborate.

A second intention of a delay response is to say to the patient, "The responsibility is with *you*. Tell me more." Delay responses often advance the relationship and may prevent the therapist from committing serious errors. While a delay response interrupts the engagement and shifts responsibility, it is not a maximally effective response. The therapist has not yet fully understood the patient's message or has been emotionally involved in the patient's expectations, and has consequently used the delay response as a tool to gain time. Since such situations are bound to occur frequently in the hour, the delay responses have a definite place and purpose, provided they alert the therapist to look for the deeper meaning of the patient's statement.

Often the therapist wants to shift the responsibility for further information to the patient. Perhaps the patient wants to depend on the therapist for advice, and the therapist can avoid getting caught in this expectancy only by using the one major tool available: delay responses. These are essentially the marks that encourage the patient to explore further to provide the therapist with more information.

A delay response by the therapist is often needed in the therapeutic process because a patient has learned that security lies in hiding information. The therapist needs to give the patient attention and time to transcend these security considerations. Delay responses are particularly useful when the patient is skillful in scanning the therapist for vulnerabilities: the patient who discovers that a therapist wants to be seen as a nice guy will use this information to render the therapist ineffectual; another patient may discover that a therapist becomes upset when talking about sex, and this information will also provide the patient with weapons to neutralize the therapist. The therapist, on the other hand, can use delay responses both to minimize the risk of giving this sort of information and to avoid engagement. Delay responses are legitimate methods of communication to indicate that the therapist is listening and wants to hear more, but is not ready to respond with more detail. Delay responses are the proper tools for the therapist to use to avoid giving a response when the therapist feels engaged in one of the patient's emotional demands.

Of course, delay responses do not always work perfectly. There are times when a simple reflection or the delay response itself is misunderstood. Here is an illustration of a rather subtle demand:

> *Patient:* I went to the store today and exchanged a pair of trousers. I just told them I did not want them. A year ago [before therapy] I never could have done this.
>
> *Therapist:* You are getting better.

To the extent that the therapist is really involved in the statement, "You are getting better," he has responded socially to the emotional demands of the patient. The patient has asked for praise, and the therapist has provided it. However, if the therapist is not caught in the patient's demand for an agreement that he is getting better, these very same words can be used as a delay statement. The response can be a reflection of feeling rather than a statement of belief. Perhaps the Rogerian recommendation that the statement should be "You feel you are getting better" is a safer way of responding to this particular message, because it reminds both patient and therapist that no value judgment is involved. To the extent that the therapist's response does not communicate personal beliefs, the therapist will be able to deal with a patient's possible misinterpretations as they appear in later statements.

That delay responses can be very meaningful in the patient's life was illustrated by Bernstein, who made up a tape of delay responses typical in psychoanalytic and nondirective psychotherapy: "Mm, hmm," "Tell me more," "Go on," "Oh," etc. He told a patient who had volunteered as an experimental subject that she should press a lever whenever she wanted the therapist to talk, and let the lever go when she wanted to respond. She also was told that the therapist would be in the next room, separated by a one-way mirror. After six hours, the patient was asked how she felt about her therapist. She said, "This was the most wonderful man I've ever met in my life. He gave me such wonderful information. He gave me unbelievably good advice. I really feel I am very obliged to this person." We cite this research to illustrate how important delay responses can be and how often they convey to patients a feeling of acceptance and responsibility for their own lives.

One of the characteristics of inexperienced psychotherapists is that they phrase delay responses in a way that arouses anger instead of providing encouragement. This is probably due to the fact that the therapist cannot as yet tolerate not knowing the meaning of a patient's statement. The delay response becomes aggressive:

> *Patient:* So I left her. I could not stand her anymore. Wouldn't you have done the same thing?
> *Therapist:* Go on.
> *Patient:* Please—I had to leave her—
> *Therapist:* (harshly) Go on.

One might speculate on the process that produced the repetition. The therapist realized that the direct question put him in danger of committing himself to a value judgment. He had learned to avoid judgmental responses, but his anger had made him aggressive. His harsh "Go on" actually told the patient, "I can't answer that. You have caught me." The words "go on" do not convey such meaning, but the adjuvant cue, the tone of voice, does. Obviously, at this point the therapist had enough information to find a response that would have been more specific to the patient's statement; he could have said, "It was a tough decision to leave her." The very fact that a patient asks questions of this kind often means that something has gone wrong. He may have sensed that the therapist cannot deal with direct questions, and so used this question to annoy the therapist. If so, the therapist's response was the one predicted by the patient: the therapist was caught in a trap by failing to disengage.

Sometimes, of course, the patient calls the therapist on a properly delivered delay response. Patients get impatient with delays:

> *Patient:* Are you married?
> *Therapist:* (with a proper delay response) You wonder whether I am married.
> *Patient:* Yes, I wonder about it. Won't you tell me?

Now the therapist must wonder why the patient is pressing the point. The patient's response suggests no lingering interest in the literal meaning of the question—the patient is concerned about confronting the therapist. The therapist who now answers the literal question would miss the most recent question in the patient's mind, namely, how much power the patient has to make the therapist answer a personal question.

The therapist could use this understanding to produce a beneficial experience. For example, the therapist could say, "You feel I am hedging, unwilling to give you a straightforward answer to this personal question?" And there is, of course, nothing wrong with the therapist's responding directly to the question with "Yes, I am married," provided the therapist's relationship with the patient permits the follow-up, "I wonder why this is of concern to you?"

Delay responses (such as repeating, "You wonder whether I am married") cannot be given indefinitely. Somewhere along the line the therapist must understand that the information given by the patient's question is changing, even though the words are not. Repeated delay responses communicate the therapist's ineffectiveness in listening. For example, in a play-therapy situation, a therapist we observed was asked by a child, "How old am I?" The therapist replied, "You wonder whether I know how old you are"—a perfectly adequate delay response. The child answered, "Yes, I would like to know. Do you know?" The therapist responded with his first statement, "You wonder whether I know how old you are." The child now got quite angry. "Yes don't you know how old I am? Do you know how old I am?" The therapist repeated his response eight times! It became clear to the supervisors that the therapist simply did not catch the changed meaning, and therefore lost the opportunity to respond to the patient adequately. The therapist should have concerned himself with the changes in the feeling tone as the patient expressed more and more anger. There are times when delay responses become a hindrance to therapeutic experience.

Teaching

Many therapists believe that the therapy hour can be characterized as a process of facilitation. Patients are motivated to seek help, and the therapist helps them "help themselves" and discover new ways of behaving. Some systems such as Rational Emotive Therapy (Ellis, 1994) hold another view and claim that the therapist must help the patient more directly by showing which behaviors are inefficient and suggesting more rational, appropriate ways of behaving. The therapist who follows this method of teaching communicates two covert meanings to the patient: (1) that the therapist expects the patient to be able to follow the suggestions, and (2) that the patient should have used his or her head in the first place.

Teaching probably is not a fully effective tool for helping people with psychological problems. The patient ordinarily cannot use directions and advice because the problems are essential to the patient's psychological economy: they serve a purpose and are not simply noxious, as the patient wishes to believe. In fact, a patient who again and again repeats a problem behavior probably obtains a feeling of control and perhaps even a sense of hope for eventual mastery by re-creating a setting that forces him to work on the problem (Shaffer, 1956). The psychological problem is a compromise solution for a patient's hopes and fears, and the patient clings to this compromise solution even while affirming the desire to overcome the problems. By giving up the problems, the patient would give up not only discomfort, but also hope. Advice has little impact on the patient because it means giving up some gratification. As the therapist shifts responsibility to the patient in a beneficial setting, the patient's problem behavior as expressed in the compromise becomes a source of uncertainty. This permits the patient to explore new choices.

Views similar to these have been widely accepted, and yet therapists who hold them often advise, guide, or direct the patient anyway, though most do so subtly and without awareness through covert cues. Teaching the patient can take a very indirect mode: just by observing that a given behavior cannot be understood in its own right.

Some therapeutic models such as paradoxical psychotherapy use covert messages to communicate indirectly to patients that they should take a look at the total situation rather than an isolated incident. One of these events is illustrated in the following excerpt from a therapy session with a woman having a marital problem.

Therapist: You tell me that you know it infuriates your husband if you cut your nails in the living room, but you are doing it! There is apparently a good reason: are you angry at him?

The therapist confronts the patient with the paradox of her own statements, in order to encourage her to speak about her anger, or perhaps to make the patient aware of her ambivalence toward her husband. The communicative meaning of the therapist's statement is to create a sense of uncertainty. The cutting of the nails is only a means to an end to pay the husband back for something she resents in him. The therapist's response is a teaching statement, whether it was given with pedagogical intent or not. It tells the patient to look at a given behavior in context with others.

In the above example the patient may respond to what the therapist said with the following:

Patient: It is my house too and if I want to cut my nails in the living room I have the right to do it. I hate to have every one of my behaviors inspected and controlled.

The patient obviously does not want to consider the therapist's lead: that her behavior has meaning beyond nail-cutting. At this point, one can discover whether the therapist can deal with a patient who does not follow his lead. The patient has clearly told the therapist that she feels that she has been misunderstood by him and that she would like to make her point more forcefully. The therapist could respond with, "You feel you should have these rights in your own home." His statement is an admission that he had not been "with her" in his earlier response. The therapist had now changed his message: he told the patient that he did not want to teach her, but respected her for expressing her feelings. He went on to state where the patient was at, rather than where he wanted her to be. With this statement the therapist successfully recovers from his misplaced teaching intention. He no longer wants to push her to speak about the negative aspects of her relationship with her husband; he recognizes that she is not ready for that. He avoided for the patient the necessity to defend her apparent "stupidity": wanting to get along with her husband, and yet annoying him by cutting her nails.

Another response could reflect the therapist's understanding yet more adequately: .

Therapist: You tell me that you know it infuriates him if you cut your nails in the living room. Yet you do it. You want to get along with your husband, but not at the cost of giving up your freedom.

Therapists need tools for the occasions when they feel they have missed the correct meaning of a patient's statement. The last response represents such a tool, it is a retreat to the time of the problem, an insightful statement whereby the therapist goes back to the place where he should have been all along.

This response suggest to the patient that the therapist respects her position and understood the meaning of her statement. Let us assume the patient now replies:

Patient: I do love him. I do love my husband. I must be an awful problem to him, doing what I am doing.

The patient's response may be interpreted to mean that she had an intense experience, perhaps a feeling of guilt: "I do not need to attack my husband all the time. You, the therapist, seem to like me even if I do get angry. My anger is a problem to me and to my husband."

The therapeutic experience was made possible because the therapist had tied the need for freedom with her "undesirable" aggressive behavior. This made her action more noble than stupid.

The intention to teach shows in many ways, particularly when the therapist teaches subtly and without awareness. Certain probing behaviors sometimes used by a therapist to bring unconscious material to awareness are often subtle teaching behaviors. For example, imagine a therapist who believed that her patient was too much of a "loner." She also felt it would be wrong for her to recommend specific social activities to the patient, as her main purposes were to help the patient help himself and to become independent. So, even though the therapist did not wish to give direct advice, she still wanted the patient to explore more adequate ways of social interaction. In this situation the therapist was like a parent who thinks she knows what is good for her child but who has learned to keep quiet so as not to stir up opposition.

The wish to lead the patient in the right direction is frustrated by the knowledge that such an attempt will not accomplish the desired end. The result of this dilemma is often a subtle attempt at leading or teaching, sometimes with and sometimes without awareness. In the therapeutic hour such leading occurs often enough. It appears in the way a statement is worded, in the sequence of questions, or in other covert ways that may betray the therapist's line of thought.

In the case just mentioned, the therapist was concerned with the social adjustment of her patient. She admitted her desire that the patient broaden his social experiences, but, since she would not give direct advice, she had to use subtle cues.

> *Patient:* It was a miserable weekend. I got up late Saturday, spent all afternoon at home reading, and then went to the movies by myself. Sunday I repeated the routine. All day I felt so lonely. I just didn't know what else to do. I had no one and I felt I didn't really want to see anyone either. I guess it was my "I hate all people" day.
>
> *Therapist:* Another of these lousy weekends.

The therapist did not know what the patient wanted to say, and so she delayed. The patient's subtle presupposition can be interpreted as having the following meaning: "I'm lonely and feel terrible. If you are any good you will suggest alternatives to me."

This hypothesis that the patient was covertly bidding the therapist to give him rather specific suggestions led to the therapist's disengaged, reflective statement.

> *Patient:* Yeah, it's getting that way too often. All week I just went to work, ate, and slept. This is something that I can do, I guess, but I just feel that there is nothing to look forward to—no relief. I did want to go to the "Y" to play chess, but I didn't have enough energy.
>
> *Therapist:* You wished you could have gone to meet with people there.

This remark is interesting because it does introduce a new concept, namely, that the patient wanted not only to play chess, but also to meet people. In that sense, the therapist's response could be seen for its teaching intention: meeting people is a concept the patient had not expressed. She singled out this concept, and said to the patient, between the lines, "Let's talk about people." The teaching implication of this statement is likely to have a negative effect on the therapeutic relationship. It probably will reinforce within the patient the idea that others will do for him what he himself feels he cannot do. It will prevent him, at least at this time, from taking responsibility for his loneliness. A response that would have shifted the responsibility for his loneliness to the patient himself would have been, "You felt too tired to go."

Calls to Reality

Other responses that fail to give the patient a necessary share of responsibility are given with the justification that they are a call to reality. Some therapists define maladjustment as a deficiency in reality testing: patients seem to distort stimuli and are not able to consider phenomena objectively. This lack of reality, of course, is most pronounced in psychotic patients, where it is only too obvious to another person. In the so-called neurotic patients the distortion is more subtle and the loss of reality less obvious. When a patient produces material that shows a poor grasp of reality, the therapist may be tempted to "straighten out" the misconceptions. It is well-known that "calling to reality" is not a very effective method to use with the psychotic patient. In fact, the psychotic patient often is driven by such methods to hold onto the distortions even more tenaciously and defensively, perhaps with the difference that he no longer feels able to talk to the therapist about them. The neurotic, however, is considered to have more intellectual control, and a call to reality may help such a patient use intelligence to break down automatic and preferred behavior patterns.

This, however, is a curious justification. The neurotic, after all, is in trouble due to an inability to use intelligence in these areas. It is puzzling to see that people treat the neurotic as if he were merely lacking in information. The neurotic uses apparently stupid behaviors to solve important problems that he or she cannot solve in any other way. Calling such a patient to reality—in effect, calling the patient stupid—can hardly have any impact other than communicating that the patient has indeed behaved stupidly. Such name-calling is not likely to be very successful in making the patient change behaviors.

Many therapists who are convinced that calling to reality is useless nevertheless engage in this behavior. Straightening out misconceptions is a conventional behavior among social persons, and it easily enters the therapeutic hour. Here is an illustration of just how such responses can occur in a very subtle form.

Patient: I was riding on Lawner Street and was coming to State Street, and the other car just ran into me. This blind bastard of a driver . . .

Therapist: (interrupting) Isn't there a stop sign at Lawner Street?

One first wonders why the therapist wants the more specific information here. After all, he is not a judge or an insurance inspector. Of course, the therapist knows perfectly well that there is a stop sign at this street, and simply wants to call the patient's attention to the fact that he had left an important element out of his story. The therapist responded in this way because the patient phrased the sentence as a demand bid: "Terrible things are happening to me because of irresponsible people. I am not to blame. Will you blame me?" The therapist essentially answered with an attempt to teach the patient to accept some of the blame: "Yes, you are to blame by having overlooked the stop sign." Rather than arousing uncertainty, this response confirms the patient's certainty that the world is against him. The statement, "These people cause you a lot of trouble," would probably have been more effective and afforded the patient the freedom to explore or even to admit his own responsibility.

Magic Suggestions

During the therapeutic hour, therapists often make "magic suggestions." In most of the examples cited so far, the therapist attempted to teach the patient more social skills and a greater sense of reality, so that the patient would be more in tune with society. With magic suggestions, however, the intent appears to be to teach the patient to think the right thoughts in order to find a solution to a problem. This subtle form of teaching probably has its origin in the magic thinking of childhood: the child learns new labels and symbols, and tries to apply this learning by manipulating events with these symbols. The child hears the word "milk" and learns that milk is not only a name but also an object that satisfies. The child's call for milk is based on the assumption that the substance will follow instantaneously.

An occasional patient relies on similar magic thinking, and introduces a demand for a magical solution by requesting that the therapist supply a password. The therapist may feed these demands by teaching magical terms: often representing the lingo of a particular theoretical position such as "you are now repressing 'the boss is really a father figure,'" etc." Instead of being a means for more efficient communication, the theory becomes an end in itself. The patient is taught to solve a problem by repeating therapist-approved labels. The therapist seems to say, "Know this ritual and you will be well."

In one hospital we visited, sex-offender patients would have to say, "I am a mentally deranged sex offender," before the staff would even consider talking to them or giving them a treatment plan. The idea so often presented in the movies that the recognition of a past trauma will change the patient's whole life is sometimes the only theoretical basis for the therapist's behavior. Following is an illustration of the use of magic:

> *Patient:* My brother came over to my house, and I cooked for him. On these occasions I miss having a wife. This time I had a chicken in the oven, and it burned crisp—black and crisp. That reminds me, the last three times I've had guests, I burned the meals, and ordinarily I do pride myself on being a good cook.
>
> *Therapist:* I hear you denying your female component. You no longer submit to your brother as the more masculine one of the two of you. Brother and Daddy are no longer threatening. You are grown up.

The therapist's response may be both an accurate interpretation and a disengaged statement. The cues in the therapist's statement that need further investigation are contained in the words "Daddy" and "You are grown up." These two symbols betray the therapist's intent of teaching. With them he tells the patient, "You must learn that your behaviors are childish. You no longer are a child, Daddy is no longer as powerful as he once was, and you do not have to be afraid of him. Accept my new labels, which imply that these behaviors are childish and you can let go of them." With such an admonition, the therapist is more likely to encourage childish than grown-up behavior. In fact, some of this therapist's patients may resent deeply the male chauvinistic implication that cooking is female behavior.

Supportive Therapy

Some therapists believe in giving support to the patient when they feel that therapeutic measures would be too threatening. Supportive statements are designed to give the patient a sense of security and to keep the patient away from the stresses of beginning a therapeutic process. Supportive work in general does not aim at personality reorganization, but at maintaining the patient's present adjustment, tenuous and difficult as it may be. Sometimes outpatient clinics use supportive therapy to keep the patient out of the hospital, particularly when and where professional help is thinly spread. The patient accepted for this type of maintenance work is supposedly too vulnerable to be placed under the stress of therapeutic work, and could generally be expected to get worse if left alone.

A supportive statement is supposed to reassure the patient. It is not merely an accepting response that communicates to the patient that it is safe to explore certain thought processes, but is instead a value judgment that offers the therapist's support for certain behaviors. As the patient's behaviors are often expressions of maladaptive symptoms, one may say that supportive statements tend to reinforce the neurotic symptoms of the patient. In this sense, supportive therapy actually communicates to the patient that the therapist has given consent to the status quo, and that the process of achieving a greater sense of well-being for the patient is fraught with danger. In other words, the patient is likely to recognize that he is seen as vulnerable and helpless.

The inexperienced therapist often uses supportive statements in the initial phase of therapy simply to find personal comfort. The therapist does so perhaps with the justification that establishing the essential rapport with the patient requires a comfortable and nonstressful relationship. Rather than accept the patient's right to express any thought he wishes for the sake of rapport, the therapist will support—that is, will approve—certain behaviors. For example, a child may throw a tantrum to avoid going to the playroom alone. In supportive work, the therapist permits the child's mother to accompany the child to the playroom so that the child can become familiar with the strange surroundings in a comfortable manner. As the child's problem may very well involve separation from the mother, the therapist's permission to act out a certain dependency behavior actually reinforces the problem. Sometimes this supporting behavior backfires. (Sometimes the therapists need to give such support for the sake of the parent, but careful attention should be given to the covert information that is thereby communicated to the child.)

When a shy adult patient is reluctant to see the therapist, some therapists feel justified in giving support. The patient who refuses to talk during the hour is apt to make the therapist take the initiative, ask questions, and probe for information. But the therapist who does so provides the patient with an experience of weakness and ineffectuality—probably an experience of success for the maladapted patient. Reflecting the patient's ambivalence would probably be wiser.

Therapists are most frequently caught in supportive statements when their own success is at stake in matters of the patient's progress. After many hours of exploration, a patient finally learns how to drive a car, find some friends, or change jobs, and then makes a strong bid for approval. The therapist is likely to give support, sometimes rationalizing that mature behaviors deserve reinforcement. Chances are that this type of support can be detrimental, as the therapist takes some credit by praising the patient as a "successful patient." The therapist not only accepts credit but also gives the patient valuable information about how the therapist can be punished, namely, by the patient's failures.

The experienced therapist will sometimes also enter into supportive behavior, but only after communicating this effort explicitly to the patient. By doing so, the therapist transforms the patient's experience of maladaptive control into an experience of uncertainty, as the patient's unconscious expectations are recognized. Ordinarily, however, there is little justification for the supportive statement besides reducing the therapist's own discomfort.

SUMMARY

The few examples given above suggest only some of the many ways in which the therapeutic urge of the therapist can cause interference. There are, of course, therapeutic approaches that endorse teaching, such as Ellis' Rational Therapy and other cognitive-behavioral strategies. Teaching, particularly skill teaching, is practiced in guidance and in rehabilitation. In fact, direct teaching is such a common human occupation that it would be surprising indeed for the therapist not to engage in it occasionally. The point of view taken here, however, is that the therapist's efforts in direct teaching are valuable only in that they teach us to understand the therapist's vulnerabilities.

8

Content Choices in the Psychotherapeutic Hour

Whether a patient chooses to tell intimate sexual secrets, reveal his dreams, report childhood memories of trauma, or laugh away the pain in a joking manner is of tremendous significance in Communication Analytic Therapy. The content of discussion in the therapeutic hour varies widely and is determined both by the thought processes of the patient and by the control of the therapist. Several broad categories of content are frequently used, and the implications for each can be usefully distinguished. Many patients, for example, present their problems as linked to past traumatic events, specifically, childhood experiences. Some discuss sexual episodes or concerns, dreams, and fantasies; others free-associate openly upon invitation.

Although the specific content presented may be important itself and may be related to the culture, expectations, or psychological sophistication of the patient, the medium of communication chosen by the patient also reveals much about the patient's wishes and fears to the observant therapist. The traditional modes of expression in therapy have become standard, we believe, precisely because they serve the needs of patients, principally safety needs.

Thus, regardless of the global format the patient's communication takes during the hour, the therapist must also be alert to the *way* specific words are used within each method of presenting material. In particular, therapists should be analyzing content for word "cages," which permit the patient to air complaints without including the possibility of taking responsibility for maintaining or changing a problem situation. Both the patient's global and idiosyncratic methods of presenting material are discussed below in more detail.

WORD CAGES

From the communication analytic perspective, the patient uses content in the therapeutic hour both to seek new satisfactions or relief from pain and, at the same time, to avoid the vulnerabilities inherent in risking changes. He wants relief, but the uncertainty of outcome and the predictability of the status quo outweigh the hope of future gains. The specifics of this conflict may be viewed directly in the microanalysis of the patient's "word cages." One common type of word cage in the therapeutic hour is what we loosely refer to as the "Popeye" syndrome. Like the sea-going cartoon character, the patient concludes an illustration of problems with a personal version of "I am what I am," thus avoiding responsibility and the possibility of change. By defining the self as static with statements such as "I've always been . . . hot-tempered . . . shy . . . a flop with . . ." or "I've never been able to . . .," the patient smothers responsibility and avoids risking change. Other word cages are quickly constructed when the patient attributes static behaviors to others or to forces beyond his control: "He is just a cold man," "The system is rigged," etc. Such word cages may provide the patient with a brief expression of frustration and a storage place for emotional weights, but little else.

The therapist has many options available when he spots the word cages. In some instances, a teaching response demonstrating the impact of the trap is sufficient. In others, the paradigmatic technique of exaggerating the patient's locked-in position is most effective. A third counterpersuasive technique of having the patient demonstrate and modulate the supposedly uncontrollable personality characteristic or feeling is also useful when it provides the patient with the experience of controlling the very emotion or behavior that has been presented as automatic and out of reach. An example of this third technique follows:

> *Patient:* (complaining) I just can't help but be furious at him when he's near. I can't do anything but be steamed.
>
> *Therapist:* Could you show me how angry you get?
>
> *Patient:* Right now?
>
> *Therapist:* It should be easy for you.
>
> *Patient:* I'll try. Well, I just don't like the guy—always brown-nosing the boss and taking credit for my ideas.
>
> *Therapist:* Nice, but I would call that only minor irritation. Can you punch it up?
>
> *Patient:* (laughing) OK. What a son of a bitch—impossible to work with! (laughing) How's that?
>
> *Therapist:* (smiling) Much better. Thanks for showing me your uncontrollable rage.

Here the patient was using a word cage, "anger," to block out other solutions. By having the patient fine-tune emotional expression, the therapist was unable to set the stage for flexibility and responsibility from the patient. The microanalysis of content is especially effective in marital, family, or group therapy—settings in which the social impact of a patient's word cages may be more clearly discernible and pointed out to the patient and recipients as they occur. Simply rewording a loaded term may have strategic power in changing the nature of a family's interaction. We can recall more than one family case in which changing "stealing" to "taking things" relieved the pressure so that family members could address other changes in the communication pattern. Sexual terms or diagnostic words such as "frigidity," "impotence," and "depression" are insidious and long-lasting. Alternative labels such as "feeling turned off" or "sad about something" imply the possibility of change and may actually be more meaningful to the patient.

CHILDHOOD EXPERIENCES

Recall of childhood events has a very special place in therapy. Freud, in fact, believed this type of production to be essential to the completion of an analysis, on the premise that such recall was significant in the process of restoring repressed ideas to consciousness. From a communication standpoint, however, childhood recollections serve a more direct need of both therapist and patient. The patient is seen as a person who wants to find new satisfactions but does not dare to become vulnerable by giving up previous adjustment mechanisms. As talking is the medium through which he wants to reach this complex goal, one might say that the patient wants to talk to the therapist, but still wants to talk as safely as possible.

The use of animal stories by children and some adults as a medium of communication has frequently been noted (Klopfer, Ainsworth, Klopfer, & Holt, 1954). A child is likely to talk more easily about the feelings of a teddy bear than about how he feels. Comic-strip characters, myths and legends, and artistic productions also achieve such "safe" communication: The individual can experience and communicate threats and pleasures without being psychologically endangered. The reporting of childhood events serves a very similar purpose. It permits the expression of self-references without the responsibility that generally accompanies such expression. The adult can say, "I hated my Uncle John," but does not face the consequences that would result from expressing hostile feelings in the present tense.

Of course, the patient may get quite involved or even anxious as reminders of past traumatic periods surface. The patient who reports past aggression by saying, "When I was small, I often wished my brother dead," may feel deep remorse and perhaps anxiety in response to this memory, but in the immediate therapeutic situation this patient is reasonably safe. The thought of aggression is only tested with the therapist, and retaliation would be absurd. Essentially, the patient uses the medium of childhood experience to scan the therapist for emotional response without having to take responsibility for feelings. Similarly, the therapist may invite discussion of childhood experience to take advantage of this safety factor.

DREAMS

An even wider range of feeling tones can be introduced via the medium of dreams. Dreams may contain intense and often violent scenes, but they are, by convention, permitted to be irrational, and many otherwise prohibited wishes may be safely introduced. Even the interpretation of a dream leaves the patient in relative safety. Although such interpretations communicate to the patient that wishes can be recognized and have meaning here and now, they still leave the defense that these wishes represent only that part of the self for which one does not have to feel directly responsible. Again, through dreams, the patient can scan the therapist's reactions to the great number of complex feeling tones and safely bring forth ideas and wishes that he would have to hide carefully were he to take full responsibility for them.

FREE-ASSOCIATION

Free-association as a medium of communication has yet other characteristics. First, it does not depend directly on memory function, but occurs mostly with the encouragement of the therapist. Thus the patient does not have the choice available with dreams and recall of childhood experiences, where the patient can simply state that he does not remember any such events at a given time. But because the patient is asked by the therapist to produce free-associative statements, accordingly there is an even greater freedom from responsibility than with dreams. Statements that are predictably illogical and unclear are elicited by the therapist, and their meaning is available only to the therapist.

They appear to the patient as bewildering, discontinuous thought processes, and generally there is some anxiety about the technique. The typical patient must laboriously learn free-association, perhaps because he feels submissive to the greater wisdom of the therapist, who can find meaning where none is apparent. The patient's feelings of submission, as well as the patient's freedom from responsibility, are important characteristics of this medium.

TEMPORAL DISPLACEMENT

Many approaches to psychotherapy maintain that memories of the past are of great significance. Other models place more emphasis upon discussion of more immediate, "real" problems. From the communication analytic standpoint, the important difference between these various uses of memory lies in the degree of responsibility with which the patient uses them. A patient may place a statement in the past because of the wish to create a distance between the present self and the past self, and in that manner express dangerous material more safely. What are the hidden meanings that such a statement of past events reveals to the therapist? By placing a memory of aggression against a father into an early phase of life, a patient is perhaps testing, not very boldly, how the therapist will react to aggression. The age of memory may very well be related to the degree of responsibility a patient wants to accept for a given feeling. By placing memories in the recent past, the patient may imply a readiness to compete with the therapist.

HUMOR

Humor may serve as a medium of communication between patient and therapist as well as a stylistic feature. As in the case of childhood memories, dreams, and free association, communicating with humor provides the camouflage and distance so often necessary for approaching taboo feeling tones or content. Transference issues, aggressive themes, and sexual wishes may safely surface in a joking way.

The patient who laughingly refers to murdering a boss, beating a child, or conducting an affair with the therapist maintains the advantages of covertly expressing feelings and scanning the reactions of the therapist without risking responsibility for the feeling of disapproval from the therapist. Often, the patient is asking, "Is it acceptable for me to have such feelings? Does the therapist have them too? Will I be punished for them?" With humor, the patient overtly owns only the joke. If the therapist does not play along with a laugh or a grin, it is the therapist who is the bad sport, or at worst, the patient who is a poor humorist with a tough audience.

The therapist, too, may introduce humor effectively into the treatment hour. Like the court jester, the therapist may catch the ear of the patient with an important message presented without the trappings of serious consequence. By joking with the patient, especially in areas where the therapist perceives vulnerability, the therapist communicates the message that it is safe and even exhilarating to play with ideas and feelings in taboo topics. The emotional climate thus created invites the patient to participate while keeping "real" feelings private. In addition, the sting of uncertainty experienced by the patient when working in vulnerable areas is anesthetized because of the "unreality" of the situation.

Humor may, however, be counterproductive. Even experienced therapists may find themselves entertaining or being entertained by a particular patient. In such cases, the therapist must assess and react to the motives of both parties who have subtly contracted this joking relationship. In order to maximize the impact of new and beneficial experiences for the patient, the therapist must often overtly explore the process of joking with the patient. The goal of this action is not to strip the patient of all hiding places, but to invite the patient to explore new options.

SEXUAL CONTENT

Messages concerning sexual behavior are of a somewhat different dimension. This topic is more daring, conventionally speaking, and the patient will often bring it up during the hour with a feeling of anticipation of great danger. At the same time, the patient can often use the therapist's reaction to sexual content to directly test the involvement or disengagement of the therapist. Discussion of psychopathic behavior and unusual sexual practices seems to make a great many people feel uneasy, including many therapists. And the patient is always deeply interested in discovering the areas of the therapist's uneasy feelings.

Paradoxically, the sexual medium is also used to test another person's readiness for greater intimacy. A discussion of sexual behaviors often serves to emphasize the close, confidential bond between the patient and the therapist. Success in discussing material in this area (with no anxiety on the part of the therapist) enhances transference phenomena, and the patient learns to speak of "my analyst" or "the hour."

PROBLEM-CHOICE AND METHOD OF COMMUNICATION

Dreams, recollections, free associations, humor, and sexual content are thus examples of media by which complex messages can safely be expressed and a large range of feeling tones scanned and explored. The structure and content of these messages permit both patient and therapist to be as much observers as participants in their discussions. The patient may ask the therapist, between the lines, "Let us assume that I am such and such a person. What would you do then?" The patient's covert expectations are introduced with an "as if" safety clause that helps disengagement of the therapist. He can adopt the role of an observer with the patient and more easily maintain an emotionally uninvolved attitude. All these methods allow the patient to create a situation for safely exploring new areas without substantially risking previous expectations. In this manner, prohibited wishes can safely be expressed and fears tested. No wonder these media have become useful tools in a wide variety of therapeutic models.

While the advantages of these content areas are obvious, there are disadvantages that come from the same sources. Both the therapist and the patient become observers when they discuss material that has only a very indirect bearing on their relationship. Once rendered observers, they reduce direct participation with each other. In other words, the possible emotional impact on one another is reduced, and the experience the patient goes through is minimized.

Although each of the media discussed here has a specific yield, content areas as such are not of singular significance in the therapeutic process. Any content area can be used by the patient to express and act out feelings that have very little direct relationship to the content itself. The sexual area can become a means of testing the social relationship; questions about vocational choice can be a means of acting out dependence feelings; reports of failure can be the manifest cues for subtle aggression against the therapist. The therapist can only try to obtain accurate information about covert cues by "listening with the third ear," in Reik's (1948) phrase, by broadening therapeutic attention to cues beyond the manifest content. The therapist must listen to the manifest cues and then ask, "Why is the patient selecting this material now, and why is he telling it to me? What is wanted from me?" Only when the therapist has formulated some answers for these questions and can point to the evidence, the specific covert cues on which answers are based, is he in a position to understand how the patient perpetuates problems. Content areas are then placed in perspective; they are essentially varying sources of covert cues. The experienced therapist will listen to content areas with only partial interest—knowing that too much interest in the manifest problem presented can lead only to engagement and a very superficial understanding.

Often in psychotherapy, the patient is given the choice of the topic and is encouraged to talk about whatever he wishes. But the influence of the therapist on the patient's selections of topics should never be disregarded, although sometimes the therapist is not aware of exercising this influence. Just as some therapists always seem to be called by patients on an emergency basis, some therapists have patients who either exclude or indulge almost exclusively in certain content areas. The therapist who reports, "My patients never talk about sexual matters; the Freudians must have a peculiar sample of patients," illustrates both selective processes and lack of awareness.

The influence of the therapist on the selection of content area should not only be recognized, but it should also be directed toward therapeutic goals. Rather than unconsciously reinforcing patient-selected topics by inserting covert cues of his or her own, the therapist should be aware of this influence and make the most adequate choice of content in terms of a theoretical model. By sampling the various content areas, the therapist can maximize both the amount of covert information obtained and the beneficial experiences provided.

The process of therapeutic gain is based on experiences that follow asocial responses of the therapist, responses that attempt to arouse beneficial uncertainty. To provide these experiences, the therapist must learn to understand the patient's increased expectations that are covertly coded. Manifest media of communication give only indirect information about this behavior. Accordingly, it does not matter very much what the patient talks about as long as the therapist obtains the pertinent covert information.

9

Extratherapeutic Incidents

ALWAYS DISENGAGE?

During didactic training and in supervision groups, our students often show strong reactions when they first encounter the following material on extratherapeutic incidents. They empathize with both the patient's plight of having no place to hide and the therapist's chore of "having" to "always" pursue even the most innocuous social convention displayed by the patient. A first impression of continual cat-and-mouse is not easily avoided, especially when we focus on isolated instances or critical moments involving extratherapeutic events. Our students often see therapists in action as "not nice" to patients. It is our sincere belief that, were it possible, most patients and therapists could not tolerate the experience of total disengagement throughout a therapeutic session, let alone the full course of treatment. The point, of course, is that not all conventional behavior demonstrated by the patient *should* be processed in a therapeutic way, even if it could. Rather, the therapist should be equipped to pursue any aspect of patient behavior and should be able to read, or at least hypothesize about, the subtler meaning of the patient's messages.

Further contributing to the portrayal of the communications analyst as a ferret breathlessly pursuing all avenues of resistance or subtle meaning are the fears of missing opportunities in therapy and of becoming unknowingly engaged by the patient's behavior. Indeed, no therapist wants to miss an opportunity to intervene in important areas. However, overall effectiveness is at risk if the therapist is working under great pressure never to become engaged or miss a chance to intervene. Under such conditions, the therapist is really monitoring her or his own performance and not the patient's dilemma.

It is not only acceptable but also necessary for the therapist to experience the engaging power of the patient's subtle conventions. For how else may the therapist disengage? It is also appropriate and advisable for the therapist not to disengage at all possible moments. Such a fully guarded posture would result in extreme distancing and would prevent the therapist's learning where the patient hurts. Whatever opportunities may be "missed" will generally appear again, especially if the therapist has responded to the engagement pattern with the desired social response. For example, the patient who succeeds in testing the therapist's love with requests for additional time at the end of the session will probably attempt a similar if not identical maneuver again. There is a drawback, however, if an engagement pattern is discovered very late in the game: an extinction burst may be demonstrated once the therapist plays the old game in a new way. After an engagement pattern is discovered to have been occurring in therapy for some time and the interaction is abruptly changed, the therapist should expect the patient to feel that the rug has been pulled out from under him. The strong feelings evoked by this eventual loss of power are, of course, an important subject to be discussed by the therapist and the patient.

Thus, it is the therapist's reading of the meaning of patients' use of convention or extratherapeutic requests that dictates the timing and nature of the asocial response. The asocial intervention becomes an arbitrary punitive device without the therapist's understanding of the function of the patient's style. Although it may be true that social conventions and conventional requests are consistent hiding places, we should remember that the patient must sometimes be permitted to hide. Without such carefully monitored permission, the patient experiences heightened uncertainty, to the extent that rigidity overtakes the experimenting process of therapy.

Rogers was once confronted with a facetious attack on nondirective theory. What does the nondirective therapist do, he was asked, when a patient is about to jump out the window? Say that you understand the feeling of wanting to jump, and then "reflect" when the patient hits the ground? The implication of these all-too-clever questions is clear: some incidents in the therapeutic hour obviously cannot be used therapeutically; extratherapeutic or socially expectant activity is sometimes in order.

On occasion, the safety of a patient, of society, or of the therapist demands attention. There is not time for reflection when the wastepaper basket is on fire. But how often do these emergencies occur? Generally speaking, the patient does not bring many situations to the therapist that cannot stand delay and inspection. Although loaded topics such as suicide, threats of violence, or unwanted pregnancy may carry a sense of urgency, it is important that the impact of these messages be processed instead of merely evoking conventional responses. When actual emergencies as determined by the therapist occur in the therapeutic hour, the therapist cannot proceed with therapeutic work. If we define emergency as an event that demands urgent action, most important events in the therapeutic hour demand therapeutic attention rather than immediate action or extratherapeutic measures.

CHANGE OF APPOINTMENTS

The predictable social response to a request for a change of appointment hour is often used by patients as a means of obtaining reinforcement for their neurotic dilemma. In trying to be sure of limiting the response of the therapist as much as possible, patients may present rather convincing reasons for this request, in a manner that discourages the therapist from thinking of a therapeutic meaning. Note that this does not imply that the patient is trying to malinger or to present convincing reasons where none exist, or that the patient is lying. But the therapist must discover not only what the patient wants, but also how the patient maneuvers. The patient who is "finally able to get a date" at the time of the next scheduled session, the "overworked" patient who has decided at last to take a day off, and the student counselor whose precarious academic situation necessitates extra study time, are doing more than making a reasonable request. They have searched for (and may have discovered) the therapist's areas of vulnerability in order to produce an emotional climate that represents more than a request for a change of appointments.

In an attempt to maintain some distance from the social expectations of the patient's message, some therapists try to detect whether the reasons given for wishing to change the appointment are fact or fancy. This judgment cannot be made, unfortunately, unless the therapist desires to become a detective. Some therapists acquiesce to the patient's demand from the conviction that patients have the right to ask for a change of hour. Our concern is not with rights, but with the information a patient may be hiding beneath a social message. Is the following message, with its highly predictable social response, designed to reinforce certain patterns of behavior?

Patient: My mother is coming in from the East and will be at the airport at 5:30 tomorrow. I have to change my appointment.

This message was designed to give the therapist very little choice but to make arrangements for changing the hour. It is the very pat nature of this type of message, however, that should help the therapist disengage from its social demand. The therapist cannot properly judge how truthful the patient's stated reason is, but still has the obligation to discover the extent to which the patient is using this information to achieve goals other than the obvious one. The general rule is that a good therapist will not take the chance of reinforcing disturbed behavior, which is what the social response might well do. This rule might be translated as "disengage first, answer questions later." The therapist must at least seize the opportunity to obtain further information. In this case the therapist continued:

Therapist: Oh, I see. Your mother is coming in at this time tomorrow and that means you cannot come to the hour.

The therapist was delaying. But the delay not only provided a chance for the therapist to think but also gave the patient the hint to elaborate.

Patient: Yes, that's right, and I thought perhaps we could find another hour this week.

The patient was strengthening the social plea. He chose to interpret the response of the therapist as one that still allowed him to hope for a conventional social reaction. He did not want his demand for a change to be treated as a therapeutic incident.

Therapist: Now, let's see, another hour? Perhaps you can tell me more about this request of yours.

In the second part of the sentence, the therapist asked for more delay. Suspicion about some greater significance to the request had arisen.

Patient: You are so difficult. What is there to tell? My mother is coming to the airport and I am asking you for another appointment, and I don't see what thought I can have about that.

The patient increased the social demand of his message. He apparently intended to make the therapist look foolish. Or was he justifiably angry? Some therapists argue that the patient has a right to be angry when the therapist asks foolish questions about the most obvious circumstances. But why should the patient's anger be called justifiable simply because the therapist is doing a professional job, and is staying therapeutic even though the patient wants a social response? It is certainly possible that the patient's anger says, in effect, "Don't dare treat this demand of mine therapeutically." The exchange continued as follows:

Therapist: It made you unhappy and angry that I didn't let this question go by, and that even here I have to psychologize.

The therapist was attempting to obtain further information. At the same time, perhaps there was an element of apologizing for being a therapist rather than a social human being. The term "psychologize" was perhaps an attempt to minimize the patient's anger by recognizing the source. It should be noted that the therapist was not angry himself. He simply maintained a therapeutic role. The patient's anger, on the other hand, probably arose because he could not obtain the highly predictable response that he had identified as justifiable.

> *Patient:* Why do you have to needle me? Why do you have to analyze everything?
> *Therapist:* That gives you no place to hide.
> *Patient:* I don't want to hide, I just want another hour. But you're refusing to give me another, is that it?
> *Therapist:* It suddenly seems very important that I give you this other hour, that I give consent for you to go see your mother.

The therapist was fully disengaged at this point. The response to the patient's comment about "analyzing everything" was probably an accurate reflection. The therapist's message to the patient said, "Let's discover what emotions are associated with your demands." But then the patient rebelled.

> *Patient:* I don't need your consent. I'll go if it's the last thing I do.
> *Therapist:* After all, it's your mother or me, John (with a smile).
> *Patient:* (Pause) I guess that is right. (Smiles and pauses for 60 seconds.) Mother wrote me that she wanted to come late in the evening, but I wrote her to take the earlier plane. I don't think I really planned that her coming would interfere with the hour. As you know, I had to face a very similar problem when my parents got divorced. . . . Father actually prohibited my seeing Mother . . .

In this illustration we notice how powerfully the patient tried to restrict the response activity of the therapist in order to make the therapist conform to the patient's demands. The patient's pressure to treat the incident extra-therapeutically was severe in this case, but when the therapist maintained the therapeutic role, some dynamics became apparent. Of course, it was possible that at the end of the exchange the patient simply wanted to please the therapist by recognizing the "significance" of his questions. But even this interpretation does not deny the necessity of asking questions. If the therapist had automatically consented to arrange another hour, the patient might have been harmed by reinforcement of his need to see Mother. Permitting the patient to succeed in such a scheme might have reinforced the very problem the therapist hoped to solve. We note parenthetically that the therapist had the habit of saying "John" at an important junction, a communication that surely was not lost on John. The patient may have learned that the therapist occasionally had to apologize for the therapeutic role and that an apology was expressed by a more intimate address. This kind of information can be useful to a patient if he later feels a need to render the therapist ineffective.

MISSED APPOINTMENTS

Although many psychotherapists attempt to sidestep the problem of missed appointments by discussing issues such as cancellation, no-show, and payment policies at the time the therapeutic contract is initiated, every therapist is faced with the issue of missed appointments. When an appointment is missed, be it without advance notice or accompanied by a desperate last-minute telephone call, the therapist must not simply rely on an automatic billing system or office policy to handle this "business" detail. There is meaning in the absence. As usual, the clue to decoding the message is the therapist's own feeling about the absence. Is the therapist angered or worried? Is he relieved at not having to face an irritating or troublesome patient? And what procedures should be followed? Should the therapist exercise detective powers and track down the missing patient? Should the absence be ignored until the patient initiates discussion? Should the therapist begin the next visit with a confrontation about the absence?

Our position is that when one session is missed, the therapist should not attempt to contact the patient or patient's family. The chased patient will experience (probably reexperience) success in creating a desired emotional response in the therapist, be it concern, anger, or disappointment. Without the new experience of failing to arouse the coveted emotion in the therapist, the patient will not grow. If, upon finding that a patient has failed to keep an appointment, the therapist finds himself terrified and compelled to step out of the role of therapist and into the role of rescuer, the patient should be referred to another helping source (see *Suicide Calls,* this chapter) after the rescue attempt is performed. By panicking in response to the message of the missed appointment, the therapist has taught the patient two lessons: (1) threats or dangerous behavior secure special love or attention; (2) the therapist has become ineffective in handling the patient through therapeutic avenues.

When the patient returns after a missed session, it is critical that the absence and its impact be discussed. Interventions here cannot take a stock form. Rather, they must be tailored to individual communication dynamics. If a second consecutive appointment is missed, the therapist is a bit over an ethical barrel and needs to take some action. Contacting the patient at this time is an act of engagement (socially prompted by the patient's passive action). Yet it can be handled with a minimum of emotional display; for example, by making the telephone contact as short and businesslike as possible and by not responding to the patient's bid to discuss excuses or other motives for missing. The therapist may simply establish whether there will be a future contact. Admittedly, the therapeutic agenda requires that the hidden reason for the absence be discerned, but the telephone is not an adequate medium for such exploration. Should a third session be missed without contact, we believe that the therapist is ethically and legally obligated to terminate the treatment contract formally, and give written notice of such intention to the patient.

PAYMENT

Remuneration for services is a generally accepted convention in our society, yet many people seem to feel that some services deserve payment more than others. Few people would argue that the TV repairman should "forget" his bill and be content with providing pleasure for others. The services rendered by the minister, the physician, or the psychotherapist, however, are often seen in a different light, almost as if charging for these services is taking advantage of people under stress. Excesses by members of these and other similar professions undoubtedly do occur; yet the feeling that these professionals should not really charge for their services seems to go deeper, perhaps involving feelings of guilt over having to buy personal attention and friendship. This feeling of guilt also affects many members of the professions, although it has not prevented a substantial increase in professional fees over the last 50 years. Psychotherapists' guilt feelings about charges can result in payment issues often being handled poorly from the psychotherapeutic point of view: payments become one of the social engagements that the patient can use for purposes of control.

Many therapists who, with some pride, defend a disinterest in fees (particularly if they practice therapy on a part-time basis and obtain their primary income from other sources) seem desirous of indicating that they are really interested only in the patient's welfare. On further questioning, some will admit that they are concerned lest the patient get the impression that they are more interested in money than in the patient as a person. Other therapists claim that payments are good for the patient and that such an exchange helps to maintain the patient's self-respect and provides a sense of independence. This line of argument can also be interpreted to mean that the therapist is not really interested in money for services, but is doing the patient a favor by charging a fee. Regardless of the therapist's attitude, the emotional involvements inherent in money matters often permit the patient to act out important feelings simply by paying or not paying the fee. We think it is important to discuss these important issues thoroughly and to separate fact from myth.

The treatment contract between therapist and patient is most likely an oral agreement reached in the early hours of treatment. The patient selects the therapist with whom he wants to work, and the therapist then decides whether to accept the patient for treatment and under what conditions treatment can best proceed. Money is often discussed during the first few hours, and the therapist sets the fee. It may be a token fee if the therapist feels this arrangement is satisfactory. It may be based on the patient's income. It may be a flat hourly fee that the therapist charges all patients. In some clinics there is no fee at all or the fee is covered by the patient's insurance without any copayment; in such a setting the question of whether a fee is indeed beneficial to the therapeutic experience becomes especially important.

The position taken here is that payment of the fee is totally irrelevant to psychotherapy. Like any other concern of the patient, the importance of a fee is in its discussion. In this sense the significance of the fee usually decreases as therapy goes on and as the therapist becomes more sensitive to other topics. That feelings of self-respect and independence are related to the payment of a fee is doubtful: a person can perceive payments as a sign of weakness ("No one will help me except for money") just as easily as a sign of strength. Even when payment of fees is not part of the contract, other topics will serve as vehicles for working on these same feelings of "giving" or self-respect and value. In any event, what the contract stipulates is not important, as long as both patient and therapist can live with it and are willing to use it as a guideline for the future.

If this contract is not lived up to, for whatever reasons, the relationship is technically dissolved and a new contract must be formed. When a contract between patient and therapist is dissolved, the therapist is responsible for either arranging a new contract or referring the patient for other help if this is judged necessary. Under no circumstances can the therapist simply overlook a breach of contract. The effect of nonpayment, once payment has been agreed on, may be as difficult for the therapist as it is for the patient, since the therapist often depends on the payment financially. In addition, nonpayments are likely to affect the attitude toward the patient, even though the therapist may not always admit this.

A contractual agreement between patient and therapist is a therapeutic event of the first order. For example, a patient may have accumulated an overall debt of several hundred dollars but, despite having contracted for regular payments, be making only occasional, small payments. The therapist who neglects to discuss the matter may reinforce the patient's unaware mechanism of involving people by making them creditors. The patient may be testing the therapist's courage, willingness to risk the total debt by challenging the patient, or even levels of trust and belief; such a need to test people's belief may be one of the patient's problems. The therapist, because of personal psychological involvement in the problem of money, may be engaged by the very conflicts that he should help resolve.

Other patients will use payment or lack of payment as a vehicle to constrict the therapist's recognition of all sorts of feelings: aggression, demand for love, feelings of unworthiness, etc. In each case, such behavior demands disengagement by the therapist and a thorough discussion of what psychological use the patient is making of the obligation to pay. Whenever a contract is not honored, the therapist should consider a new contract to replace a defaulted one. The decision regarding a new contract should be based on the therapist's judgment of the conditions under which the best work may be done.

The following example illustrates the potential significance of the topic of payments for patient and therapist:

Patient: Sorry, Doctor, I don't think I can pay you the full amount this month. My child needs an operation, and with the hospital expenses I am running terribly short.

The tendency of many individuals brought up in our culture would be to sympathize with the patient who has had these special expenses. The message is (by emotion) specifically designed to evoke just that reaction, and the person who disregards such a request is in jeopardy of being seen as inhumane and greedy. The patient's message is designed to extend a strong emotional force, one likely to arouse highly constricted thoughts in most respondents brought up in our culture. Some readers will surely protest the insinuation that such a statement must be a manipulation. After all, what if it is true that the patient had these expenses? What if the child needs extended hospital care? Is the therapist not also a human being who should sympathize with the patient? It is precisely the readiness with which many therapists accept these considerations that indicates most clearly how powerfully such a message structures an emotional climate in the respondent. The therapist's role is to help the patient, and proper understanding is the best tool. Sympathy or any other emotion must not stand in the way of one's best effort as a therapist.

Therapist: You state this in a way that would make it very difficult for me to say no to you.

The therapist here refused to react to the immediate social demand of the patient. Instead, he stated his recognition of the emotional design of the plea, providing the patient with an opportunity to express any deeper significance of this event.

Patient: Well, I have paid my bills most of the time and this is a real difficulty. I mean, the child needs the operation and I just don't know how I could pay you this month.

The patient was still aiming at a conventional end to the discussion, but one may note that no solution other than nonpayment was offered.

Therapist: It would be inhuman if I said that my payments come ahead of hospital expenses for your child.

The therapist disengaged from the demanded impact of the convention.

Patient: Well, I'm really sorry about it, but I think I can make it up next month. I will have to do some extra work, I guess; I've already arranged to do some work in the evenings.

The patient then discussed the issue and was not concerned only with consent.

Therapist: I thought you didn't want to give me much choice. In a sense you didn't really ask me a question. But I believe you are asking now if you could delay one month in payment.
Patient: Yes, I felt you would understand that something like this can happen to everyone.
Therapist: And I was unreasonable to hesitate . . .
Patient: It seems to me that you're questioning whether my child really needs an operation. I'd be happy to give you the name of the physician. He said that it was absolutely necessary. He must have the operation. There certainly is no question in my mind.
Note that the patient again made a bid for consent from the therapist, rather than deal with the issue.

Therapist: Again you're placing me in a position where I am inhuman if I'm not ready to help you in an emergency, like a friend who lets you down.

The therapist exaggerated again. He was impatient; he wanted the patient to look beyond the reality of her request.

Patient: I guess you are right. For a moment I thought you didn't believe me. But the child does need the operation.
Therapist: How am I holding up the operation?

Patient: Well, I have to pay you, too, and I cannot pay you both at the same time. While I think this hour is terribly important to me, I think the operation is even more so at this time.

Therapist: What is really endangered then, is not the operation, as you would pay for it anyway, but your hour with me.

Patient: I don't want to give you up. I have no one. You are the only person who will understand, and it is in these hours that one needs . . . (pause) . . . friends, people who will stand by when one really needs them. (pause) I suddenly realize what you meant before; that I did not give you much of a choice.

Note that the patient then gave up trying to evoke sympathy in the therapist, and instead attempted to create a different emotional climate to oblige him. We may call it flattery or a play on the sense of obligation. She apparently believed that the therapist would respond more favorably to this message, but we should note that she still wanted to force him to consent to see her by using emotional impact. She was not yet discussing the therapist as a person who has the right to say no.

Therapist: You want to find out how much I want to see you?

With this response the therapist was again disengaged from the new impact (which he himself has perhaps elicited). He attempted to give the patient the experience that neither forcing her friends nor seducing them is a necessary mode of behavior.

Patient: Perhaps I can make arrangement with the hospital and pay in installments. Would it be all right if I pay you about half the amount this month and spread the other half to next month? I think I can handle it that way.

Here the patient has experienced that she could not get results by an emotional impact on the respondent, but had to deal directly with the issue.

Therapist: That sounds like a reasonable offer.

Patient: Of course, I could have asked my folks, too, but I don't like to. With them it is always fight, fight, fight. My mother . . . (etc.)

Here the patient was no longer forcing the therapist through emotional impact to do her bidding. The therapist has used the information provided to the best advantage of the patient. Had he responded to the social demands of the patient and immediately agreed to the delay in payment, he would have reinforced her neurotic behavior, perhaps the one of "forcing" people to do her bidding with an emotional impact solicited through sympathy and seduction. But the therapist was now in a position to tell the patient whether he was willing to engage in a new contract. The patient could leave with the experience that she must deal with the issues involved rather than try to overwhelm others with emotional stimulation.

In summary then, treating payment as a therapeutic incident does not spare the therapist from making decisions about money. However, these decisions will be based not on the patient's manipulations but on the therapist's estimate of how best to treat the patient.

GESTURES AS COMMUNICATIONS

Patients engage in gestural behaviors—specific body movements, habits of speech, specific ways of sitting, means of smoking, and so forth—that can only too easily be accepted by the therapist without further thought. However, these gestural behaviors may be safe ways of expressing significant information. In some cases, the patient perhaps has experimented with them and established them as a successful means of communication. A person who habitually talks very softly may use this gesture to create a climate of being in partnership with the therapist, as well as to force the therapist to listen very attentively. Or a student closing his eyes during a lecture may wish to create a futile sort of anger in the teacher. The use of gestures, then, can serve to control the respondent's response activity without permitting counteraction in a meaningful way.

Therapists, too, react to the emotional climate created by certain gestures, often without recognizing them clearly. By doing so, they subtly reinforce the patient's schemes rather than arouse beneficial uncertainty. The significance of some of these gestures—apparently so harmless and yet so controlling—will be elucidated with an illustration.

A patient had the habit of standing next to her chair in the office until the therapist asked in a friendly way for her to be seated. This ritual had become rather thoroughly established, and the therapist had not given it any thought until he described the patient in detail to his control therapist. When asked if he did this with all his patients, the therapist realized that the ritual might be of some special importance to this woman. He began to suspect that she acted out her feelings of dependency with this gesture. An excerpt from the interview, after the therapist was alerted, follows:

Therapist: Good morning.
  Patient: (looks at the therapist and seems bewildered) Good morning. (still standing)

Therapist: (sits down) You are wondering . . .
Patient: You seem to be very short this morning . . . Oh, just an impression. (still standing) I don't know, I really have nothing to say today. (pause)
Therapist: Nothing to say? I notice you are still standing.
Patient: Oh, yes, I guess I was. (sits down)
Therapist: You look dissatisfied. Is there something you don't like?
Patient: I don't know. I just feel disappointed.
Therapist: Disappointed? In me?
Patient: No, I am not disappointed in you. In myself. It's all very confusing.
Therapist: It seems that I am doing the wrong thing today.
Patient: I don't know. It just is an off day. I feel blue.
Therapist: I should do more for you.
Patient: No, you do all you can. It is me.
Therapist: That leaves me out. As if I really were not here at all.
Patient: (laugh) I wonder if you like me.
Therapist: I did not prove it to you today: you had to sit down without my offering you a chair.

Here the therapist gave his punch line, but it should be noted that this bit of "insight" was not really necessary. Therapists simply are verbal creatures.

Patient: Oh, yes, I can sit down on my own, I guess. (She cries.) Lytha [her sister] was really mean. She said that I should get out of the house and grow up. I felt so small but I could not say anything and she kept nagging me. She does this once in a while. I wish she would leave me alone. I am not doing anything to her and I don't know what she wants from me.

The patient had little awareness of the meaning of the sitting-down gesture. But the fact that the therapist did not reinforce her subtle bid to have him invite her to sit down (and in that manner give consent to her depending on him for the chair) brought forth exploratory behavior in the area of dependency.

In the following weeks this patient was able to assert herself more readily in the hour ("I can sit down without you"). Obviously, the discussion of her gesture alone did not accomplish this, but it was a beginning. The therapist's recognition of the meaning of the gesture did result in his being more alert to the parts of her behavior that were designed to have him take the initiative in their relationship. When the therapist gave his punch line, he probably wanted to reassure himself that he had, in fact, understood. He had permitted the patient the experience that taking the initiative was not as dangerous as she had feared. The uncertainty aroused in the patient by responding to her gesture apparently served its function.

GIFTS

Another avenue of behavior that is often not recognized for its therapeutic importance is the patient's use of gifts in relations with the therapist. Gifts have a conventional connotation of friendliness, with the expectation that the respondent will be grateful. The receiver is not to "look a gift horse in the mouth" and should not inquire into the value of the gift. Instead, one should gracefully accept the present and play the role of a pleased person. This role is so definitely expected that any deviation is likely to arouse painful and embarrassed feelings. When a seven-year-old girl brings the therapist a bouquet of flowers she has picked in the garden, the first impulse of any recipient is to say "Thank you" and feel very pleased about this expression of gratitude and friendliness. Yet within the therapeutic situation, nothing could be more wasteful. It is just because the gift is such a safe way of expressing feelings and setting up structures that some of the most therapeutically important feelings are likely to be hidden behind these expressions.

The therapist is placed in a situation that demands disengagement from powerful social conventions if the gift-giving is to be treated as a therapeutic incident. In some cases, the therapist's disengagement will motivate the patient to take the gift back, while in others the patient may continue to offer it even after the therapist has disengaged from the imposed convention. The therapist might accept the flowers from the child, but only after exploring the giving with the child, lest significant problem behavior be reinforced.

Gifts need not always be objects. There are gifts like invitations, compliments, referral of other patients, and, more subtly, gifts of the therapeutic "productions" demanded by the therapist. For example, a therapist wants the patient to talk about oedipal feelings, so the patient obediently talks about them—they are now gifts, to which the therapist may unknowingly respond with pleasure and thus reinforce submissive behavior patterns in the patient. Such motives are the most difficult to recognize in this context, but the well-trained therapist will recognize his own pleasure and be able to disengage even from these subtle schemes.

The patient not only gives gifts, but also demands them. Demands may involve conventional and seemingly trivial gift objects such as cigarettes or matches, special privileges such as permission to smoke, or they may involve the therapist's services. The patient may complain about the heat or cold of the office, or the noise outside. Sometimes the patient's demand to be pleased will even involve the way the therapist conducts the session ("Please shut off the tape recorder," "I can't hear you," or "Don't talk so much"). The demand of a patient often seems rational enough, a justifiable request from one person to another. In fact, it must seem rational for the patient to achieve desired ends. In some instances, the therapist must deal with the rational demands extratherapeutically (as in a case of fire), but for the most part he or she can afford to look for unaware sources. We shall present an example that took place at the end of a session that deals with a patient asking for matches to light his after-therapy cigarette.

> *Patient:* I forgot my matches. Do you think you could find me one?

The patient demanded a gift that cannot easily be refused. Most people automatically respond by offering to help. Here the therapist disengages.

> *Therapist:* I would be quite a heel if I refused you (does not offer to find a match).
> *Patient:* (laughing) Well, for the money I am paying you, I guess you can afford to give me one.

The patient persists in his request by trying to shame the therapist.

> *Therapist:* You are telling me that I owe you this.
> *Patient:* You are a hard man. You don't let me get away with anything. All I wanted was a smoke, but I am losing my appetite for it fast. Can't you ever give?

The patient was angered because he could not get his wish. Note that he threatened a loss of appetite, which happened to be one of his more consistent problems. The therapist picked up on this.

> *Therapist:* You are disappointed because this safe way of making me give was not so safe after all. You even try to make me feel bad by your loss of appetite because I didn't jump at the opportunity.

Note that the therapist disengaged from the demand but was not fully disengaged from the anger. The phrase "jump at the opportunity" was not without anger.

> *Patient:* Now, about this woman I have been telling you about . . .

The patient changed topics. He had experienced that his problem of using a threat against himself to get his wish did not pay off. If it had, the therapist might easily have reinforced the very problem he was trying to help.

The following is an example of a patient who mailed a Christmas gift to the therapist. The therapist brought the wrapped gift to the next hour.

Patient: (sees the wrapped gift on the desk) Oh, I have to tell you about a dream I had during the vacation. It was recurring and quite disturbing. (etc.)

This was an unusual opening, and the therapist believed that the patient was bringing up material that he felt was important enough to prevent the therapist from discussing the wrapped gift.

Therapist: I wonder why you start off the hour with something so very important. Has this something to do with the parcel here on the desk?
Patient: I saw that you hadn't unwrapped it. Well, you handle it your way. Why didn't you even unwrap it? It would embarrass me if you unwrapped it in front of me.

The patient expressed some feeling of discomfort but still wanted to avoid the issue.

Therapist: To discuss this present would be more difficult than discussing the dream?
Patient: I just went by the store and I saw that thing and I thought since it is Christmas time I wanted to enter the spirit of Christmas giving. I am disappointed that you didn't unwrap it, because I expected that you would enjoy it very much.

The patient justifies the gift as an act of kindness. This, of course, is the conventional meaning of gifts, but the therapist was aware that an act of kindness can serve other ends. He then attempted to understand better the reason for the gift.

Therapist: Expected?
Patient: Oh, I bought it for you and I expected you to be happy with it. I just now thought that it doesn't seem to fit anymore—it's past Christmas and all. It is sort of a Christmas-y gift. Why don't you unwrap it and see for yourself, or don't you want it?
Therapist: You seem to feel now that I don't quite deserve your gift. I am making too much fuss about it—bringing it here still wrapped.
Patient: Well, do you? I mean, your bringing it in here wrapped, and not saying "Thank you" or anything else. You are treating it

as if it were poison or shit or something. Don't you want to see it? (laughing) For all you know, of course, it might be shit.

The patient felt cheated of his pleasure and acted out his aggression.

Patient: It struck me funny, if you must know. You haven't looked, and it might be a piece of shit all wrapped up. Just my sordid sense of humor.

Therapist: Are you saying now that this gift could also have been something I might not have "enjoyed" so much?

The therapist was now working on the hypothesis that the hostility was at least partly associated with the gift itself and not only with his nonacceptance of it. Perhaps there were ambivalent feelings in the patient's giving of it. Perhaps the patient wanted to express subtle aggression unnoticed, which was indeed one of his problems.

Patient: It's a lighter, not shit. I bought it because you always seem to be looking for matches. (reaches for the parcel and places it in his pocket) Permit me to take it back. I thought that it embarrassed you that you waste so much time with matches. Mind if I keep it now?

Therapist: I think you already made up your mind.

Patient: I will keep it as a reminder.

The presentation of a gift carried important meaning that could easily have been overlooked if it had been treated as an extratherapeutic incident. By neither accepting nor rejecting the gift, the therapist opened up the patient's behavior to inquiry. He did not reinforce the patient's secret wish to please or hurt by simply accepting it.

DEMANDS

Many hard-to-refuse demands may be made on the therapist, designed to tempt him to provide services outside the hour. Such services include requests for reading material, for fee reduction, for changing the hour, for decreasing the number of therapy hours, or even for the name of a prostitute. Each of these events should be looked at as a therapeutic incident and not as simple "after-the hour" comments.

Some might argue that the patient can legitimately ask some questions that deserve an answer, e.g., "How long do I still have to come?" Although this is not denied, it must always be remembered that the patient has learned to communicate vulnerable wishes under camouflage of the obvious. The patient who requests the therapist to estimate "How long do I still have to come?" has selected a question that can express many meanings. The patient may want to express fear, make an outright demand, display anger, apologize to the therapist, or even threaten to quit. Of course, the request itself must be dealt with on its own merits, and then answers can be given, but the more subtle meaning of the patient's communication must first be understood. The ever-so-rational demand itself is at times the means by which the patient attempts to perpetuate maladjustment by forcing a reinforcing response. The therapist should not be overly concerned with the rationality of a given request but, as elsewhere, with the emotional climate it creates. Once the covert meaning of the request is understood, appropriate responses can be given.

An illustration of a "service demand" and one way of handling it follows.

> *Patient:* It is terribly noisy in here. Of course, it has been noisy all along, but today it just gets on my nerves. I don't know why they have to blow their trumpets so hard. (a band was marching by the building in which the office is located) No thought comes to my mind. Don't you think that this is true—I mean outside my neurosis? I wonder if we couldn't close the windows?
>
> *Therapist:* We?

The patient made a rational demand; the therapist did not unthinkingly fulfill it but inquired for meaning.

> *Patient:* I thought you'd want to close them. After all, it's your office. Would you mind closing them? I don't think I make that sort of request often, and you can see for yourself, or I should say, hear for yourself, that this is quite impossible. I can hardly hear a word you're saying.
>
> *Therapist:* I should close the windows because it's my responsibility to take care of my office.

This was a delay statement, but the therapist recognized that the patient was using the noise to justify a bid for controlling the therapist's behavior. It happened that the patient had many problems with people because he made demands on them that he conceived as justified (and this, of course, is why the item was presented). Were the therapist to jump up and close the window, he would reinforce the problem behavior.

> *Patient:* No, that won't be necessary. (gets up) I think I can close them myself. (closes one window) Well, now isn't this much bet-

ter? At least it cuts out most of the sharp tones. (goes to the other window) Well, this one is more difficult. (attempts to close it but cannot do it) For Christ's sake, I can't close this one. What is the matter with it? (leaves the window open, returns to the couch, and speaks very softly) I don't know what happened, I just can't close it. (begins to cry) I couldn't close it.

Therapist: Makes you feel sort of helpless that you need me to take care of you.

Patient: Leave me alone. I tried it, didn't I? It really is your responsibility. I don't know why I should close your windows. I did it just because I did not want you to have to get up. I tried it, but I couldn't do it. (cries again)

Therapist: There should be something left for me to do. Why should you have to do it all? When you give a finger, who knows, I might be asking for the whole hand.

The therapist operated on the hypothesis that the patient's demanding behavior was a way of not allowing others to make demands of him. He had perhaps learned that those making demands of him were insatiable. The therapist worked on this therapeutic objective even though the social "window closing" demand appeared justified.

Some will argue that the patient's unhappy feelings arose from the therapist's refusal to respond to the justified demand. After all, the patient politely asked to have the window closed, and the noise outside made this a reasonable demand. Rather than close it, the therapist proceeded to talk while the window remained open. The argument might go: Why shouldn't the patient be angry, since his reasonable demand was not acted upon? No one likes a reasonable request to be forgotten under talk; in fact, one may ask what right the therapist has to refuse the reasonable demand of a patient and to avoid the responsibilities of his office.

The fact is that the therapist did not close the windows, but neither did he refuse to close them—he merely insisted that the demand be discussed. What is more, it is very unlikely that the patient actually became angry because the therapist lacked politeness. It is much more likely that he was anxious rather than angry—anxious because the therapist was not manipulated by the patient's "justified" demand that he play a social role. Instead, the asocial response of the therapist made the patient uncertain about his making demands on people.

Of course, the therapist could have closed the windows and protected the therapeutic gain by discussing the demand later. The actual way of dealing with the problem is not as important as the therapeutic attitude toward subtle cues. We feel that the therapist did increase the impact of his asocial response by not obliging the social demand immediately.

VACATION

The patient's request for a vacation or time off can be difficult. The therapist may have taken a vacation himself, during which time patient and therapist had not met. The patient now comes and asks to be excused for a week or a month. The request is based on the convention that everyone has a right to time off. But we should note that the patient is also asking for the therapist's consent to do so. He wants the therapist to agree to take time off, the implication being that if the therapist consents, it will not interfere with treatment.

As the patient has the right to accept or reject the absence of the therapist, so the therapist has the right to refuse or consent to a patient's demand for a vacation. The therapist should not be influenced by the fact that there is a waiting list of patients or by his own vacation history. An absence, for whatever reason, demands a discussion of the contract the therapist has with the patient. The therapist, therefore, must deal with a request for time off as a demand for consent. This turns the request into a therapeutic incident.

NUMBER OF APPOINTMENTS

The patient sometimes demands a change in the number of hours he is seen during a week. How does the therapist arrive at an adequate number of therapy hours in the first place? Practices differ widely. Some therapists insist on seeing their patients a set number of weekly hours, while others permit the patient to choose. Some therapists use yet other criteria, such as the patient's financial resources, their own time schedule, the estimated amount of resistance seen in the patient, or the level of anxiety. Some therapists adopt flexible schedules, telling patients that the number of hours will decrease as treatment progresses, while other therapists do not change the number of hours over time. There apparently is no agreement on meaningful criteria for determining the necessary number of hours for maximum benefit.

Some therapists see their patients monthly (such as in rural mental health clinics) and believe that these visits have a benefit, while others work a 24-hour schedule on occasion and ascribe maximum benefits to this intensive effort. With the encroaching influence of managed care, the insurance "plan" itself often specifies the structure and duration of treatment, complicating the process of both reading the patient's wishes and pacing care.

It is easier to say which criteria are inadequate than to point to adequate ones. It seems inadequate to use the financial resources of the patient as a criterion for determining the number of hours for maximum benefit. It is true that a patient's financial resources have to be considered and that a given therapist may want to reduce rates or not accept a patient, but it is difficult to justify consideration of financial resources in determining the desirable number of hours. Nor should this decision be left to the patient's judgment. To do so is to imply that the patient has more adequate criteria on which to base this judgment (a doubtful implication, to say the least) than the therapist. The therapist is certainly in a better position in this respect and should not pass on responsibilities that are rightfully his. The therapist must discover reasonably defensible criteria for the number of hours during a week or month to see a patient. The decision should be based on an estimate of maximum benefits under the specific conditions of the setting.

Psychological theory does give some clues for predicting rapport and transference. Many therapists, for example, agree that it is very hard to work with patients classified as having "personality disorders." The anxious patient who is very desirous of help may present a different problem from the involuntary patient sent in by a referring agent. The patient with somatic complaints often needs more time to establish rapport than others.

When a patient demands a change in the number of hours he is to be seen, the therapist again must understand the demand in its therapeutic context rather than in terms of the "reality" of the request. Changing hours inevitably changes the contract. The demand may have many subtle meanings. A request for a reduction of hours may imply a wish for reassurance of improvement; a wish to increase the number of hours may imply a wish for greater dependency, or even the patient's desire for the therapist to say that progress is not adequate. When this demand is treated extratherapeutically, the therapist often misses a significant therapeutic opportunity. Simply referring to the managed care plan limits or the instructions of case managers is also a sign of abdicating an important arena of therapeutic work.

INTERRUPTIONS

Therapists have established various ways of handling telephone calls, knocks on the door, noises outside the office, and other interruptions. Such occurrences may give the patient significant information about the therapist's way of looking at the therapeutic relationship. For example, a therapist may answer a telephone call at length, apologize too profusely for a call, or refuse it altogether, with obvious anger.

It is impossible to avoid all disturbances, and the therapist's only safeguard is to be aware that disturbances, when they do occur, are an interference in the interpersonal process with the patient. One must discuss them with the patient, and in this way use them for therapeutic gain.

The helpless look given to the patient while the therapist is engaged in a long telephone conversation, the apology, or even the disregard of the interruption will all give the patient information. Aware of certain biases in the therapist, the patient will be in a position to arouse feelings in the therapist and thus to constrict his response activity when danger to the self is sensed. Having another professional observe the practitioner's office habits— responses to interruptions in the office setting, for example—often provides some insight into idiosyncratic behaviors that affect the therapeutic relationship.

OUTSIDE CONTACTS

For many years it was considered improper to talk to any member of a family other than the one in psychotherapy (see Chapter 11). The rationale was that such outside contacts would disturb the relationship with the patient. Many therapists, therefore, have made it a practice to insist to a person calling on the telephone that the information conveyed must also be made available to the patient; it cannot be treated confidentially. While we agree with this conclusion, the original rationale for avoiding confidential contact seems faulty.

That the patient may experience suspicion, fear, or a sense of lack of responsibility is not really the critical consideration in therapeutic contacts with outside sources. After all, the patient can attach fear to any half-worthy object, and the therapist cannot remove all such objects from the patient's life. These feelings are subject to therapeutic work and will yield many important experiences; the therapist must be prepared to discuss them with the patient.

There is, however, a more valid reason for avoiding confidential information from outside sources. Such information, accepted under the banner of confidentiality, limits the therapist's response activity with a patient, for the therapist will have to weigh what can and cannot be said. There can be no "getting in cahoots" with a worried father, an upset wife, or a concerned schoolteacher.

However, there are other, proper means of bringing outside information into the therapeutic hour, as we shall discuss in the following chapter.

What are the responsibilities of the therapist when the patient calls between hours and wishes to talk? Some therapists engage in therapeutic discussion, some hedge, and others discourage such calls altogether. The call itself, however, has a very special message: "I am worried and I have the right to ask that you talk me out of my worry. Think of me, now." The message stands in the service of a plea for a social engagement. For example, a woman may call at 2:00 A. M. and say, "Please, it is urgent, see me now." We follow the practice of not responding to the patient's therapeutic material over the phone precisely because the act of phoning (and its plea to impose on the therapist during nonscheduled hours) may be one of the patient's problems. We reason that a response from the therapist would reinforce the behavior of getting extra time (love) by referring to special suffering (the reason for the call). From a social point of view, this argument sounds cruel and cold. (Who wants to let down someone in their hour of need?) However, the asocial response ("Thank you for calling. I'll see you at the appointed hour") provides the patient with the needed experience that extra suffering does not bring extra love. This asocial response has its justification in the observation that by giving the engaged social response the therapist would actually maintain and perhaps increase the patient's suffering.

SUICIDE CALLS

Is there a point at which the therapist must become a social human being rather than a therapist? What if the patient threatens suicide? Should the therapist not undertake the social role at this crisis point and rush to the patient's aid?

We believe that suicidal behavior is often a learned behavior. Through thousands of messages, the patient has learned to force others to do his bidding by arousing guilt with threats of personal suffering or destruction or by threatening others to be the party responsible for their suicide. A patient who has been reasonably successful over time in engaging others' sympathy for suffering may, under particular stress, feel able to be successful with the therapist by threatening self-destruction. The therapist who accepts the social role and gives extra attention would not only reinforce such behavior for the future, but also increase the possibility of the patient's following through with the threat at the present. It should be noted that the therapist must use good clinical judgment in deciding when to respond in the expected social manner to special calls or requests. Major accidents, family illnesses, and emergencies do occur and should be treated socially unless there is some reason to believe that this behavior is not rare and is part of a pattern. The patient's state of mind is such that arousing guilt or threatening another person is more important than survival. If the patient experiences success, a situation is created where he or she can commit suicide as a symbolic act: to die to be loved and remembered.

Some argue, however, that the patient is under great stress, and giving some extra love is important even if it does reinforce maladjusted behavior. Furthermore, the argument goes, the rejection experienced by the patient when a desperate bid for love is not answered may provide the final push toward a self-destructive act. The argument surely holds true for a new patient or a stranger who calls a suicide center. However, the patient with whom a therapist has worked for any length of time in a beneficial setting is not so likely to misread the therapist's cues ("I will see you at the appointed hour") as a rejection. This patient will also get the message that the therapist wants him to pull through under his own strength, and the show of confidence is more likely to discourage a suicidal action than a show of guilt.

However, there are occasions when the therapist does not trust the patient, and when the therapist will act in a social role either to provide extra help or to advise a protective environment. After the emergency is handled in such cases, it is important to refer the patient to another source of help, because the therapist, by responding socially, has now shown the patient that the therapist has become ineffectual in handling major problems therapeutically. If the therapist does not refer the patient, the future of the therapeutic contact is likely to be dim. The patient has experienced the fact that with desperate measures he can manipulate the therapist.

BREAKING OFF TREATMENT AND TERMINATION

A patient's request, threats, or demands to stop treatment are important enough to merit a detailed discussion. Many models of psychotherapy imply to both patient and practitioner that psychological problems have specific origins, and that, with careful work, a "cure" means that behavioral excesses or deficits will be eliminated, internal stress will be reduced, unconscious conflicts will be resolved, self-actualization will take place, or, in some cases, the proper scream will be expressed. Thus, the end of treatment in most theoretical models leads us back to some form of the health idea: that there is a problem (illness or pain), and the successful end of psychological work occurs when this problem disappears. In the communication analytic model, the health perspective is replaced with the idea that new styles of adjustment, behavior, and feelings can always be explored in hopes of gaining further flexibility and efficiency. That is, there is not a specific point where therapy will be of no further value. An individual can always desire some assistance to explore new choices. This formulation is particularly useful when we consider that individuals in industry, government, education, and private life (who are not maladjusted) seek to improve their communication skills. We believe that our model is equally useful for patients and nonpatients.

We are not suggesting that therapy should require a lifelong commitment from the patient. Instead, the question of breaking off therapy may be viewed as a communication related to the theme of the patient's acceptance of responsibility. Borrowing from Zen philosophy, the patient who needs to evoke a reaction and perhaps seeks to obtain reassurance from the therapist that he is ready to leave is really not ready to break off treatment.

Of course, therapy does and should end. The hypnotic routine of frequent visits may too often produce an unquestioned dependency covertly hidden from patient and therapist. Rather than keeping the same pace throughout the course of the work until "health" arrives or is discovered, we prefer to space contact hours at greater intervals as the patient exhibits greater freedom in exploring choices in the area of his vulnerability. We are building into the system the patient's increased responsibility for his own life—and our own disposability. Usually a patient will enter treatment with conflicts and problems, often without awareness that he helps to maintain them. During the course of therapy, the patient is continually thrust into a position in which the therapist's responses no longer evoke familiar rewards. In a safe and caring atmosphere this leads to a feeling of uncertainty. When the patient permits himself this feeling of uncertainty in the area of his vulnerability, he will necessarily seek out new choices and become creative. The communication analytic therapist will typically not approve or disapprove of any of the patient's choices. This nonjudgmental attitude of the therapist has its limits. Should the therapist be convinced that the patient is in fact dangerous to himself or to others, it would be the therapist's obligation to evaluate the patient for a propensity for violence and then act to protect the patient and society.

In most voluntary therapeutic relationships the patient has a right to terminate a contract with the therapist at will. It is this understanding that seems to make it plausible to treat the demand for termination extratherapeutically. In communication analytic therapy, however, such demand is treated as the patient's wish for engaging the therapist possibly for his consent. In fact, in our experience many patients who come into the hour with a request for termination may be more concerned with the therapist's consent than with leaving. The patient may not really wish to break off treatment, but sometimes wish to obtain the therapist's refusal, try to arouse the therapist's anxiety by threatening to quit, or just get the therapist to commit himself about the patient's progress. Any such demand must be discussed therapeutically. And yet that still leaves us with the question, Should there be a time when we use our expertise in human behavior and give the patient our consent, our estimate that the patient's best interest requires further therapeutic work? Let's look at the following illustration:

Patient: I am through. (pause) Instead of getting better I am getting worse. I think that therapy has not helped me at all I am sick and tired of giving up the little money I have and wasting hour after hour coming to your lousy office. There is no sense to it. I still can't live with myself any more easily than before I came here. It's gotten worse. I don't know what I am going to do, but one thing I am sure, this is the last time I will see you.

Was the threat to break off the treatment used here as a vehicle to express other meanings? Did the patient really want to stay in treatment but want to show anger and aggression to the therapist? Our answer to this question is yes. We reason that with such strong feelings, the patient would not have come in at all if she had given up the thought of further treatment. The underlying meaning is not yet clear. The patient may have been using aggression to cover up her increased (and deeply prohibited) wish to have a more loving relationship with the therapist. In the present case however, there was some evidence that the patient wanted the therapist to take a stand with regard to her progress. Discussing termination at the start of the hour was designed to elicit such a report.

The patient sets up the therapist to respond either by defending himself ("There has been some progress") or by agreeing ("We got nowhere"). She tries to force him into a role of either accepting or rejecting her. Note that this demand for a black or white commitment could be a problem of the patient, one she should be helped with. If the therapist's response were indeed to the social demand of the message (agreement or disagreement), it would reinforce her problem. We wish to restate that in the communication analytic model the therapist's consent for termination is seen as the essence of the patient's question. Therefore, whenever this question arises, the therapist's consent will be the object of discussion. However, the therapist will only withhold consent when the patient is seen as dangerous to himself and/or others. Patients who do not fit this description will learn that they do not need consent and that their question represents a remnant of dependency or stands in the service of other needs. The therapist responds here to the feeling tone.

Therapist: I wonder what you are so angry about.

By asking for further associations, the therapist did not commit himself by either accepting or rejecting the demand to break off treatment, but implied that termination was not the issue.

Patient: Angry? I have a good right to be angry. I am spending all this dough and nothing comes of it. Wouldn't you be angry? In any case, I just told you, and I am sick and tired of your asking me these silly questions.

The patient reacted to the therapist's lack of engagement. Unwilling to experience uncertainty she tests the therapist with her attack to see whether she can make him angry.

Therapist: You really are angry today.

Here, the therapist was floundering. He apparently was surprised that the patient had not abated the intensity of her hostility, so he simply repeated his previous message. He lost sensitivity. His response was an expression of his own irritation.

> *Patient:* Sure I am angry, but this is the last time I will be with you. I am sick and tired of your face, of your voice, of this office. I want to go.

The patient almost gleefully took advantage of her success. She seemed to enjoy her ability to arouse irritation in the therapist.

> *Therapist:* Why don't you go then?

This comment implied that the therapist had recovered and paradigmatically shifted the responsibility back to the patient. It was a gambit that involved certain risks, namely, that the patient would take his response as a challenge, particularly as the response was worded too harshly. (Smiling would have softened it sufficiently.)

> *Patient:* Okay, can I go now? (gets up)

The patient saw an opportunity to make the therapist ineffectual: she acted as if she had his consent for termination. At this point, the therapist adequately followed up his paradigmatic statement. He avoided the comment that she probably feared even though she had asked for it: ("Well, if you want to"). Instead:

> *Therapist:* I believe you feel that you are not ready to leave as yet.

We should note that the therapist carefully shifts the responsibility for a decision to the patient but this time without irritation.

> *Patient:* (sits down) I don't know what else there is to discuss, but have it your way if that is what you want.

The patient in turn placed the responsibility for staying back on the therapist.

> *Therapist:* You want it to be my wish that you stay in treatment. That I would tell you I want to work with you.

The comments indicate the therapist's disengagement, and returning the responsibility for leaving to her.

> *Patient:* (laughing) I don't know, I had this uncontrollable anger . . .

While in the above illustration the statement "This is the last time I'll see you" is clearly representing other demands than that for termination, we do have patients who make that statement extratherapeutically, i.e., they wish to terminate. The patient may still ask for our consent but it is clear that he has made the decision to leave.

Here our clinical judgment plays a major role. Should we be convinced that the patient is sufficiently disordered to be dangerous, we would have to state that we disagree and feel that continued treatment (if necessary, with another therapist) is essential. If our estimate of danger is of great certainty, we are obliged to discuss with the patient that we need to protect him by contacting outside agencies and any intended victim. Sometimes it is useful to repeat this statement in writing to the patient.

If the patient is in good control of himself, we would treat the statement therapeutically during this last hour, to give the patient the opportunity to reaffirm his decision. With a patient under fair control, but one who would greatly benefit from continued treatment, we should first of all be aware that (provided we are charging the patient), we are in a possible conflict of interest situation when we suggest to the patient to continue treatment. Our major choice would be to respond to the patient therapeutically and explore the consequences of termination. Under the circumstances it may be wise to suggest a month or longer intervals before the next treatment is scheduled to assure that the patient knows that his leaving does not have to be final. We found that such an extended meeting date can be of great benefit to the patient.

It is not only the patient who might wish to terminate treatment; there are three reasons why therapists might wish to do so:

1.   The therapist believes that the patient has benefited and further contacts would be of little value. Under these circumstances, we believe that the therapist may want to discuss the patient's dependency needs and possibly suggest to schedule increasingly extended meeting times.

2.   The therapist believes that the patient does not respond to him and that future meetings would be of little value. Here we believe it particularly valuable for the therapist to test for his own engagements patterns with a control therapist. A referral may be necessary if these patterns are too well established.

3.   The therapist has a very strong aversion to or attraction to the patient. The therapist may be working on his engagement pattern with his control. Ordinarily a referral would be useful.

The therapist's readiness to listen is the major instrumentation in the therapeutic hour, and when the instrument is dulled by strong feelings, positive results are elusive.

OUTCOME

The problem of more objective evaluation of therapy outcome has not been satisfactorily resolved. Higher self-esteem, better social relations, more adequate productivity, better coping with stress, better sexual functioning have all been suggested as adequate measures of therapy outcome. We feel that such measures are useful but probably less suited for a general theory, which should include such changes as can also be observed in well-functioning people. Recently, some studies have used outcome measures based on the communications process. These studies analyzed patient's messages at the beginning and termination of psychotherapy. As stated, Murray (1980) analyzed the blaming attributions of a patient's speech and found that successful treatment resulted in reduction of such characteristic patterns. Brokaw (1983) measured the patient's ability to increase his choices after the therapist's asocial responses and reported positive findings. It would be useful to analyze pre- and posttreatment samples of speech of patients for language usage. A sensitive study may well uncover important messages, as language usage would be related to change in life-style. We feel that such measures would be more fruitful in the evaluation of the psychotherapeutic process and less subject to the problems related to a definition of an abstract state of mental health.

10

Technical Problems in the Therapeutic Process

PATIENT PRESELECTION

Selection of patients may actually take place long before the first hour. Many therapists decide whether they can help a person from neurological and historical data, often without having seen the patient. An independent practitioner may exclude psychotic patients, patients afflicted with organic brain disorders, some problem groups such as alcoholics or drug abusers, or members of certain age groups. Criteria for selection vary from therapist to therapist. The use of some criteria is probably helpful, as the therapist will then select patients whose problems fall within his areas of competence and experience, and patients with whom the therapist will feel comfortable.

However, there are unfortunate consequences of preselection. Some patients who may very well be helped by treatment are denied treatment by therapists because of their neurological classifications. For example, it is generally accepted that personality disorders are hard to treat on a private basis. This notion is probably due to the fact that patients with personality disorders are exceedingly skilled in the game of manipulation and understand very well how to immobilize the therapist through their skillful engagement patterns. Some therapists do not accept homosexual patients, claiming that goals with such patients are unclear or that the work makes them feel uncomfortable. Homosexuality, of course, is not a psychological problem at all, although it may be a social problem; the homosexual who comes into treatment most likely has problems like anyone else, rather than the desire to change his sexual orientation. Consequently, it appears to us as if this type of selection is based on prejudice rather than on evidence that homosexuals are an especially hard group with which to work in a private setting. There are a few homosexual patients who report that they want to change their sexual orientation. We have found in working with some of these cases that gay or lesbian patients who have been sexually abused as children, often by a parent or family member, have been successful in changing their orientation. We need to point out that it is important that the therapist should work to be neutral as to the question of homosexual orientation.

Surely, there are some patients who cannot be treated in a private setting, who need the protection of a hospital environment. However, when we speak of the population that would be suitable for the private setting, we believe that preselection, i.e., a choice made before a patient is accepted for the first hour, is often based on hearsay and faulty, preconceived notions. Unfortunately, there does not seem to be a properly designed test for patient treatability or prognosis, though there are some claims for certain indices derived from tests like the Rorschach test, the Minnesota Multiphasic Personality Inventory II, and the Thematic Appreciation test. At present, testing by and large will not help therapists select the patients whom they can expect to help best. The therapist must rely largely on contact with the patient during the first few hours to estimate whether help can be made available to the patient and whether the patient is responding positively.

INTAKE

Even if not part of the preselection program, the first few hours should serve two major functions: (1) they should help the therapist make a reasonable estimate of how this particular patient can be helped by this particular therapist, and (2) they should give the patient some idea of what to expect in the treatment hour.

Fundamental decisions about the therapist-patient relationship are often made during an "intake" session. During this time, demographic information is collected, the source of the referral is identified, necessary release forms are signed, fees are discussed, and a general inquiry is made into the medical and psychological history of the patient. The therapist will also want to discuss the number of hours recommended for the patient's treatment and the time available. Occasionally, the therapist will also want to discuss the length of the contract with a patient—that is, how many hours the patient may need to be seen. A time for evaluation of the outcome of the relationship may also be set. Even if this sort of evaluation is not desirable, it is needed if only for the reason that managed care insists on it.

Many patients now come to the psychotherapist with insurance coverage, and the therapist has to enter a DSM-IV code for the patient. It is probably useful for the patient to know how many hours the insurance will pay for the particular code mentioned. This type of information should be available to the therapist and certainly should be made available to the patient. Additionally, a frank discussion of exactly what information the managed care company requires needs to take place early in treatment.

Some psychotherapists give the contract discussions very little time; others devote a whole hour to it. It may takes just a few minutes at the beginning of the first hour, and patients may spend most of the remainder discussing the problems that brought them to seek help. Still other therapists make extensive use of an intake or orientation form, which they ask patients to complete and sign as part of an agreement for treatment.

The therapist confronting the patient in the first hour should be aware of being "the stranger," and any stranger is generally perceived both as a threat and as a possible object of gratification. The patient's first impression of the therapist is based on scanning. The patient wants to discover how the stranger may present a threat, and the therapist should realize that she or he threatens the patient's present state of adjustment by virtue of being a therapist (hence the "head-shrinker" label). The perception that the therapist may be a threat determines some of the behavior of the patient.

We can learn about the nature of this behavior by looking at similar events in everyday life. If we meet the salesman selling us a used car, we feel vulnerable if we suspect that he has no concern for us but is merely interested in getting rid of the "white elephant" on his lot. He threatens not only our pocketbook, but also our sense of accomplishment and self-esteem in dealing with others. We must read the salesman accurately to be sure that we will not be taken. When we meet a stranger at a party we may not have a financial stake to protect, but typically we feel we need to protect our integrity. If the person appears to engage in behavior that leads us to sense danger—be it in intellectual competition, seductiveness, charm, wit, or whatever—we are likely to assess him or her as a danger to us. So we run, flatter, engage the person in a field where we are safe, fight him or her, try to outdo him or her, etc. In other words, when a stranger threatens our psychological security, we bring forth typical and consistent behaviors to deal with the threat.

Even when on first impression we assess a stranger as likable—a person who seems attractive and worth cultivating—we respond conventionally. To reach out for another person, we may show indifference (letting the stranger do the wooing first), possessiveness, or any other coping behavior we have available.

The patient, being by definition vulnerable, often sees the therapist as a source of danger during the first hour, and consequently reveals information concerning how the patient typically deals with threats. The therapist must be alert not to become engaged. The patient will use with great skill the engagement patterns with which he is most familiar. This is the patient's battleground, to use a martial comparison.

When a new patient arrives, it is important that the therapist obtain a written release permitting access to available information from medical and psychotherapeutic sources. The therapist must be as certain as possible of treating a mental and not an organic condition; information about the neurological and medical condition of the patient is therefore important. If the patient has had previous psychotherapeutic experience, the therapist will want to discover whether the patient has separated from the former therapist.

A patient who intends to employ several sources of help presents not only a therapeutic but also a delicate professional problem. While the patient certainly has the right to change therapists, the decision to change may be motivated by the patient's desire to play two therapists against each other in order to maintain the present state of adjustment. The right of the patient to change therapists must be respected, but the patient's welfare must be the therapist's greatest concern. In some cases a therapist may refuse to accept a patient who has been in treatment with a colleague if treatment would not best serve the welfare of the patient. This becomes particularly significant if the colleague is a close friend and the patient is aware of this fact.

The first hour presents the therapist with a unique opportunity to assess what "hurts" the patient, and the therapist should assess the hurt by observing the patient's covert message components, which are designed to elicit an emotional response from the therapist. A patient starts with a description of how she has been "let down" by a previous therapist and has spent all her money without results. She may add that she knows the new therapist to be excellent—a friend of hers has been helped. Instead of becoming engaged in the emotional climate of the flattery, the therapist could learn that this patient approaches the stranger with flattery designed to seduce the stranger into competition with a third party. This is probably the patient's approach when she feels she has to overcome her apprehensions about relating to others—a significant behavior pattern of which the therapist ought to be aware.

Another patient may describe his problem in highly technical terms, telling the therapist how he had "reexperienced [his] Oedipal complex with a great trauma," etc. This patient deals with the stranger by trying to impress him and compete with him in an area of the stranger's own competence.

A third patient may be depressed and withdrawn, incidentally creating an emotional climate in which the therapist is expected to take the initiative in any discussions and, of course, reinforce the patient's depressed state. Still another patient may be on the verge of leaving the office when first entering, perhaps showing that flight is the patient's typical response to danger.

The interpretations of these subtle cues are conjectures at this point, and they must be treated as such. Nevertheless, the cues give significant information, and the observant and experienced psychotherapist will often be able to make accurate predictions about the course of therapy from them.

During the early contact, the patient will develop an image of what to expect from the therapeutic hour. The patient will try to make an estimate of what the therapist can do, and will make some assessment of the value received. Most patients have already tried—either with another therapist or on their own—to live better lives. They come to the psychotherapist and often make a considerable financial investment to find yet a better quality of life. To the extent that they can be brought to experience more hope for the future and for a higher quality of life, the early hours can be successful.

Hope is not easily arrived at by praising or supporting statements; it is rather a function of the experience of mutual respect. The therapist earns respect by understanding the patient's dilemma and helping the patient make new choices. Even in the first few hours, there has to be some movement in that direction. We do not believe that rapport-building such as advanced by English (1966)—"comfortable and unrestrained relationship of mutual confidence"—should be specifically encouraged during the first few hours, but it should be the nature of the relationship throughout. Rapport-building seems hypocritical. Should one have to pretend that the hours are comfortable because such pretense would permit the patient to better withstand the discomfort of the later hours?

Every therapist has a personal style, and it is within this style that the therapist must convey understanding and respect to the patient. Some therapists laugh a lot; others work with undertaker faces. Some are silent; others talk more. Some dress conservatively, others dress flamboyantly. By and large, styles appear to be discounted by the patient, who looks for attention and some sense of caring. This quality is communicated by listening, and the job of the therapist in the first few hours is to listen attentively to both the overt and covert components of the message and to respond in a manner that enhances searching for new choices. Hope is the outcome of work well done.

From a communication analytic viewpoint, the danger is that the therapist becomes so used to a set routine of treatment that he is no longer aware of it and how it affects the patient (we only need to think of the hospital where the patient is wakened routinely to take sleeping pills).

THE ORDER OF THE THERAPEUTIC PROCESS

Some therapists have tried to discover an inherent structure in the classic therapeutic process. One of the most outstanding efforts can be found in Wilhelm Reich's *Character Analysis* (1976), written before Reich became obsessed with the Orgone. He saw a lawful relationship between the individual's character layers and neurological and physiological structure. Each given character layer was thought to be responsible for certain behavior and was seen as specifically related to the organic structure of the person.

Reich wrote that problems that have occurred early in a person's life could not be resolved in therapy unless more recent character structures and their physiological correlates had first been worked through. This theory was designed to bring order into the therapeutic process by establishing a proper sequence. Unfortunately, perhaps because of the unhappy later development in Reich's career, this contribution was not as thoroughly discussed as it deserved to be. Horney (1945) tried to bring order into the therapeutic process by suggesting a "hierarchy of symptoms," an interesting attempt based not on the person's history or learning but on the interrelationships among the patient's defenses.

Analysts are concerned with the problem of order, and often use both a historical model and the analytic relationship to establish a proper order within the analysis. By paying attention to the patient's earliest childhood memories, the analyst has a source of information that gives clues for interpreting later patterns. In terms of the relationship, the analyst's first concern is with understanding the initial nature of the relationship and learning about the patient's use of resistance; only later does the therapist proceed to work through resistance and, incidentally, transference. The analyst does not wholly follow the patient, but selects communications and behaviors believed useful for responses. Rogers, who had much impact on therapeutic procedures in the United States, originally was not concerned with altering the process, and suggested that one should always follow the patient. In his later books, however, such as *On Becoming a Person* (1961), he introduced seven stages of the therapeutic process that are thought to follow each other in successful psychotherapy:

1. There is an unwillingness to communicate about one's self. Communication more easily concerns external factors.
2. Expression begins to flow regarding non–self topics.
3. There is a freer flow of expression about the self as an object.
4. The patient describes more intense feelings of the not-now-present variety.
5. Feelings are expressed freely as in the present.
6. A feeling that has previously been struck or has been inhibited in its process quality is now experienced with immediacy.
7. New feelings are experienced with immediacy and richness of detail, both within and outside the therapeutic relationship.

Like others, Rogers saw therapy as an orderly process, a function of the development of the therapeutic relationship, a process specifically related to the personal growth of both the patient and the therapist. This description of the sequential stages of personal growth probably fits some cases but not others. We cannot agree that the suggested process has universal application.

The most recent attempt to bring order into the therapeutic interview is the imposition of contractual arrangements and informed consent to treatment. These range from determining the specific nature of the therapist's responses to the number of hours required to attain the therapeutic goal or to dictating periodic evaluations of outcomes. Some contracts also include discussions of ethical considerations. We believe that caution is in order when contracts are administered to a patient who may not be knowledgeable about psychotherapy, or about the nature of psychological problems in general. Many patients may be poorly equipped to understand the nature of contracts in general. Unfortunately, in the era of tightly managed care, contracts are often imposed upon both the patient and the therapist.

To our knowledge, no research has yet assessed the value of an ordering device for psychotherapeutic process. In the absence of additional research, hope appears to lie in the increasing perceptiveness of the therapist, whose first duty is to be a sensitive and increasingly knowledgeable instrument. The therapist may encourage certain messages or discourage others, but the focus of attention should be in becoming knowledgeable about where the patient hurts and which of his messages provide the patient with the possibility of discovery and evaluation of new choices.

Here is an example of how the growing awareness of the therapist regarding the meaning of the patient's statement can affect the therapeutic process.

A patient says, "This chair is very uncomfortable."

The therapist may read this statement as, "I am not so sure I should be here." The therapist might respond, "You were not sure you wanted to come today?"

The therapist may now get the response, "Oh, no. I am happy to be here."

To the therapist who disbelieves the patient, the patient's denial would mean that the patient does not want to be recognized as aggressive or self-assertive. On the other hand, were the therapist not convinced that the patient's statement revealed more than an opinion about the chair, the therapist would interpret the patient's response as a correction. This interpretation would indicate a self-assertive patient. By increasing the accuracy of such interpretations, the therapist certainly can bring some order into the therapeutic process: the therapist will show an increasing awareness of the covert meaning of the patient's messages and also be fully aware of the nature of his own impact upon the patient. Knowing how accurate the interpretations are and gauging their impact on the patient is an ordering device that speeds up therapeutic recovery by the fact that each response is more knowledgeable.

HABITUATION

Through thousands of messages, the patient is made uncertain of his former adjustment mechanisms. The patient can tolerate this uncertainty and will actually seek it out (by coming to the hour) because he is learning to be daring, courageous, inventive, and even creative. In therapy the patient can test a repertoire of emotional and intellectual endowments and psychological skills without great risk to the self. He is in a pseudorealistic situation: one made not of the gross realities of the world but only representative of them. The therapy hour is a sanctuary and at times even a playland. The question is really not why a patient becomes dependent on the hour, but why the patient would want to leave this situation at all. Partially because psychotherapy can be experienced as pleasurable by patients, the negative effect of requiring that payment be made to someone considered "an honest friend" is experienced by many patients, especially if they have developed a positive relationship with their therapist. In the successful therapeutic hour, patients may finally feel they have someone with whom they may let their hair down. The clash of feeling here, evoked by the two different forces of a caring acceptance and requirement of payment for services, may result in reducing the effectiveness of or stopping treatment.

Leaving psychotherapy is not easy for most patients. We are not implying that patients are biologically prepared, as John Bowlby's (1973) ethological theory might suggest, to remain in the cocoon of treatment, but we do know that patients in hospitals often seem to have trouble leaving the protective atmosphere (hence the treatment potential of an "open door" policy). We also know that many patients become habituated to the therapeutic process or to a given therapist, and stay in these relationships for a very long time.

Is habituation an inherent part of the therapeutic process? Dependency on the therapist and habituation to the hour are probably symptoms that have their origin in early learning. Separation anxiety or the fear of abandonment, as Rank (1973) so cogently pointed out, is based on the fact that the child depends on the mother in order to survive. The fear of losing a person on whom one depends is probably one of the universal early experiences among humans. Responses to the loss of a loved person include feelings of misery, inadequacy, and incompetence. A child who has experienced trauma in this area may have learned to use these negative moods in an attempt to forestall the anticipated loss. The classic work of Mary Ainsworth (1973) demonstrated that the roots of attachment styles may be observed early in the interactions of infants and strangers. The patient may have learned how to turn loss of love into attention and perhaps even caring. This lesson may become the basis of dependency relationship with the therapist: the patient may believe that only misery will produce love.

Freudians feel that the transference neurosis—that is, the introduction of a historic love relationship into the hour—is a dependency phenomenon essential for treatment, and that this relationship has to be worked through properly before the patient can act independently. Rogers (1951) tried to discover a therapeutic relationship that did not involve dependency feelings. He felt that his model of a patient-therapist relationship would eliminate dependency by avoiding the authoritarianism of a doctor-patient relationship. This was apparently an erroneous view. Later, in 1961, Rogers stressed the importance of a close relationship in which dependency feelings are more readily accepted.

The behavior therapist does not typically accept dependency as a phenomenon, but sees the therapist as a contractual helper to a given end. Yet it is not unlikely that the patient, even in spite of such theoretical considerations, grows dependent on the helping hand.

The Gestalt therapist sees the practitioner essentially as a teacher, and the theory says that the dependency ends when the class is over. However, the Gestalt therapist recognizes dependency as a phenomenon and would not want to terminate the class without due consideration.

Paradoxically, then, the patient comes to the therapist to get well, but knows that getting well will bring the loss of the therapist. The patient does not wish to give up the therapist because this loss would reactivate separation anxieties. The result is habituation to the therapeutic hour.

The resolution to the habituation problem lies in the pseudoreality of the hour. The patient may love or hate the therapist, may test various ways of involving the therapist; but the patient knows that these feelings are not really reciprocated. Both the setting of the therapeutic hour and the therapist's communications give the patient the information that the therapist is concerned, wants to help, wants the patient to be free to explore new choices, and wants the patient to experience life with greater pleasure. But through thousands of asocial responses, the therapist also reminds the patient that the therapist is not really the person the patient wants—not really a friend or a lover, not someone who exists outside the hour. In other words, while the patient experiences a bond with the therapist, the patient also learns that this sanctuary is transitory.

It is this experience that works against dependency and habituation, and encourages the patient to direct the newfound courage toward new objects and toward people with whom the patient can have a reciprocal relationship.

This analysis of the state of dependency may help us to understand the cause of unresolved dependency feelings in relationships where habituation has set in. What is likely to have happened is that the therapist has stepped out of the asocial role and appears to have become a friend, parent, or lover to the patient. The therapist may not act out these roles overtly, but through subtle messages of which the therapist may not even be aware, the patient may be led to experience at some, possibly unaware level that there is a future in their relationship. The possibility that the therapist may not be aware of maintaining dependency and contributing to habituation is one reason we recommend that a therapist maintain a professional relationship with another qualified person—someone who would go over several hours of transcripts and discover continuous engagements or responses indicating that the therapist has dropped the asocial role. To get on a therapeutic track again, the therapist would have to learn how to disengage.

IDENTIFICATION

Readiness to try out new behaviors discovered in the therapeutic process can be traced directly to the asocial response that allows a state of beneficial uncertainty. The direction of this change, however, needs further discussion. We have stated that we do not believe the wish for maturity is inborn and simply liberated in the therapeutic hour (Rogers's growth principle is probably wrong). A model of psychotherapy can only sow confusion if it tries to explain the aim of the change as an inherent part of the model. Change and the direction of change are clearly two separate considerations.

We once listened to an anxious bank robber who went into therapy. He evaluated himself and his capacity. Cracking safes was his métier. During therapy, he calculated that he had gotten caught only twice in 193 robberies. So, in his therapeutic work he decided to continue the probability game that had provided him and his family with a better-than-average income. Did the therapist fail him? Therapy had apparently helped him reduce anxiety even though the direction of the change was not toward better citizenship. We did ask our patient what he thought the worst scenario would be if he ever got caught, and he said that he would lose his wife and would be in prison for many years. We felt that was as far as we could go to help him to think of other choices in his livelihood. Therapists like to justify their work by thinking that they produce not only more effective persons but also better citizens. What is it that affects the direction of an individual's choice? Some who hold the view equating therapy with moral education might believe that therapy with the bank robber was incomplete. As a result of treatment, he may even have become a bank robber more at ease with himself and his career. We can only hope that the patient accepts responsibility for his actions. Therapeutic goals do not guarantee good citizenship. The question of when a behavior is a "sickness" or an irresponsible choice cannot be answered here.

While we trust that the bank robber did not choose his direction from identifying with the therapist, many patients seem to do just that.

The young child chooses goals through a process of identification with one or both parents. This identification may be positive—the child wants to be like the parents—or negative—the child wants to create a distance from the parents. As the child matures, he makes choices that are far less influenced by this early dependency. In therapy, however, it seems that the early developmental state is reactivated. The patient experiences a sense of courage and explores the world anew, but has not yet found a direction. The new direction is often found in the person of the therapist, from whom the patient tries to borrow some "piece" of identity. The patient may start to smoke a pipe, decide to become a psychotherapist, take up the therapist's favorite sports, and even use similar phrases and synchronic gestures. The patient looks at problems with the therapist's eyes. One therapist even reported that a patient dreamed dreams similar to the therapist's own.

There are, of course, other role models, past identifications from redis-covered inner resources, religious conversions, or just impactful books available to the patient searching for a new identity. However, identification with the therapist represents most often a first attempt of the patient to fill the vacuum in a search of identity, and its therapeutic importance should be a subject of discussion in the therapeutic hour. The therapist should not shy away from confronting the identification process with the same tact, timing, and dosage consideration applied to other important interventions.

The child who says she wants to become an engineer like her father implies certain motivations. The girl may want to show that she is as great as and can compete with her father; she may want to show that she is a failure compared to her father—that is, unfit for competition; or she may even voice her disdain for her parents' treatment of her because she is a girl. The patient who identifies with the therapist also communicates certain motiva-tions. The identification may ask, "Will you accept me as a person who is equal to you?" "Will you accept me as a person capable of competing with you?" or perhaps even "Will you accept that I go beyond you in certain of my aspirations?" The therapist must be sensitive to these messages and disengage from them. In doing so, the therapist will assist the patient not only to work through these dependency feelings and to mature, but also to find a personal identity.

REPLACEMENT BY OFFERING ANOTHER PATIENT

A special case of the search for identity occurs with the patient's wish for incorporation or replacement. This desire reflects the wish to maintain the connection with the therapist. Replacement fantasies often take the form of a wish to find a replacement patient for the therapist. These behaviors bear an important message to the therapist, but here again, one has to distinguish the message from covert cues. Some patients want to flatter or please the thera-pist. By finding a very difficult patient, other patients may hope to test the therapist's strengths and qualifications. Some patients seem to be motivated to test the therapist's personal preferences. Will the new patient receive more attention and love? Will the referring patient be able to become an adjunct therapist and help out with background information? We should note, however, that replacement can also be a simple "Thank you."

Patients also aim at time to be the therapist, either talking about other people and how they helped them or employing therapeutic-type responses during the hour. These communications are often a sign of exhibiting their coping skills, a sign indicating "I am ready to be on my own." In some cases, this behavior might be connected to an earlier pattern of behavior. It may have been learned with a parent to test whether a parent would accept the child's growing maturity. Children often assume a hypermature status or act especially grown-up to scan for parental approval for maturation.

The therapist should be sensitive to communications that imply replacement. We have seen a number of beginning therapists in whom such statements evoke an emotional climate of threat and discomfort from which they must learn to disengage. Not all therapists seem to be ready to accept competition in the area of their own competencies. The therapist's failure to disengage at this stage of the process can prolong therapy indefinitely. For example, a therapist may feel threatened by a patient's newly found courage and respond with a typical behavior under threat—that is, the therapist may minimize the patient's strength or maximize his own status to accentuate the differences. However, by doing so the therapist is likely to reinforce the patient's feelings that the replacement fantasies are powerful and dangerous indeed, or that the patient cannot aspire to equal or even better the qualities of an authority figure.

When we talk about replacement desires we speak of a widespread phenomenon that occurs in many different situations. Replacement fantasies are often perceived to be dangerous thoughts. In the biblical story, Joseph's actualized fantasy about colorful clothing, which made him outstanding and set him above his brothers, almost terminated his career at the bottom of a well. It is always dangerous to want to be bigger than you feel you are. In therapeutic situations, the therapist should be aware of the daring, searching behavior of the patient, and attempt to help the patient see that this struggle is being recognized. In fact, the therapist should help the patient realize that the wish to replace does not necessarily mean to kill, that there is enough room at the top. The therapist might want to explore with the patient the consequences of these replacement fantasies—the actual and imagined consequences.

Communication Analysis in Family Group and Group Therapy

The documented effectiveness and economic efficiency of group treatment as reflected in traditional methods of working with individual patients have increasingly given way to group therapy. Slawson (1950), Ackerman (1972), and George Bach (1954) were the pioneers and early writers on group therapy, and they showed that high-quality services can be rendered to either a natural or a synthetic group. Later, other methods continued to demonstrate the effectiveness of procedures that allow services to be made available to a large number of individuals at the same time. Some such efforts use principles of mass psychology, as for example in religious group experiences, in which a group may include hundreds or thousands of people. We have witnessed psychotherapy on television programs and national radio shows for an even larger audience, although to our knowledge the effectiveness of such methods has not been properly demonstrated beyond their obvious entertainment value. Much current group work for individuals troubled with problems of addictive behaviors or a host of other au currant personal problems such as codependency and dysfunctional family life is being conducted without traditionally trained health care professionals. The work is being done in 12-step groups or self-help groups in which member support is an important ingredient of change or maintenance of a problem. Some individuals appear to be assisted by these programs, especially by the religious or spiritual components, while other members find this aspect of 12-step type groups a hindrance to effective group work. Data appear to support the success of 12-step programs for alcohol addiction (Alcoholics Anonymous) yet are less clear in other applications such as coping with eating disorders or sexual behavior problems.

One of the most effective methods of improving the mental health of a large number of people has very little to do with psychotherapy. It is administrative action on every level that changes the environment and with it the individual's quality of life. We all should be aware of the administrator's power to influence the psychological well-being of people, be it the

President of the United States, a school superintendent, or the police sergeant. We should not look at psychotherapy as the single or the most forceful way of altering the self-concept or the world in which a person lives. Today, psychologists are serving in various administrative layers, including Congress, city government, and police headquarters, where they consult on decisions that are likely to affect the mental health of thousands of people.

The method we shall discuss in more detail here is family group and group therapy. A large variety of techniques have been developed: psychoanalytic groups, Rogerian groups, Gestalt groups, groups that are designed to give as much catharsis as possible, groups where people act out their particular problems, primal-scream groups, imaging groups, encounter groups, sexual-dysfunction groups, even groups that look simply at tranquilizing wallpaper. Because the more traditional theories of mental health were devoted largely to explaining individual dynamics, efforts had to be made to find theories for the interactive processes of group therapy.

A new picture of the patient seems to be emerging: the patient is no longer mentally sick and, in fact, is not even necessarily seen as a malfunctioning individual. Szasz (1961) has led the field in viewing the person afflicted with mental problems as someone who learned the wrong behavior, as all of us sometimes have. In some instances, the patient may have had a genetic predisposition toward such selective learning and needs retraining. All the older theories now begin to haunt the theoreticians. The words "patient," "doctor," "ill," "health," "sick," "treatment," and "therapy" seem dated. The major difference, if one listens carefully to Szasz, between a client/patient and others is that the client or patient seeks help. According to Szasz, we all have problems, and yet not all of us seek help. The words that once designated mentally sick people and old treatment procedures have had a useful history, for they replaced words such as "tainted personality" and "insane." They brought the patient out of the snake pit; they were labels applied to the patient by the doctor rather than by the judge, and they implied both treatability and a need for shelter and protection.

The present attempt to discard the word *sick* and maybe the sick role altogether has many arguments on its side. The sick role was doing its job so well that it often became a life sentence; patients became habituated to the role and developed "hospitalitis"; they wished to remain forever in the safe hospital environment or in the psychotherapeutic relationship. And the sick role was used by too many people, victims and victimizers alike, as an excuse, an alibi for unacceptable actions and criminal behavior.

A "dysfunction" role may alleviate these disadvantages by viewing the patient as only temporarily in need of a protective environment. Indeed, the temporary use of mental hospitals is reflected in the increased admission and discharge rates. The distance between a severely malfunctioning person and a mildly malfunctioning individual is no longer as great as when the sick role was in vogue. Retraining is equally applicable to well-functioning individuals who want to change certain patterns. Thus, training groups for executives, engineers, sales personnel, university administrators, and school principals are now using therapeutic techniques. The revolution in the mental health field that narrowed the distance between the functioning and the nonfunctioning individual has made it possible to use therapeutic methods in everyday life. There is certainly no shortage of books explaining in popular language to parents, lovers, and loners how therapeutic modes can be of help to them. Basic to all treatment processes is the communication exchange, with its analysis of channels of communication, its principles of impact, and its definitions of persuasion. In this chapter we shall describe two important operations of these methods from the communication analytic point of view.

FAMILY GROUP THERAPY

Ackerman (1960), Jackson and Weakland (1961), Bateson (1961), Bell (1961), and Berne (1961), among others, can be credited for the very sudden impact of conjoint family group therapy. They presented evidence that seeing a family as a unit and working with individuals' interactions with the other members of the family is a more useful tool for helping a disturbed family than treating them individually. This approach relies on the theory that the malfunctioning member is part of a system, and that the system itself is enhancing the disturbances (Alexander and Parsons 1982). All members of the group have some investment in the malfunctioning member, and often they do all they can to protect their investment: they work hard to keep him malfunctioning.

In conjoint family group therapy, a disturbed family is viewed as one in which communication among the members is severely disturbed. Each family member is given a chance to discover his contribution to the family problems, often through coalitions where two members of the group vote together, regardless of the issues.

The success of conjoint family group therapy requires an increase in pertinent communication and perhaps a decrease in peripheral communication. That is to say, the group has to learn about things that help them solve the problems rather than talk around them. The therapist typically analyzes those cues in the communication process that each member sends to constrict the communication of other members (see Bateson, Jackson, Haley, and Weakland 1956). In the language of communication analytic psychotherapy, the therapist "catches" the family member in the act of using cues to achieve certain types of emotional engagement within the family. The therapist is effective because there can be no denial that the one family member has said something or used a certain procedure that has created a certain emotional climate in another member or members.

The art of catching the person in the act, of course, works only after the therapist is established as a person who is not siding with any of the family members. At the beginning of the hour, the therapist typically asks the members of the family to discuss their problem with each other rather than with him. Although this is a somewhat difficult task at first, most families quickly adapt to it. It places the emphasis from the start on communication, and avoids the referee's role for the therapist. By staying with an analysis of the process of communication among the family members rather than with its content, the therapist avoids entering into the group dynamics and is less likely to become a partisan.

We have adopted five guidelines for the therapist in such a setting, all designed to enhance communication of pertinent information among group members:

1. *The therapist intervenes when a member uses blaming behavior or says or implies that someone else must change to solve a problem.* Blaming and demanding that others change are devices people use most frequently to shift responsibility away from themselves and thus maintain the status quo. When a wife says, "If John would only stop drinking," she uses this device. The therapist responds with, "John surely knows your feelings in this matter. The question you should ask is how come you have a husband who drinks and how are you contributing to his drinking?" The therapist's message, "What do you as a member contribute to the conflict of this family?" is essentially a communication analytic statement. This question, asked of all participants by a therapist who is seen as nonpartisan, will arouse uncertainty and focus the patient's attention on her own problem. The positive implication of this intervention is that the patient has more power and more control over her environment than she believes. The negative implication, of course, is that she is to blame. The therapist has to guard against using the intervention to shift blame.

2. *The therapist intervenes when any member makes a statement that is designed to maintain the status quo.* A husband says, "My wife wants me to be more aggressive, but I am what I am. I can't help it." The therapist responds asocially to this communication device with, "You are saying, 'I am the way I am. I am not willing to accept the possibility of making any change in myself.' Perhaps you could ask yourself, 'Am I contributing to making my wife angry?' Please understand me. I am not saying that you should not be contributing to this. Maybe you have good reasons to make your wife angry. I just want to get you away from the idea that you are a victim, and that there is nothing you can do about these things." The thera-

pist thus attempts to create uncertainty in the husband by questioning his favored hiding place, epitomized by the "I am what I am" statement. Historical remarks ("My mother never loved me") are also regarded as just another way of holding on to the past, and the therapist arouses uncertainty in such cases by gently pointing out that a patient is using blame as an alibi. Patients may also refer to their feelings to maintain the status quo. A wife who came in with her husband said to us, "I just feel cold toward my husband," and the therapist replied, "And I am sitting where your husband is sitting, and I feel that this was a very, very angry, and even cutting statement. Perhaps your husband deserves it, but why not discuss why you deserve to have no pleasure with your husband." The therapist intervened to reopen a question that had been shut out by the communication device.

3. *The therapist intervenes when a member constricts communication by asking loaded questions or by conveying messages of which the member may not be aware.* A husband gruffly tells his wife, "We always talk things over, don't we?" The therapist intervenes: "I can see that you want to avoid hostility and fights, but did you give your wife any freedom to answer this question? You are asking a question, but are discouraging the answer (laugh). Will this increase your knowledge of where you stand with her?" A mother nags her child to speak louder, to sit still, not to lie, etc. The therapist intervenes: "I know you want to help your child to be a better person. You repeatedly tell him that he is not living up to your expectations. You also know that the procedures you use to improve your son have not been successful at all. Why do you repeat them again and again?" The mother responds, "I don't know what else to do." The therapist gets up and shakes the mother's hand. "I have to congratulate you," he says, "because now we are off to a new start, aren't we?"

It should be noted that in such situations the therapist analyzes only the communication patterns and does not judge or take sides in the argument proper. The therapist also has to be especially careful not to come across as supercritical, and always to recognize the patient's conscious motivations, which are often noble and well-intentioned, before accounting for the inadequacy of the procedure the person is using to reach a noble goal.

4. *The therapist must make a distinction between motivation—that is, the way the patient interprets an act—and procedure—the way the patient tries to reach for the goal.* The therapist's actions must tell the patient that he is not being criticized, but is being accepted and understood. They must also lay the groundwork for the patient's reevaluation of his motivation. The thought processes here are as follows: "If I am always desiring to have a good relationship with my wife, but if I am also always using a procedure to make her angry and disturb her, then perhaps my interpretation of my motivation is wrong. Perhaps I do not really want a good relationship with my wife—or I should change my procedures."

5. The therapist must maintain balance within the session. Throughout the hour, the therapist must be alert not to get caught talking only to the
most responsive group members; all members must receive an equal time
allotment. In this manner, the therapist conveys nonverbally that all members contribute equally to the disturbance in the family. Typically, a family
with a member who is seen as having "the problem" will quickly learn that
the "black sheep" among them serves a function for all members of the
family. Often the black sheep's function is to provide a distraction from the
severe tension existing among other members of the family. Not infrequent-
ly, after the first few hours of family therapy, the tensions among the other
members become the focus of their discussion. At the same time, the black
sheep begins (sometimes reluctantly) to lose his or her problem. Owen
Henninger, Jr., used this method at the Metropolitan State Hospital in California with groups of patients. He invited all close relatives of the ward
patients to attend meetings and reported that these sessions were very successful in restructuring family interaction, because the hospitalized black
sheep, in a communication analytic setting, could no longer be seen as the
only person having a disturbance.

Communication analysis in family group therapy uses the language of the
family as its source of information. The family members do not have to learn
a new language to fit the therapist's theories and professional stereotypes.
The therapist analyzes communications—be they words, gestures, or
innuendos—to discover the hidden roles of the family, the family laws and
rituals. The therapist responds to the family's processes of hiding, not to
what is hidden. During work with a whole family that shares a history, any
one of the therapist's responses is likely to create uncertainty in all members.
This seems to increase the members' readiness to try out new interactions.
We have noted that many families seen for fewer than 15 meetings have
made marked changes in their interactive patterns. This result is partially
achieved by the fact that the therapist helps to establish goodwill among the
members, and the other members then become adjunct therapists in the
family home, where they check themselves and are in a beneficial sense
checked when they fall into a pattern that formerly created disturbances.

GROUP THERAPY

While family group therapy is concerned with natural groups that are
cohesive and maintain continuous interaction outside the therapeutic hour,
groups formed of individual patients often have neither a mutual history nor
outside contact. In such cases, the members learn to interact with each other

in an exploratory way. One therapeutic benefit to being cast into a group of strangers is that the patients can be more daring in testing each other, since there are only limited consequences to this behavior. Rules regarding confidentiality and limits of association outside the group setting assist in regulating these consequences. Also, there are no fears that the group members will punish them if they explore new ways, a fear that is quite relevant in the family setting.

However, differences between family and other therapy groups occur not only in historical patterns and forces, but also in the motivational states of the patients. While family group members have an investment in each other, and often a goal of keeping the family together, the nonfamily group member has only a minimum and temporary investment in the other group members, and ordinarily no interest in the group's staying together. Both the historical and the motivational differences have their consequences; the therapist will respond to interaction patterns differently. In a family setting, the therapist can assume that members are familiar with the impact they have on each other, while in a group setting, impact and emotional climate have to be explored from the beginning.

C GROUPS

C (communication) groups are different from ordinary therapy groups inasmuch as the members are familiar with each other but do not live in a family setting. For example, plant managers having communication problems within a large industry might join a C group to improve their communication patterns.

The essential difference between C groups and other groups is that in a C group catharsis and deep levels of self-disclosure are not used. In other types of groups, catharsis serves to deepen the involvement of those present and to provide opportunities for relief of stress and tension. In catharsis, information may be revealed that is not particularly flattering to some group members, and in a family situation these types of honest interchanges are perhaps useful because they encourage others to supply similar information. In a C group, such information would not be encouraged. The basis of the group is for the individuals to learn about each member's impact on the other members. For this purpose, more sensitive and intimate information is not required. In many situations, the therapist might even thwart high-level intimate disclosure by warning that the information about to be revealed may not be useful for the purpose of learning about one's impact on others.

This type of protective behavior by the therapist has been criticized by some as serving to overly constrict group activity. But it is also a useful tool because it permits the group to center specifically on their interactions and what they do to each other unknowingly, rather than on information that might be used in later gossip. C groups are particularly useful in industry and in school settings, where a number of leaders and students interact and learn what interpersonal impact they have on each other.

THE GROUP THERAPIST'S ROLE AS COMMUNICATION ANALYST

The group leader is not just another group member, as some group thera- pists like to assume. Just as a father cannot be a child's pal without betraying the parental trust when responsibility for and authority over the child must be taken, a group leader would be hypocritical to proclaim that he is just a group member. The leader's purpose in the group is not to progress toward better functioning personally (though this sometimes can be a result) or to discuss personal problems. The leader has a major voice in determining where and when to meet, and though meetings can go on without some members, the group is likely to fold without the leader. Even when a group continues under its own power, it changes in character once it is leaderless. (We believe that a leaderless therapeutic group is likely to be beneficial for some members at the expense of others. We reason that engaging or involv- ing another person is the patient's greatest skill. Unless the group contains a person trained to disengage from the strong social demands made by some individuals, one who can show by example that disengagement is possible, the chances for therapeutic benefits are reduced to a minimum.)

As a communication analyst, the group leader will serve neither as a group member nor as a direct participant. The leader will occasionally interpret the emotional climate the group has created for itself, or respond to a member's bids for engagement. The leader's interest will be in analyzing the group members' communications for their subtle meanings and impacts, not to enter discussions of subject matter, to become a referee, or to try to bring the silent member into the group's conversation (though the therapist would try to do this in a family group). The leader will respond to the impact of silence on the group and verbalize the emotional climate it creates.

At the start, the leader will typically comment on the group's having been formed because all members had some issues to cope with. After such a general statement, one member may begin to talk, and others will remain silent. The therapist will not make any further structuring comments. Should the group remain silent, the leader will comment on the emotional climate this silence creates. As group members begin to participate, the leader will respond to the subtle cues, always concerned with both the emotional climate producing these responses and the impact his statements have on the group.

For maximum effectiveness, the therapist usually responds to an individual and deals with the individual's impact on others (including the therapist). This procedure has been subject to debate in group-therapy circles, and some have argued that therapists should avoid responding to an individual lest they only accomplish individual therapy in a group setting. However, we fail to see how individual therapy could ever be done in a group setting, since the entire group is necessarily involved with each exchange, be it between the group leader and a member or among group members.

When the therapist responds to an individual member, the others become participants in the exchange, though they may not add a word. The subtle meaning involved in singling out one member, the jealousies involved, the covert attempts of the member to use his prominence, and the member's wish to create a specific emotional atmosphere are all cues of importance to the group. These cues will affect the emotional climate of the group, engaging some of the members and thus restricting their response activity. The therapist will be on the alert to discover, *in situ,* any such imposed limitation on the communication exchange, and will use it to give other group members the experience that one can disengage from similar involvement.

We once worked with a group of near-dropouts, and the youngsters were in a sullen mood. One boy started:

> *Marcus:* I don't know why I should be here. I get laid every night.
> *Therapist:* Indeed, you live a happy life.
> *Marcus:* And I drink, too, a six-pack every night.
> *Therapist:* You live a regular sort of existence, too.
> *Marcus:* (desperate) But I smoke too!
> *Therapist:* So? (The other boys laugh).
> *Marcus:* That was some trap.

This opening speech was certainly important, and not only to the boy who made it. The other boys indicated with their laughter that they had recognized Marcus's need to find the enemy, and that they also were relieved to find the therapist able to handle this gambit. The asocial responses of the therapist gave them hope. It was a novel experience in a friendly, beneficial setting. The boy probably felt that the therapist was not easily manipulated. Marcus's response, "That was some trap," likely had more impact than a technical discussion about the emotional climate Marcus had sought. The response showed the boys that one of these games had not worked well, but that this failure did not appear to have grave consequences. The game was on, and the testing of the therapist continued:

> *Tony:* Why should I go to school? It's only for wimps. I think they teach you a lot of crap anyway.
>
> *Therapist:* (paradigmatically, in an exaggerated tone of voice) There is really no earthly reason to go to school. It's a ridiculous requirement.
>
> *Ramon:* You can't be anything but a dishwasher if you don't go to school
>
> *Therapist:* What's wrong with being a dishwasher?

We note that Ramon could no longer stand the lack of authoritarian demand. He was forced to intervene with such a demand on his own. The therapist still responded paradigmatically and asocially, giving the boys the experience that values have to come from them. Their antivalues, tested against the imagined enemy, were not achieving the desired emotional involvement of the "authority figure," the therapist, which allowed the boys to learn that these messages were not really necessary to feel safe with adults, and that the therapist did not fit the expected authoritarian mold.

> *Marcus:* Yeah, what's wrong with being a dishwasher?
>
> *Ramon:* Nothing wrong really, but I just don't want to be one.
>
> *Lou:* (to Marcus) And neither do you.
>
> *Therapist:* (to Lou) You are telling him what he should do, sort of ganging up against him. Will he be able to listen to you?

Here the therapist went into the second phase of his work: he alerted Lou and the group to the impact their statements had on each other. He now made the impact explicit.

> *Marcus:* I've got a girl and beer. Who cares?
>
> *Willie:* I'd like to have a girl, too.
>
> *Ramon:* I think Marcus is a sad case, bullshitting all the time. He wants to finish school like the rest of us. I know that.

The therapist recognized the dynamics of the interaction: Marcus, upon the reintroduction of authority by Ramon, withdrew to his girl-and-beer image, and in this withdrawal was joined by Willie. But Ramon himself wanted to face the issues. The therapist did not discuss these dynamics with the boys. He wanted them to experience what sort of responses they had elicited in each other and what type of emotional climate they helped to create for the group. The therapist responded to the last message.

> *Therapist:* (to Ramon) You want him to know that you know Marcus is putting on an act.

Ramon: He doesn't seem happy with that girl-and-beer stuff. He's just talking.

Willie: I would be happy if I had a girl.

Therapist: (to Willie) I got the impression you want to make friends with Marcus.

Willie: He's OK. He's got everything I want.

This seemed to be a detour from the main theme. But the theme does not matter. What matters is that the emotional demands inherent in their statements were made explicit and were recognized. Generally, it does not really matter what is being talked about. The only qualification is that the therapist understand the impact demands of each of the messages. Here the therapist intervenes with:

Therapist: (to Willie, with a smile) If you could only get him to share his riches with you.

Ramon: I think I am going back to school.

Therapist: (to Ramon) I hear you say that the guys are too far gone. You have to go it alone.

Ramon: They are fuck-ups. Girls are okay, but they are no reason to foul yourself up.

Marcus: (to Ramon) To hell with school. I hate school. Don't tell me what I should do.

Therapist: (to Marcus) To hell with Johnny. He's just talking like the teachers!

Ramon: I don't give a damn what you do.

Willie: To hell with school.

Therapist: (to Willie) If I could only have Marcus as a friend.

The therapist began to cue in to the subtle language of the participants. He became sensitive to Marcus's desire for an enemy, to Willie's need for reassurance of his rebellion, and to Ramon's need to align himself with a friendly authority, and the need of Tony and Lou to remain in the spectator role, unwilling to commit themselves one way or another. This sensitization to the subtle communications used by group members helps the therapist to make explicit the hidden impact of their statements. The therapist's purpose is to provide each boy with the experience of uncertainty regarding his automatic way of sending messages.

In summary, the therapist provides the group with an experience of disengagement by giving asocial responses wherever the therapist discovers inexplicit demands for engagement. The therapist hopes that each group member will experience beneficial uncertainty whenever one of them is caught in the act. The therapist thus attempts to create a beneficial emotional climate in the group, an environment in which the boys no longer find themselves reinforced in their automatic, preferred behavior patterns, but are able to discover new choices.

THEMES IN GROUP THERAPY

Disregarding the nature of the topic or even the silence, the skilled therapist discovers the way an individual member tries to engage another person to fulfill expectations. Even talk of the weather can provide such essential information:

> *Group Member 1:* Nice weather today.
> *Group Member 2:* Oh, yes, I love a blue sky.
> *Therapist:* And the clouds are beautiful, and the wind is blowing so sweetly, and the sun is sparkling, bright, and handsome.
> *Member 1:* Let's get going.

The paradigmatic response of the therapist was made with the intent of providing group members 1 and 2 with the experience that they were using the weather to maintain, conventionally speaking, a superficial level of conversation. Had the therapist's intervention been given in a severe tone, it might have sounded heavy-handed, and members 1 and 2 might have read the therapist as being impatient and critical. Giving paradigmatic responses in just the right way is an art, and the inexperienced therapist may very well choose not to do so with regularity until learning the impact these responses have on others.

We have been associated with a hospital where the technicians were given permission to act as group leaders, with instructions to stay within a particular theme such as racing cars or sports. These instructions were thought to be safety measures that prevented the technicians' hurting the patients. Such limitations, of course, are nonsensical, though they may provide a sense of status to those who invented them. To some, it may appear that talking about sports cars is somewhat inferior to talking about one's ego. Yet by giving the technicians what could be conventionally termed inconsequential themes, the authorities conveyed to the patients and the technicians the notion that the paraprofessionals were less prepared to deal with delicate topics such as sex, religion, politics, and child-beating—which, of course, is a debatable proposition. We firmly believe that restricting topics is of little significance. In fact, research on group process (Lieberman, Yalom, & Miles, 1973) indicates that style of group leadership, especially an aggressive or challenging style, leads to group casualties—not the topic of the discussion. If being too authoritarian is a person's problem, this person will use any topic at hand as a vehicle to boss someone else around. If a patient operates with a covert pattern of seduction, the patient display this engagement pattern whether the topical content is the weather or the stock market. Each of us has areas where we are more likely to be engaged than others, and it would be wiser to think of the particular deficit a given person has and help that person explore their stylistic vulnerability than to forbid discussion of certain topics.

Some therapists try to lead the group to deep and meaningful discussions, and even speak of "peak experiences" within some sessions. We have already stated that we do not believe in the value of such selections; we are more concerned with how these themes are used than in what they are about. Our wish to minimize the significance of themes should not be read as meaning that one specific theme cannot yield more information than another once the therapist understands the patient's language. The therapist should be aware than a given theme may be of great significance to one group member but peripheral to another. In other words, we feel that the therapist cannot afford to become interested in any given theme, not even Hill's so-called "work theme," lest the therapist become engaged and ineffective in reading the impact one group member has on another, whatever theme is serving as a vehicle.

Hill (1961) and Hill and Hill (1961) devised an effective method of measuring the group process. It involves evaluating the statements made by participants to determine whether they are self-centered, group-centered, work- or issue-centered, etc. Although this attempt permits vigorous measurement of the group process, one could ask whether such categorization makes sense altogether. A work-centered group may simply use a different theme to work out their problems than the self-centered group, but any communications can be effective in helping a patient make gains, provided the therapist recognizes just how these communications are being contribution by introducing a systematic method of evaluating the group process, but we are far from convinced that their choices are based on the right principles.

SILENCE OF GROUP MEMBERS

When a group member remains silent, group therapy leaders tend to become concerned. This worry probably results in part from the therapist's having learned that talking is a good and therapeutic thing. But silence can be an important means of communicating to the group and to the therapist: with it, the patient can arouse concern, he can create an emotional climate of guilt (because the group has been neglecting him), anger (because the silent member remains an outsider despite some missionary efforts on the part of the group), or even fear (that the silent member may incur harm by participating).

That a silent group member has less of a therapeutic experience in the group than a talking member has never been demonstrated. In school, the silent student certainly can earn as high a grade as the noisy one. Why, then, do so many therapists assume that the patient must talk to get a beneficial experience?

We suspect that the silent group member makes the therapist and the other group members feel uncomfortable. The therapist often becomes engaged because verbal verification of the therapeutic hypothesis does not come from the silent member. The therapist is apprehensive about the silent group member because he needs the familiar verbal cues to define what type of engagement is occurring. The talking group member is always aware of taking the risk of revealing intimate information to the group, intentionally or otherwise, and of therefore being vulnerable to those present. Silent participants may in fact give an equal amount of intimate information to the group, although they may be unaware of engaging in the same degree of risk-taking behavior.

The silent member dampens the spirit of the group and generates an emotional climate of apprehension and caution; the therapist wants to encourage more restraint-free interaction. Consequently, many therapists give special attention to silent members, exert special efforts to "make" them talk. However, we believe the therapist sacrifices the welfare of silent members by singling them out. The word "sacrifice" is used because we believe that special attention reinforces the silent behavior rather than giving these members an experience of uncertainty through a disengaged response. We believe this reinforcement to be an error. The therapist should respond to the silent member in the same manner used with more talkative members, indicating that the therapist understands the subtle information communicated by silence. He will then allow the silent member to see that the wish to engage others via silence has been recognized. With such an intervention, silence is not likely to succeed in constructing the group's behavior in the expected manner, as it is essentially as risk-taking as verbal behavior.

By treating the silent member as an equal in the group rather than as a person who is not playing the game properly, the therapist will give all members the information that they are in a beneficial, protected environment. They will learn that they cannot fall into disfavor because they behave differently from other group members. This "democratic" acceptance (love of the least) is probably a better guarantee of restraint-free interaction than rejection of the silence. Silence has to be dealt with as a communication, a behavior like other behaviors, from which the therapist must be on the alert to disengage properly.

THE CUES CREATING AN EMOTIONAL CLIMATE

Individuals appear to behave differently when they are members of a group than when they are alone. Although many people have thought about this problem of mass psychology, the nature of these differences is not clear. An otherwise decent citizen participates in a lynching as a member of a group. A miser contributes to a cause when the emotional climate of a group demands it. A mildly religious person admits to being reborn at an evangelical meeting. A soldier is braver and more effective when part of a daring unit. In times of stress, a whole nation—millions of individuals—commits atrocities that each single individual rejects as uncivilized.

What are the forces that cause the individual in a group to perform an act contrary to the individual's values? How does the group arrive at this change in values, and how does it cue the individual as to when the new values are to be used? We believe that communication analysis offers some understanding of these phenomena. Our particular interest lies in the previously isolated concept we called "shift of responsibility." We shall analyze the subtle communication that occurs among the members of a group in an attempt to discover just how an individual contributes to a given group climate, and how the shift of responsibility takes place.

Individuals join groups for many reasons. Merely to join is to give up certain rights, and to adopt in one form or another the standards and rules of the group. The group member hopes for certain gains: joining a group is always a communication to oneself as well as to others. One who has, for example, been accepted by an exclusive country club has enhanced his self image and has probably also tried to enhance the image others have of him. Becoming a group member sometimes means adopting group values for which the individual is not directly responsible. The new member of the country club may now profess detestation of outsiders or behave arrogantly to servants because these are the norms communicated by the group. In groups such as churches or even nations, and also in smaller groups such as street gangs, the person who has selected such a value system may hold the values of this group above life itself. In fact, an individual may face death with a sense of glory when death is believed to help the group—the club, the nation, or mankind—to survive.

What sort of information must an individual receive to make such judgments? What sort of cues does the group give so that the member can make such significant choices? One answer that appears plausible lies in the identification process. The individual receives information about group values and belief systems, just as such information was once communicated by parents. After accepting these values, the group member begins to create a new self-concept round them—that is, the group member develops a new identity. Joining a group is like joining a new family. The new group setting permits the person to share responsibility with the new family.

Over the past few decades, modern communication and transportation systems have led to increased awareness of the diversity of existing groups, and this exposure to multiple value systems has probably reduced our willingness to identify only with a single value system: exposure to a large variety of groups is likely to reduce allegiance to one's own group. It is for this reason that certain religious cults try to keep their flock from intermingling with others, especially in the phases of indoctrinating new members.

The motivation to belong to a group apparently results from the hope of sharing responsibility with others as well as from the fear of isolation. The individual chooses to join a group because the promised sharing of responsibility offers advantages. The would-be member may become aware of the economic advantages most groups provide for their members, becomes acquainted with the group's credos, pledges, bids for secrecy, punishments for leaving, romantic opportunities, clothing or food taboos, and common language. After accepting the information, the prospective member develops a sense of belonging. The individual may also be motivated to join the group by strong fears of isolation, loneliness, and uncertainty, and by the hope that the fears will be relieved by the new group values and the new positive feeling of belonging.

Belonging also increases one's sense of power and direction. Being in league with others, and possibly with powerful people, provides a sense of honor. Increasingly, the overt and covert communications offered by the group to the individual will affect the individual's attitudes, and the individual will shift personal values toward those of the group to feel increasingly a part thereof.

Similar forces are at work in group therapy, though the goals of this group are different from those of many other groups. This claim for uniqueness is based on the rather peculiar objective of the therapy group: it aims at its own dissolution. This objective demands that the group members perform entirely different tasks than they would in most other groups. Instead of permitting individuals to obtain solace by shifting responsibility, this group is designed to facilitate members' acceptance of responsibility for themselves. The group leader provides members with information that encourages at best only a temporary dependency on the group and that challenges each member to become increasingly self-reliant. The very structure of a therapy group in which the members do not know each other and meet for only a limited time provides each member with the information that there will be no benefit of attendance other than personal growth.

Another unique quality of most therapy groups is that each group member defines personal goals in the group. While a member may join a group because of a sense of isolation, the information received in this group teaches that isolation is avoidable and that available choices allow all people to overcome it.

A major portion of what transpires in a group depends upon how the group is identified to its members. Suppose, for example, a therapist decided to select for a group at a children's home six children without parents who had arrest records. What would happen in this group would depend heavily upon whether the group members were told, "This is a group of juvenile offenders," or, "This is a group of orphans," or, "This is a group of your peers." A group that has to meet on the order of a judge in order to avoid going to jail is likely to start with a different emotional climate than a group composed of volunteers seeking help.

The location and size of the room also are factors in determining the emotional climate. The group that meets in a school building probably begins differently from the one that meets at a mountain resort. The way the leader sees his role further determines the emotional climate in the group: an active group therapist creates a different climate than a passive one; a therapist who intervenes often and for extended periods differs from the one who mostly listens. Male and female therapists are often perceived differently.

While these factors help determine the initial climate of the group, their significance typically decreases as the group works together. The orphans talk about items other than their parental losses; the schoolroom is no longer of much importance; the frequency with which the therapist intervenes is largely discounted; and even the voluntary (or involuntary) aspect of group attendance no longer plays a major role. The group member becomes familiar with the new engagement patterns.

SHIFT OF RESPONSIBILITY THROUGH ENGAGING THE GROUP

One purpose of engaging another person is to shift responsibility. The child who is fearful and does not want to fight the neighborhood boys may try to engage elders and elicit from them prohibitions against fighting. With this tactic the child needs neither to fight nor to feel responsible for a failure to stand up to others. In the child's mind the parents are responsible for preventing the fight; and even though the prohibitions give the child some comfort, he may still berate the parents for them.

A group member typically wants to shift responsibility for certain unacceptable acts to the group and will try to engage the group in very much the same indirect manner. The processes of engagement will provide the group member with the experience of identification—either positive or negative identification by siding or disagreeing with the member who is addressing the group. For example, a patient in a hospital setting complained long and bitterly about the injustice of the hospital administration, which would not permit him to go home. With this message he elicited sympathy for his trials; he was trying to elicit positive identification of the other group members with his cause. Once he succeeded in arousing this emotional group climate, he had found an alibi, proving to himself and the group that he was a victim, an innocent bystander without responsibility for his fate, that he was detained against his will. In spite of this ploy, into which he had put much energy, we knew that he would not have dared to leave the hospital even if the staff had let him go, for he also knew that he could not yet trust himself on the outside.

The therapist in this case failed by not helping the group to disengage from this climate. He reinforced the ill man's adjustment by allowing his "They keep me here against my will" message to create an emotional climate for the group. Once the patient had been successful in sharing responsibility with the group through group engagement, other members felt highly encouraged to try their skills in engaging the group in their problem areas. The very existence of an intense emotional climate within a group should alert the therapist that he must guard against becoming ineffectual.

The group therapy session in which intense engagement patterns have occurred can offer the therapist an important opportunity. Because of the intensity of feeling, disengagement can be extraordinarily meaningful. Intense emotional engagement provides for a very strong in-group feeling and an overwhelming sense of identification. When it is not properly used for therapeutic gains through disengagement by the therapist, it strongly reinforces the behaviors the group process is supposed to make uncertain.

The group member who has helped create an intense emotional climate and who becomes aware of the therapist's disengaged response will first try to deny or fight the disengagement that interferes with the member's plan to share responsibility with the group. Communications designed to maintain the emotional climate are particularly useful when the therapist remains disengaged and can clarify the struggle to shift responsibility to the group. This beneficial use of disengagement is most often achieved by the therapist who masters a sense of timing. Such a therapist accepts the emotional climate and allows the group engagement to become intense before helping the group to disengage from it. The therapist's own disengagement—the labeling of the group climate—must be done gently in order not to create alignments within the group.

Timing is important. An entirely adequate therapeutic response may be rendered useless if a therapist miscalculates the impact of the response on the group. Timing in group therapy differs from timing in the individual therapy hour because the therapist has to assess whether the disengaged response will be properly understood by at least most of the group members: a therapist with poor timing may make a disengaged response that is comprehended by too few group members. If, in the process of therapy, the therapist directs asocial comments too often to this small group-within-a-group, the others suspect that the group is proceeding at their expense, and alignments in the group are reinforced.

The therapist's response to the patient who complained that the doctors unjustly kept him in the hospital might have been paradigmatic: "They keep you chained here, locked up behind heavy doors." The patient was, in fact, in an open-door ward, and such a heavy-handed response would have been designed to suggest to all group members that the emotional climate created by this patient was a bid to justify his wish to stay in the hospital. Yet if we assume that only some of the group members might have been aware that the patient was in an open-door ward, the response would have divided the group into those members who comprehended the intended meaning and those who did not. Timing in group therapy sessions demands that the therapist take into account the members' knowledgeability on certain issues.

We do not expect that all responses will provide desired experiences simultaneously to all members of a group. There will always be some differences in knowledgeability and comprehension, and, of course, group members are likely to pay different degrees of attention.

ON GROUP FORMATION

A given statement at the right time can inspire laughter, tears, a sense of serious purpose, a climate of relaxed play. A French nobleman about to be hanged from a lamppost by a revolutionary crowd during the French Revolution is said to have remarked, "It won't help enlightenment to darken the lamp with my body," and the group suddenly changed its ugly mood and let him go free. He had been able to engage the group, and the response was instantly adopted by the entire group. The possibility that a single response can account for changes in group attitudes can be observed in many places. For examples, skiers who do not know each other but stand in line for the lift will very quickly become an angry group when they see a skier trying to break into the line. The resultant overwhelming group engagement can sometimes lead to violence.

In group therapy, group engagements often occur based upon equally intense stimuli. A group member who has preempted much time may stay suddenly quiet and create a vacuum, the consequence of which might be confusion among all group members until a new leading voice emerges. In another group, a person given to friendly smiles and a lot of head-nodding may create an emotional climate to become the best-liked person within the group. Should this person suddenly change and say a critical word, the effect on the group might be instantaneous. Another member of yet another group, through gestures or manner of speaking—perhaps through personal excitement—may create exhilaration within that group. Not all persons are successful in creating an intense climate. Some, of course, would like to create a climate in which they are noticed; yet each person at certain times will contribute to the climate within a group.

Most often the individual is not conscious of the emotional climate he is bidding for, and being assigned responsibility for the bid is an interesting experience. Frequently, the first reaction of the group member who is caught in the act of creating a particular climate is denial. The group member will often even claim to prove active dislike for the climate he has helped to create. Whatever the claim, the group member has to deal with having been discovered influencing the group.

Some group members, perhaps unconsciously, desire to engage by polarizing the group. They often do so by exaggerating their own belief or value systems. The group splits into alignments, the members are divided in their feelings about the stated beliefs, and the essence of their engagement is in the polarization itself. Sometimes splits in the group are due to an emotional climate that has been created by at least two competing members who look for followers. It is the therapist's job to disengage from these emotional climates. They will always restrict the communicative process within the group; the construction will distort the interaction and previously established behavior patterns will be manifested.

The following example illustrates the sharing of an emotional climate by a group of "juvenile delinquent" boys (aged 15 to 17), with particular emphasis on the contagious effect that is the basis of group formation. During the third session of this group, one boy began to relate an event in his life that apparently had bothered him greatly. With tears in his eyes, he told the group that he was responsible for the death of his mother. The past Christmas Eve he had refused to do an errand for her—to get her some drugs from a "connection" (he had done this before). His mother, furious, had stomped out to get the drugs herself. On her way back, she apparently stumbled over the curb, lost consciousness, and froze to death in the gutter. The presentation of the message was partially designed to arouse sympathy in the group— an anguished plea to share the burden, to have the boys and the therapist share responsibility for the speaker's part in the mother's death. The message had an almost magical effect. Group members who had been cynical before began to relate to the boy and reassure him of his innocence, expressing their own feelings that maybe they had been guilty of committing acts of violence themselves. They all spoke with great intensity of feeling. The hour was characterized by a deeply stirred emotional climate, by talk of violence, reassurance, and self-abuse. Every member participated somehow in this meeting; all wanted to be heard. The emotional climate represented an extremely strong group engagement. It permitted not only the boy who started, but the others as well, to shift responsibility away from themselves to the group. This sharing also created a sense of meaningfulness, of belonging to the group, and initiated an instantaneous relief system. By describing their many self-incriminating acts, the boys also laid the groundwork to repeat them in one form or another.

As soon as the therapist became aware of the sense of intimacy and intense feeling that had been produced in the group engagement, he responded to the group's emotional climate in a disengaged fashion by reflecting on the climate at this point. Some therapists commit the error of becoming intensely interested in, even pleasurably involved with, the group when there is a deep involvement. With such attention, the therapist communicates approval to the group and is likely to reinforce cathartic confessional behavior rather than uncertainty. The members of this group, in their confessional mood, obtained relief by disclosing the violence and crimes they had committed. In this particular group, had the therapist shown subtle approval and pleasure by merely providing supportive therapy (see Chapter 7), the members would have learned that talking of violence and crime is an exhilarating behavior, that reports of deviant acts are a basis for friendship and feelings of belonging, and that confessions of violence enhance status in the group. Yet had the therapist censored such discussion, he would have communicated to the group that he was an outsider, one who could not understand the sense of belonging that came from their involvement. The therapist wanted neither to approve nor to censor. He wanted to help the group separate out the sources of their experiences, to help them disengage from the climate in order to be open for new choices. He had to stay disengaged in order to communicate to the group that he could understand the values, the sense of belonging, and the sense of daring the boys experienced. The therapist had to provide the boys with the experience of uncertainty, to let them discover that their wishes to belong, to share, and to find friendship were not necessarily related to behaviors involved in committing crimes.

The therapist's responses were designed to accomplish this task. He re-mained disengaged from the emotional climate created by the group, and by his very attitude and presence trained the boys not only to share respon-sibility for actions with the group, but also to assume responsibility for their own behaviors. One boy said, "When I saw my father beating up Sis, I threw that pan with hot boiling oil right into his face, and after that we didn't see him for another two years!" The therapist responded, "You chased him out of the house to protect your sister, and you felt good and strong at the time. For some time you were the man of the house." This response was an asocial, disengaged, response, since it did not follow either the boy's bid for approval or his fear of disapproval.

The response subtly alerted the boy and the group to the fact that the violent act reported was not completely altruistic, not just designed to help the sister, but that the boy got some pleasure from it: he committed the violent act to feel like a man. Very subtly, the therapist's response forced the boy to look at his behavior in a different way. Perhaps he was able to ask himself, "Must I really commit a violent act to be a man?" The therapist's response was disengaged but subtle, and in that sense counterpersuasive: it permitted the boys to view their group experience as something other than simply an act of sharing. The boys learned that these group sessions were a challenge and that they entailed a new way of looking at their behavior. The therapist was able to create a sense of uncertainty in the group, but a sense of uncertainty that was tolerable and challenging rather than threatening. He had created a sense of beneficial uncertainty.

ON SIZE AND DURATION

Psychotherapists have strong opinions about how large a group should be and how long contacts should last. They were reluctant to give up the one-to-one relationship as the most effective model for psychotherapy, and only hesitatingly accepted slightly larger groups for psychotherapeutic efforts. Psychotherapeutic group work is often planned for groups of 6 to 15 individuals, though today they can include mass meetings such as religious support groups, or mass audiences such as those available through radio and television programs.

The attempt to reach large audiences is not new. We need only to think of the emotional impact of some church services or even political addresses, or powerful stage plays that have been stirring people and causing them to think about their lives and their behavior for a long time. The proper information can arouse beneficial uncertainty in a group regardless of its size. Unfortunately, research into therapy with very large audiences is presently lacking, even with regard to methods used or results obtained. We need to discover the variables that could be used to help people in very large groups, and we need to evaluate such efforts effectively. We also need to learn to guard against their misuse.

The same comments apply to the problem of how long the psychotherapeutic contact should last. By and large, the amount of contact required to help a particular individual is dependent on the therapist's viewpoint. Among different therapists, the desired amount ranges from short-term contacts (between two and six meetings) to five- to seven-year plans with five meetings each week. Although in the era of managed care, brief therapy is the rule, the individual therapist typically has a fairly consistent view on the number of contacts required. Present managed care requirements set constraints on the number of contacts with limited or nonexistent flexibility for different diagnostic categories. Unfortunately it is usually the case that problem type or therapist viewpoint typically has little impact on plan limits.

The compression brought about by managed care neglects the two end points on the continuum of care: on the one hand, very brief contacts such as 15-minute or even 5-minute meetings, and on the other, lifelong contacts. It is important to review the value that the two extreme points might have on the treatment process. We do not always know whether contacts at these two ends of the contact range are of any value to the patient, though the derivation of benefits at these extremes is certainly conceivable. It may be that some people can be helped best by seeing a professional person for a very short time over a span of many years. It may also be that some patients need to establish a lifelong contact in order to maintain their psychological adjustment, and that such very long contacts do not necessarily indicate failures in therapeutic skill or lack of responsiveness in the patient.

A third form, of course, has been recommended in communication analytic psychotherapy: using the hours themselves and the scheduling of these hours as means of making the therapist dispensable for the patient. Such phasing out can occur by seeing a patient intensely for a given time and then eventually phasing into biweekly and even monthly and eventually bimonthly contacts. These phasing-out procedures themselves give a message to the patient, subtle as it is, that might be useful in preparing the patient to take responsibility for termination.

Continuous contacts have been viewed as failures in therapeutic skill because of the mental-health goals typically set for the patient. When the goal was to "cure" the patient, an exceedingly long treatment time was looked on with suspicion, and the critics would say that an unwholesome dependency had taken place or that a transference phenomenon that had not been "worked through" was hindering termination. But if psychotherapeutic efforts are viewed as teaching sessions whereby people discover consequences of their behavior and are confronted with a discovery of their automatic behavior, such "schooling" can go on for a lifetime without making an individual feel unduly dependent on another. Just as a professional person will continue to accumulate knowledge by reading the appropriate journals, attending lectures, and enrolling in occasional refresher courses or institutes, it is conceivable that the wish to be an "artist of living" (*Lebenskunstler*) may lead an individual to want to continue to keep up with this "field" throughout the years by continually seeking out related opportunities.

The concepts of "completing one's analysis," of "being cured," of "mastering one's own problems" are based on the idea that there is a state of optimum mental health that can be reached. This state is sometimes defined as one that permits the individual to have self-correcting devices at his disposal—methods of recognizing problems and making adequate corrections. In view of these definitions of the state of mental health, one might believe that help should be needed only temporarily or until the patient has succeeded in establishing these self-correcting attitudes. This view of mental health, however, is highly doubtful. Most individuals cannot be categorized as being either "self-actualized" or "self-correcting" or, on the other hand, as "sick" or "not self-correcting." The chances are that a vast majority of people are self-correcting with regard to some of their problems, while they are constricted in others. In our experience, even the adequate and healthy person can profit from engaging in a therapeutic relationship, from looking at the self and discovering personal responses in the presence of another person, and from inspecting personal patterns of automatic behaviors and constrictions. Not everyone may need psychotherapy, but everyone can, nevertheless, occasionally profit from the experience.

Continuous contact of many years' duration, even though some years may entail attendance at only a few meetings with a therapist, seems particularly profitable as a preventive measure. In fact, the field is slowly moving away from exclusive occupation with disturbed individuals or people in great pain, and much therapeutic work today includes seeing normal individuals who present specific problems, such as stress-reduction. These individuals have problems in mind when they begin therapy, but are also essentially interested in developing their resources and their potential. At this point we refer to a remarkable book that has summarized hundreds of researches in the area of group therapy and group treatment: Meltzoff and Kornreich (1970). In this book are reports of research on most of the questions that people want to ask about group therapy and group leadership, and even some questions that we do not particularly wish to ask. Yet even these studies do not include research on very large audiences.

The present focus on biological health is no longer exclusively concerned with sanitation, nutrition, and medicine: changes in a person's life-style, including emotional style of life, are included as an essential element to achieving well-being. The question of how a large number of people can be helped to affect such changes is a vital research question.

12

The Child's Communication in Therapy

Silent language is an important characteristic of all human interaction. The child, not yet fully accomplished in the nuances of language and therefore not yet the master of hiding behind words, relies even more heavily than the adult on silent language to express wishes and fears. Many of the subtle meanings that later will be incorporated into verbal language are acted out by children.

In exploring children's behavior and its effects on later life, parents, therapists, and other social scientists often focus too narrowly on the factors influencing the direction maturation may take. Typically, the child's behavioral idiosyncrasies, biological predisposition, and family dynamics are taken into account. Often neglected are the communications from surrounding influences such as peers and the political-cultural environment. We shall attempt to examine these additional forces, as well as to isolate some of the skills of the child in interactions and to explore therapy with the child from this point of view.

CULTURE, PEERS, AND BEHAVIOR

Although basic stylistic features of the child's communication style evolve within the family unit, we cannot discount the profound influences of peers and cultural phenomena on the developing child, especially during the critical stage of adolescence. One has only to review the influence of life-styles and behavioral patterns on youth during the past thirty-five years to document the power of culture. From the antimaterialistic hippies and flower children of the late 1960s to the narcissistic acquisitiveness of the 1980s to the generation X "slackers" of the 1990s we have witnessed profound impacts from the larger culture on the behavior of individual youths. We cannot dismiss as simply so much cranky myopia what leads many parents to exclaim in the consulting room, "I never would have dreamed of behaving this way when I was a child!" Times really have changed and continue to do so. The child entering the consulting room with multiple tattoos and body piercings is a different cultural entity from the hippie adolescent of 1969. In fact, it may be the therapist who has lost perspective when parents are automatically assigned responsibility for the child's behavior.

The predisposition of adolescents to be biologically and psychologically receptive to new directions in life-style and rebellion is well-recognized: young people are ready for movement and ripe for cultural influence. The effects of culture involve a host of economic, social, and intrapsychic factors. This should not serve to discourage the individual practitioner. Rather, he or she may choose to view these factors as important areas for exploration in working with the younger patient. The complexity of the interaction between social phenomena and individuals may be exemplified by reviewing elements of the hippie/antiwar movement of the 1960s and early 1970s. Where did the flower children and (quoting Bob Dylan) "mystery tramps" come from? Very few tuned in, turned on, and dropped out from ghettos and lower socioeconomic strata. The hippie movement was largely a white, middle- to upper-class experience. Youths from other segments of society, particularly lower socioeconomic situations, rejected the counterculture and were often angered by the carefree attitude of relatively wealthy, young, white people who *chose* to shop at thrift stores and rejected the advantages for which the poor were longing. Culture can obviously make powerful differences.

A smaller yet equally powerful segment of culture, the peer group, also helps to set the stage for much of the behavior of youth. Research on personal values (Feather, 1980) and moral development (Hoffman, 1980) reveals that adolescents are more influenced by parents than peers in these areas. Yet face-to-face encounters with young people will lead most observers to conclude that daily personal and social behavior is, to a large extent, chosen from if not determined by the peer group (Brittain, 1968). Through the critical stage of identity-versus-role confusion (Erikson, 1985), the adolescent continues to rely upon peers for social reference.

There is a strong case for considering the impact of physiological, cultural, and peer influences on the behavior of young people. Yet this consideration should not be confused with blaming. Therapists ought to recognize the powerful pulls of a culturally or peer-dominated path, yet should not resign themselves or their patients to it. Such passive resignation becomes too powerful a hiding pose for young patients, their parents, and their therapists. Young people must still be considered responsible for their own choices (conscious or unconscious) and their behavioral consequences. As Mary Cover Jones (1965) has said, the adolescent is also a "constructive actor" who actively creates new situations to explore.

THE PARENT'S POSITION

Children are usually brought to the office of a therapist. In most cases, we can be quite certain that the child has managed to deeply concern at least one parent about the child's welfare. The child has given the parents the feeling that they are incapable of handling the situation, that whatever they are doing only aggravates matters, and that time and money have to be expended to recover from this family trauma.

To elicit such feelings in the parents, the child does not need to behave within the limits of a particular pattern of aggression or defiance. A withdrawn child, a child with more than his share of accidents, a child with psychophysiological somatic complaints, or a child who is suicidal may prompt these reactions. Whatever the problem, the parents in their bewilderment and perhaps desperation are willing to delegate at least part of their authority to the therapist and pay a price in effort and care. If we assume that the child wants the parents to expend extra effort and care, we must admit that the child has been successful.

We often do make this assumption. More specifically, we assume the child has learned that certain behaviors will arouse anxiety in parents, perhaps making them feel impotent. By pursuing the "sick" or maladjusted role, a child will get the parents' extra attention without demanding it directly.

The child need not consciously scheme for such a reward or be unloved. Through many thousands of messages, the child has learned that a given behavior will have an unsettling effect on parents. To the extent that he wants to upset his parents (for whatever reason), the child is in a position to do so, even though some pain or punishment may be connected with this behavior. The upset of the parent apparently becomes rewarding, and the pain or punishment accompanying it is peripheral to the child.

Thus far we have suggested that a child is able to upset and emotionally engage parents at will, simply by using the information given daily. One parent may be particularly involved in early toilet training. Young Justin senses, through hundreds of repetitions, that wetting his pants creates great disturbance and involvement from his mother. When "mother is upset" becomes a desirable goal for the child, so he will use his knowledge and engage in the very behaviors he knows will gain this end.

The question of why a child should want to have upset parents is a little more difficult to answer. Were the child to openly admit wanting to upset the parents, the "why" question would be simple enough to answer. (The adolescent coming home late is often aware that she wants to "worry mother.") If such an admission were possible, we could then suggest that this child probably had a specific reason to "get even" with his mother. Perhaps she felt he was getting less candy than his sister, or was being unjustly yelled at, or had to stay alone too long, or was dominated too heavy-handedly. But we have found, in general, the child creates upset with two qualifications: (1) he is not aware of why he is doing it; and (2) he also experiences something that is personally upsetting—a spanking, rejection, physical pain, or loss of a valued object. It is almost as though the child creates the upset in the adult at the same time he provides a personal alibi—an alibi based on the assumption that no one would voluntarily seek pain. With the wetting behavior, the child expresses the belief that he did not intend creating the upset or being wet any more than he intended being punished or feeling pain. "I cannot be held responsible for this action," his pain tells himself and others.

Consequently, explaining the child's habit of creating upset in terms of simple retaliation is inadequate. One must also consider the fact that the child wants to retaliate safely for wrongs received, but cannot afford to be accused of doing this and eliciting further retaliation from the parent. Perhaps he has learned that overt retaliation against parents not only upsets them, but also makes them truly dangerous. Aggressive, retaliatory behavior, then, must become subversive. It must occur without the parents' having a legitimate way of fighting back.

This sort of subversive behavior can be observed in every home in one form or another. One child accidentally drops mother's best china; another forgets his schoolbooks just before a test; a third becomes the victim of the neighborhood children. While it would be absurd to claim that all such conditions are motivated, unconsciously or otherwise, in some cases there does seem to be sufficient evidence to call this a "safe" impact behavior. The child beaten up by the neighborhood bullies may sometimes be observed seeking out and teasing the bullies. The child carrying mother's best china may take it by way of the route most likely to cause a stumble. Some parents may respond with anger, disgust, or anxiety to these behaviors. It is highly probable that the child has learned to find such negative responses rewarding and reads them as "concern," as a way of engaging the authority figures.

This "concern" that the child bargains for eventually culminates in the parents' recognition that they can no longer deal alone with these problems. They feel a loss of competency and are ready to make some extra effort and go to some extra expense to bring the child into therapy. Thus the child has been doubly successful in arousing the parents: they have become upset and they have sought the professional concern of a therapist.

The "concerned" parent, then, is our first clue to the family interaction. The focus of our work is on why the parents responded to the child in a particular way and what the child encounters to prompt subversive retaliation.

Aside from the dynamics of concern and the child's unconscious wish to incapacitate parents, there are sometimes other feeling tones and motives mentioned when a child is brought for treatment. Bringing a child to therapy is simply not as accepted in our culture as making an appointment for the repair of a child's chipped tooth.

Parents may also act out their own subtle motives by bringing a child for treatment. Powerful messages are sent when a child enters treatment—messages to the child, to a spouse, or to another family member. Such messages may translate into the common theme, "I'm the only one who really cares about this child; the other parent doesn't really want to help." Bringing the child for treatment may provide a safe outlet for these feelings and a subtle means of controlling another family member.

Making the child into a patient is common in divorce situations, where demonstrations of concern about a child's mental health become a means of acting out feelings toward an ex-spouse. The child becomes a psychological pawn in the parents' game of expressing hostility or maintaining closeness with each other. Our research has demonstrated that divorced parents often misread their children's level of adjustment (Young, 1983a), and that they have a tendency to see more pathology than actually exists (Young, 1983b). The communications analyst must explore on several levels the meaning of bringing the child to therapy and declaring a particular child the patient (see Chapter 11).

THE CHILD'S PLACE IN THE FAMILY

While the therapist may want to see the child in play therapy alone, it is nevertheless useful to meet together with child and parents, and possibly with other siblings. One or more such group meetings give the therapist information that may otherwise be missed. But these meetings do not replace the intake session in obtaining information on the specific problem with which the family is concerned. The intake session is also useful in obtaining releases for information from previous professional contacts, for assessing previous medical and psychodiagnostic information, and for discussing the necessary number of contacts and fees. The family group meetings are designed to give the therapist firsthand information on the idiosyncratic rules and laws of interaction and communication patterns in the particular family (see Chapter 11).

In one family, a boy of nine had run away for the fourth time. The parents and a younger brother came to the first session and, upon the suggestion that the family discuss the problem among themselves, all three started to lecture the "prodigal son" on the evils of having the wrong friends. To a remarkable extent, the discussion was led by the eight-year-old, who assumed a very serious mien and told his brother Johnny that he should always find out whether his friends come from respectable families. The therapist not only learned that this family was preoccupied with respectability, which perhaps explained in some measure the particular "unrespectable" behavior in which Johnny was engaged, but also gathered information about the cohesiveness of the three-to-one alignment. This alignment, hypothesized from this first interview and verified in future sessions, sensitized the therapist to the sort of frustration Johnny was experiencing. In the work with Johnny, the alienation from his family became an important issue, particularly Johnny's contributions to maintaining the very alienation he so hated.

We once interviewed an 11-year-old girl who, for the most part, lived in a world of her own. She described with detail and imagination the beautiful garden she inhabited. In her thick referral folder she had collected a variety of heavy diagnostic labels. She was in a class for disturbed children on a third-grade level and was described by her teacher as extremely inattentive. Her mother had been interviewed and was described as a tense, well-educated woman who was overly concerned about her child. When we asked the whole family to come to a session, the mother told us that her two older sons could not come, as they had moved out of the home at the ages of 14 and 15. They lived with friends, and she sent them money each month. However, the father, Ruth (the patient), and a younger brother would come. The interaction of these four people during the first group session showed that the parents did not talk to each other and apparently had not done so for many years. The 9-year-old brother, with support from his mother, was "bossing" Ruth in a truly remarkable manner: he would strike her hard when she refused to play with him, and if she tried to play, would then yell at her and beat her for playing badly. The only responses from the mother at these goings-on were a shrug and the remark, "These children."

When the therapist commented that the mother and father had not said a word to each other, the father responded with tears. "How can I talk to her? Any word I'd say she would take as an offense or an insult; she'd run out of the house and take the car and go racing through town. After our boy was born, I just could no longer talk to her."

The mother yelled back, "You know what you did to me before Tommy was born! You have no right to talk to me in this manner!"

The children were so astonished at this exchange that they stopped fighting. The son went over to the mother, and Ruth made gestures implying that she was planting flowers in her garden.

From this dramatic exchange the therapist obtained useful information for a hypothesis regarding Ruth's place in this family. She apparently had learned that communication among family members has very dangerous consequences, that her father had "sold her out" to maintain peace, that her brother (acting out the father's wishes?) would enslave her, and that the one way in which she could retaliate was to escape and worry them. With this behavior, she would have an impact on the family and be a person in her own right.

We do not claim that there is not more to this behavior. There is the possibility of a genetic or biological predisposition and deeper historical sources, but we do believe that an analysis of such interactions does give the therapist important clues for future work. At this point, we wish only to show that full family sessions preceding play therapy are indeed useful in sensitizing the therapist to important problems of the patient.

One therapist saw a child of five who was very dependent on his mother. When the child was separated from her to be taken to the playroom, he resisted and cried violently. Working under the assumption that he must have the child present to work with him, the therapist carried the boy into the playroom. Although views on this type of intervention differ, a case can be made for this procedure. After all, the mother had come a long way to get treatment for the child, and permitting the child to control whether he received treatment would have its own hazards. The therapist believed that he ought to let the child know that he understood his feelings of anguish, but at the same time he wanted to set clear limits regarding this behavior. At that point the child began yelling with such intensity that his mother rushed in, grabbed the child, and left, thus ending the contract.

One could easily argue that the mother was not ready for separation and used the conventional "My child suffers too much" to justify withdrawal. This argument is too pat. It would probably have been wiser to show concern for the mother's anxiety by inviting her and the child into the playroom for a family session. While one would temporarily be giving into the son's need for control, through this gesture one would also communicate to him that the fear of separation is a family problem, not his alone. In addition, one would enhance the probability that contact would continue.

In analyzing unspoken language of the family, one must consider not only vocal stereotypes and the nonverbal properties of speech, but also relevant information that is presented through contextual cues, which include the setting, and also that which is given to the child by the parents prior to the contact. The therapist is frequently asked by a parent what to tell the child before the first session. We usually suggest that the child be told that the parent is worried and that the child is being taken to see a therapist to help both the child and the family overcome their problems.

Discussing this question with parents is important even if they do not bring it up themselves: how they motivate the involuntary patient to come is significant. The parents of some patients we have treated paid their children for going to see the therapist; other parents bribed their children with a bike (to be given after getting a good "report card" from the therapist); still others referred to the therapeutic hour as a school session, and to the therapist as a teacher. Our intention is not to correct the parents or to avoid misconceptions, but to point out the possible significance of the subtle information introduced into the therapeutic session through these suggestions. Threats or rewards will surely influence the child's approach to the therapist. A therapist sensitized to this information will become more effective in understanding the child.

The therapist must also remain aware of parental feelings: first, because the therapist will then see the child's problem as it relates to the interaction within the family; and second, because the continuity of the relationship with the involuntary patient is dependent on the parent.

ACTION LANGUAGE

In adult psychotherapy, the therapist has to make an effort to transcend the social meaning of words and try to understand their implied meaning. In play therapy, the therapist has an advantage because the child has not as yet mastered the adult ability to hide behind words. Instead of or in addition to words, the child may use gestures, silences, and facial expressions to express emotions. The child may even use spatial relations to be close to or far away from the therapist, and will use all these behaviors with less inhibition than adults. Toys, too, can take on a communicative meaning. The attentive therapist will become sensitive to the unspoken language of the child and will be able to extract the subtle information it conveys.

Most therapists prefer simple toys to complex ones. A therapist will find it easier to understand the meanings expressed in play with a wooden hammer than with, let us say, an erector set. In addition to a few simple toys such as finger paints, dolls, blocks, soldiers, cars, planes, a punching bag, and sand and water, we have successfully used masks and a small house or tent in which the child could hide. While the adult can successfully hide behind words, the child should have more direct means of disappearing whenever the need is felt.

THE CHILD: AN INVOLUNTARY PATIENT

The child essentially is an involuntary patient. This fact by itself presents some contextual information. The therapist's final decision is sought. Accordingly, the child who is brought to us by the parent does not present a problem in treatability, but rather represents a case where the child's awareness of needing help has not been established. The therapist should be sensitive to this distinction. When we call the child an involuntary patient, we do not imply that he does not want to be helped. All patients are ambivalent about obtaining help, whether or not they report they want it. This is an observation on which Freud built his theory of resistance. Even the patient who claims that he wants help still clings to the present libidinal position, though its desirability may be denied. The voluntary patient is often unaware of a wish to cling to problems. The involuntary patient, on the other hand, is unaware (or denies) that he has any problems. Although there are ethical problems involved in giving therapy to a person who believes it unnecessary, whether a person clings to problems with or without awareness probably makes less difference to the effectiveness of the therapeutic interventions than we might think at first glance. In our experience, hospitalized patients exposed to a therapeutic milieu, delinquents referred by a court, or children brought in by their parents all seem to respond as well as voluntary patients. The therapist cannot accept the assumption that only the patient who seeks help can be helped. Communication will be effective as long as there is a person present who receives the information. Communication principles maintain that covert information can have a emotional impact on another person regardless of whether this impact was sought consciously.

This decision regarding a treatment contract for the child rests on the parents in most cases, and so contact with them is necessary. Our procedure has been to have all contacts with the parents in the presence of the child, so that there is clear understanding by all family members as to what exchanges took place. The parents often seek contact with the therapist because of their concern about the progress the child is making. Sometime they want to discover the "magic" the therapist uses to produce changes in the child, and at other times they seek advice on how to solve specific problems. They may wish to direct the therapist's attention to certain goals that are important to them ("Can't you help me make the child want to go to church?"). The therapist's attitude toward the parent during such contacts will convey important information to the child. Our practice has been to suggest in front of the child that the parents talk directly to the child about matters of parental concern. The therapist who becomes advisor or referee risks being directly identified with the parents and loses the unique relationship with the child.

STRUCTURE

Therapists differ in what they tell the child upon entering the playroom. Some prefer to start the hour with a long list of dos and don'ts, while others refuse to provide any structure. In our opinion, verbalizing a given structure essentially serves the therapist rather than the child. The message, "You can do what you want here, but you cannot hurt yourself or me," is likely to give the rebellious child ideas, the docile child the feeling that the therapist is too strict, and the withdrawn child, at best, the information that the therapist is somewhat uncomfortable. The message, "You can do anything you want and you can trust me," is even more inadequate, for it invites the child into cahoots without consensual validation. The child's best guess about this message is the way we feel about a book title: will it fulfill its promise? The true structure of the interview will, of course, emerge within the treatment hours; and it is during the sessions that the child will find out how much to trust the therapist, what the limits are, and what he is expected to do.

Structure can be imposed not only by action, but also by the therapist's silence. The child may believe that the silent therapist is playing a waiting game to avoid taking responsibility for the first move. In such an unstructured setting, every gesture of the therapist will be of great importance to the child.

One often unnoticed gesture is the establishing of distance between child and therapist. The child may stay at one end of the room, with the therapist at the other. The question of who will make the first move to close the gap may seem inconsequential to the adult, but appears to be clearly perceived by and important to the child. The adult's immobility may be interpreted by the child as indifference. In some cases, a move toward the child may be seen as a threat. We maintain that each spatial move has specific meaning, and the therapist should be aware that such motions, ordinarily unimportant, are likely to be meaningful to the child. Therapists for adults are typically sedentary in their practice and might want to explore movement options and their impact when working with younger patients.

Another subtle gesture often overlooked by the beginning play therapist is the child's use of silence. The adult can use silence effectively, but also has the skill to cover up silence with small talk. The child ordinarily has a somewhat smaller repertoire of behaviors to cover discomfort. He may play silently, thus leaving out the adult; stare into space as if the adult were not present; or engage in self-talking. These are all gestures that tell the therapist that the child wants to avoid the responsibility of seeking a relationship, perhaps because he is afraid of the consequences. The child may feel hostile, or may simply be silent because of the wish to find out what approach the adult will use. We cannot know the reason without further evidence. To properly structure the interview, the therapist must read these subtle gestures and give child patients the understanding that they are not lost—that there is an attempt being made to understand them.

TYPICAL PROBLEMS

There are some specific problems often encountered by the therapist working with younger patients. What about rapport? Should the therapist try to be nice in order to elicit the child's response? Predictably, our answer is no. We feel that the therapist should not make any special social effort or pretend that the hour is designed for the pleasure of the child. He should interact with the child and try to understand the child's hurt. At the same time, the child should be provided with experiences that will permit new choices, both at the beginning and throughout the contact.

Some therapists sit in their chairs and let the child come to them, while others sit on the floor with the child. Some always let the child originate the play, and enter into it only on demand; others refuse to enter the play even on the demand of the child. Still others are willing either to originate the play themselves or to play with some objects such as finger paints in order to stimulate the child to explore these toys. We feel that none of these variations is of great significance by itself, but that each presents a different structure to the child. The therapist must use the approach with which he feels most comfortable. We encourage our students to try out some of the more unfamiliar approaches, approaches with which they can explore their own limits. The important point is whether, with a particular approach, the therapist finds a way to help the child experience the freedom to explore new choices.

Another problem that often bothers the therapist is the child's leaving the room. The child may repeatedly ask to go to the toilet. He may make a plea to leave or just make a run for the door. Within reason, we believe that the child should be kept in the room, even if the therapist must sit in front of the door. It is true that this gesture communicates to the child that the therapist is bigger and that the child must therefore remain in the room. However, the therapist's desires to maintain the relationship and help the child are also communicated. Guaranteeing the child's presence enhances therapeutic effect. Some therapists deal with the child permissively, with the assumption that the child will eventually accept responsibility for staying when given the power to make the decision. These therapists are taking the risk that the parents will be content with a five-minute visit; more seriously, they simply have postponed the handling of *limits.*

Even the most permissive therapist must set limits at some time. Many unspoken rules regarding the interview itself are in actuality standard operational procedures that impose immediate and direct limits on the contact. A therapist is ordinarily unwilling to see the child in a local bar or see a child for four hours at a time on demand. We are inclined to make the presence of the child another such standard operating procedure. We recommend enforcing this presence and using the child's behavior to learn about problems.

The child is trained to accept responsibility by testing the limits of the environment. Testing limits is also an essential part of play therapy: the therapist structures a new territory for the child and presents the child with unique boundaries. We will analyze the problem of testing limits from the standpoint of communication theory.

When the child or the therapist is endangered, or, to a lesser extent, when the play-therapy room equipment is placed in jeopardy, the traditional limits are tested. The therapist ordinarily deals with these situations by acknowledging that the child wants to do a certain destructive act and stating that permission for such an act will not be granted.

In a playroom where the windows are not secured by a safety device, the child may attempt to climb out the window. What does this behavior mean? One could speculate that the child has learned that "taking chances" will arouse the adult's anxiety and constrict the adult's behavior to prohibitive, punitive responses. If this guess finds support, the therapist can infer with reasonable certainty that the child has learned the use of this high-impact behavior because milder behavior such as jumping from a chair did not elicit the desired response. We do not know yet why the child wants to constrict the adult into a "worry response," but we assume that he expects to obtain it. The child has learned that climbing onto the windowsill creates anxiety in a mother (who would not be likely to say, "Oh, Johnny, I see that you want to climb out the window"), and that she will order a stop to this behavior. The therapist who responds with a similar anxious and restricted response would most likely reinforce the child's testing behavior and enhance the chance of its recurrence. At this point the therapist has to set limits in a different manner than the mother and others have previously done. The response should be designed to give the child the experience that testing the adult is all right, but that the particular testing behavior chosen is not acceptable. The therapist may say, "You want to frighten me, but you cannot climb out the window." If this limit is not successful, the therapist will have to constrict the child's behavior, but again with firmness and no anxiety. The communication involved in this gesture must say, "I will accept having to prevent you from killing yourself, but your thought of testing me in this manner does not frighten me; you have the right to think any thought."

A child throwing sand at the therapist may attach certain expectations to the gesture. In showing so much direct aggression, the child may assume (by convention) that the adult will get angry and punitive. The therapist who acts out the expected social role may reinforce the inappropriate aggressive behavior. The child may perceive the expected response of anger and punishment as a reward. By separating the wish for aggression from the aggressive behavior proper, the therapist recognizes the right of the child to feel aggressive but limits the aggressive behavior itself. The therapist may say, "It is really fun to throw that sand at me, but you cannot do it here." Should the behavior persist, the child is essentially telling the therapist that this testing behavior is extremely important and is possibly being used to convey a meaning other than aggression.

The inexperienced therapist is given to repeating statements when the child repeats a behavior, but such a repeated response quickly becomes inadequate. The experienced therapist may respond to repeated misbehavior with, "You wonder when I will get really mad at you." If the child persists, the therapist might ask what we have called the existence question,

"You wonder when I will give up and let you go?" With this type of response the therapist recognizes the legitimacy of the child's wish to be aggressive but attempts to limit the behavior. In some cases no verbalization will stop the child from hurting people or destroying objects. Then, physical restraint is necessary. If the therapist is anxious about or unable to provide such restraint, a referral may be in order.

Neill (1977) has claimed that a child who is left relatively unrestricted will eventually find his or her own limits. The child allowed to break windows will discover that there is no need to do so to establish himself. We do not share all of Neill's assumptions. When the child learns to obtain a punitive response from the adult, he also learns that the controls for behavior lie outside, and that one does not need to accept responsibility for behavior since some adult will do this. However, when the expected response does not follow an act, the child is faced with an experience that demands that control come from within.

One could agree with Neill to the extent that broad limits help to retrain the child. However, whether the child's experience must in fact include testing all limits with actions before accepting personal responsibility is questionable. Does such a model perhaps confuse wish and deed? We believe that the *wish* to destroy the window is actually as significant as the deed itself. It is the wish that motivates the testing behavior. The deed becomes necessary only if the wish itself is not dealt with. With the therapeutic responses, "I can understand how you would want to feel strong and break the window. That would show me," the child can learn that there is nothing wrong with the wish itself, but that the deed may not be necessary to prove this point.

In this connection we can comment on the contradiction in the educational goals to which the child is so often exposed, particularly in reference to aggression. The male child, according to social expectations, is supposed to be reasonably aggressive, willing to compete, and ready to assert himself. Yet the responses to his messages connoting aggression, competitive feelings, or self-assertion not only leave him unrewarded, but actually punish him. The punishment would be understandable were it administered only for aggressive deeds, but more often than not he is also punished for his wish for aggression. Typically, punishments seem almost designed to "throw out the baby with the bathwater." The parent says, "You are a bad child; you should not hit your brother." The statement, "You are a bad child" is designed not only to discourage the boy from hitting his brother, but also to make even his wish to hit his brother suspect. "You are a bad child" means just that: "You and your behavior are unacceptable." Perhaps the boy has just been hit by his brother or has seen his brother preferred by having received some reward from his parents, and his wish to hit is simply a manifestation of his desire to assert himself. He wants to compete, and his aggressive act serves his need for self-assertion. "You are a bad child" is a statement designed to discourage these feelings.

What the child should really learn is not that he is bad for wanting to hit his little brother, but that the actual deed of hitting him is unacceptable, and that there are more adequate ways of asserting himself. The trouble is that the parent may not have guided the youngster toward more adequate ways of expression, and the child simply learned that he is not permitted to be assertive himself when he feels that an injustice has been experienced. When his parents discourage even his wish for self-assertion, the child is placed in a double bind. He is expected to be self-assertive, but cannot afford to be self-assertive enough to have such behavior seem meaningful to him. By differentiating the wish from the deed, the therapist helps the child escape this double bind.

A related problem with which play therapists have to deal is the destruction of property. Trained to be permissive, many beginners tend to constrict the child as little as possible. This permissive response is often of great importance to the therapist but probably somewhat less so to the child. For example, in allowing the child to squeeze the whole tube of finger paint instead of a limited amount, the therapist may think he is in a unique, asocial situation where acceptance of the child is mandatory. Actually, the quality of this therapy is not dependent on the number of inches of finger paint the child is permitted to use. The child who squeezes the whole tube on the paper does so either because of the understanding that this is permissible or because of a wish to challenge the therapist. If the act occurs because of a lack of instruction to conserve, a simple limiting statement corrects the child's behavior. If the child squanders because of a wish to discover or exceed limits, the problem becomes an interpersonal one and is no longer related to the finger paint.

At this point a statement of limits—"I know you like to use more of the paint, but that is all I can let you use"—would set the limit in much the same fashion as when the child wanted to climb out the window. If the child were trying to elicit a scolding or punitive response by squandering paint, the therapist's setting limits without scolding is indeed a new experience. A child will frequently persist in testing limits as though obtaining the punitive response was of great importance. This increased challenging activity, vociferously demanding the expected response, is designed to test adults, many of whom grow impatient with the test and become punitive. The therapist who becomes anxious rewards the child with the expected response, thus reinforcing the problem: an anxious, punitive therapist tells the child quickly that the therapist's acceptance of the wish to assert is only skin deep, and that this adult, too, has to be engaged and controlled by more subtle means.

The child's testing of limits does not necessarily directly involve threats against the self, others, or property. Challenges are often much more subtly introduced, as the following exchange will illustrate:

    Child: Can you spell my name?
    Therapist: You wonder if I can spell your name?

This was a simple delay response that asked for further information. Like all delay responses, it avoided the social response (J-o-h-n-n-y) this message was set up to elicit.

    Child: Can you spell it?
    Therapist: You wonder if I can spell it.

This response was a preservation. It no longer was a quest for further information, but communicated to the child that the therapist was having some difficulty in responding. Possibly the child had the feeling that the therapist was not permitted to give a direct answer, and so wanted to challenge the therapist's involvement with this restriction.

    Child: Can you?
    Therapist: You wonder if I am able to spell it?

Here the therapist becomes engaged in the demand of the child. True, the child's name is not spelled, which would also have been an act of engagement. But at this point the child most likely was no longer interested in having the name spelled, and appeared to want to "call" the therapist on not giving a direct answer. The ineptness of the repetition permitted the child to sense having succeeded in being one-up in rendering the therapist ineffectual. One might say that by being repetitive, the therapist reinforced the child's notion of being able to get satisfaction by confusing an adult. The child apparently enjoyed the victory and continued the role:

    Child: Why don't you spell it?
    Therapist: You want me to spell it.

At this point the therapist played the role of the confused adult to perfection. The child might very well ask, "How dumb can you get? I told you four times that I want you to spell it."

    Child: (angrily) Yes, spell it.
    Therapist: You are quite angry that I haven't spelled it yet.

This reflection was more adequate. Apparently the therapist has begun to pull out of the engagement. The response shows that the therapist realized that spelling the name was no longer really significant and that the real question was of control.

> *Child:*   Please spell it for me.
> *Therapist:* It is very important to you that I can spell it. It would show
>   that I care for you.

The therapist responded to the sudden change of pleading in the child's voice. He introduced his interpretation (the translation of "Can you spell it?" into "Do you care for me?") with skill. His response told the child, "Your challenge ('Can you spell my name?') is a substitute for words such as 'Do you like me?' What is so dangerous about this inquiry?" Thus, he stopped reinforcing the child's belief that receiving responses of affection can result only from controlling and misleading adults. Had the therapist spelled the name at the beginning of the exchange, the child's problematic behavior would have been reinforced.

Of course, the child might have had little awareness of the meaning entailed in the first question ("Can you spell my name?"). The subsequent reluctance of the adult to answer turned this exchange into a question of control and then into one of affection. Even so, it would have been an error to spell the name at the beginning of the exchange, as the therapist was still unclear as to what this question implied.

After the therapist had disengaged, the child responded.

> *Child:*   If you like me you will spell my name.
> *Therapist:* That would really prove it to you.

The therapist was fully disengaged at this point. The child still wanted to force the therapist to like him, and the therapist responded to this minor attempt at blackmail.

> *Child:*   I think you like me a little.
> *Therapist:* You are not quite sure, but it seems that way.

In terms of providing the child with the experience that subtle methods are an unnecessary means of coercing others to express liking, this was a good response. Now, the therapist could even have spelled the name without an overlay of meaning, though the behavior would probably have met the therapist's need for completion rather than any needs of the child.

In this exchange, the child tested the limits of the therapist in a more subtle manner than by destroying property. The chosen testing ground was the area of the therapist's self-restriction. Again, the child's benefit did not derive from unrestricted freedom, but from the asocial responses of the therapist who managed to disengage from the social demand of the message.

THE ASOCIAL RESPONSE IN PLAY THERAPY

While the disengaged response used with an adult is predominantly verbal, a disengaged response with a child can more readily take a nonverbal form. We have already mentioned that the spatial relationship between the child and the adult plays a role, as do gestures such as sitting by the child on the floor or cooperating with the child in play. We once worked with a student and a very withdrawn child who sat very still at the far end of the room and stared at the wall. The student apparently grew bored and pulled some papers out of his pocket and started to read, occasionally looking at the child to see if there were any changes. This gesture of inattention was certainly most inept, as the child's testing behavior was possibly concerned with the meaning that his presence would have to the adult. The therapist perhaps became engaged in the child's attempt to elicit a response, and confirmed the child's view that "adults just do not care."

Many therapists work with children who come to the room and sit inertly in a corner, presumably in a state of self-preoccupation. Assuming that we know the child is medically sound and of normal intelligence, we can use the information presented by the child's apparent inertness for a tentative answer to the question, Where does this child hurt? We can speculate that a child who ignores the stranger may have learned that any show of interest or participation indicates some kind of commitment. Commitment may appear dangerous—the child may have experienced that "they will take the whole hand if offered a finger." Or the child may have found that commitment is typically met with indifference, and that inertness not only serves a defensive purpose, but also has the effect of eliciting commitment from the adult—it serves to arouse feelings in the adult, perhaps anger or love and sympathy.

In view of these speculations, we would want to be careful in committing ourselves by using methods such as encouraging the child to talk, responding with indifference or anger, or hiding behind reading material to make a point of our inattention. We would want the child to learn that ignoring us arouses neither sympathy nor resentment. A verbal delay response might be:

Therapist: You wonder what coming to this playroom is all about.

The therapist attempted to disengage from the idea of commitment, and tried to let the child know that silence is all right. The response was probably more adequate than those we often come across in our transcripts: "It is hard for you to get started," or "It is hard for you to talk to me." These two responses show concern for the child but have the ring of engagement, as they imply that the child in fact wants to get started or wants to talk. They certainly imply that the therapist wants words. The silent child all too easily can read these responses as encouragement to talk or as sympathy, perhaps the very responses desired from the adult. Their occurrence would reinforce the child's silent behavior.

A verbal response is not really necessary, and probably serves more as a means of anxiety reduction for the adult than as a method of help for the child. With the act of talking itself, the therapist defines the structure and communicates to the child, "One ought to discuss events here." It is questionable whether this communication is actually beneficial. An alternative would be to sit quietly, with interest centered on the child, provided this can be done without anxiety or a sense of failure. We do not claim that the therapist's feelings will mysteriously be communicated to the child, but we believe that such waiting behavior, with one's interest maintained in the child, is an indication that the therapist is in the proper frame of mind to disengage from the child's silence. By avoiding gestures of restlessness and by showing interest even in the face of silence, the therapist helps the child experience that adults do not necessarily either have to talk or impose themselves on youngsters.

We generally find that with such responses, the child eventually admits an awareness of the presence of the other person by glancing furtively and perhaps by reaching out for nearby objects. The therapist's silence, combined with attention and interest, is a disengaged response under these circumstances. After the therapist obtains additional information, he can soon enough label what is going on and talk to the child at a time when verbal communication would help. Eventually one may want to respond to a furtive glance with, "You wonder what I am doing," or "You wonder why I am not talking." Yet, we know that even this behavior of labeling the child's state of mind is an invitation for a reply, and the therapist would have to be concerned lest it be perceived as coercion. An acceptance of the furtive glance with both interest and continued silence is probably more adequate, but more difficult for therapists to accomplish.

A variation of the silence theme is presented by the child who comes to the playroom and is immediately occupied with the finger paints, thus ignoring the presence of the therapist. In this variation, the message is more ambiguous. The therapist does not know if the child really wishes to ignore or merely perceives the play situation as an event similar to the kind of supervised play experience in school. In that case, a verbal response may be indicated to clarify the child's motivation:

Therapist: You like to play with these paints.

This response again represents a mild invitation to recognize the therapist's presence, and the therapist can gauge from the child's response (or lack of comment) what sort of feeling was involved in the ignoring behavior.

A nonverbal response can be useful for disengagement in a situation where the child tries to hide. Some playrooms have tents or playhouses where the child can hide; some therapists provide masks for the child to use. Without physical facilities for escape, hiding may be attempted with an act that symbolically represents the desire—for example, simply not looking at the therapist. By constantly staring at the child, many therapists do not permit hiding. The nonverbal gesture of keeping one's gaze on the child can be most disconcerting to him. There are times when it would be wise to shift one's gaze to other objects. This gesture is actually not very different from the behavior, used in adult psychotherapy, in which the therapist does not always give the interpretation or the response that comes to mind, but times the responses so that the patient has the feeling of proceeding at his own speed, of being able to take time to rest and time to hide according to personal needs. The child also needs this freedom, and the nonverbal gesture of averting one's eyes, minute as it is, can communicate the therapist's understanding of such a need.

This gesture would be particularly important if the therapist were to become engaged with the child through visual cues. A little girl had performed a dance for her therapist, and the therapist became aware that he had been quite caught up by the beauty and grace of the child. She expected this response, and it is likely that her very seductiveness was part of her problem. Were the therapist to be seduced by her gesture, the child would most likely be reinforced in using it. Therefore, the therapeutic objective was to give this girl the experience that she could be liked without resorting to seduction. With this goal in mind, the therapist said, "You like it when a lot of people admire you for dancing so prettily." Since the cues have been visual, the therapist should be cognizant of where he directs his gaze in order to help the child experience that he is not engaged by her exhibition.

One extra verbal cue we have observed many times in the supervision of play therapy is the use of children's talk by the therapist. Many adults have adopted a particular way in which they approach children, whereby they let the child know with every message (in terms of adjuvant cues) that they think of him as immature. This behavior probably derives from a generalized feeling of uncertainty that many adults have when they deal with children. Most adults have learned to make some allowances for the child's behavior, and the child in our society does have certain rights of exploration that we do not allow the adult. He can be a little more dirty, and vanity is considered cute; crying is not a crime, and even yelling on occasion is permissible. Furthermore, children, along with drunks, are considered people who tell the truth: if they do not like you, something must be wrong with you. Consequently, children are often seen as a threat by adults, and many feel uncomfortable with the child's greater freedom. Some therapists bring such feelings into the therapeutic hour. A therapist may talk down to the child. To the extent that the therapist is not aware of the subtle information transmitted, he will be a blunt instrument.

Sometimes the therapist faces a different dilemma in play therapy. As a verbal creature, the therapist will use words beyond the understanding of the child. Play therapy is a real challenge in this respect but, in essence, no different from therapy with adults. The therapist has to leave the academic way of talking and think of the impact that comments may have on the patient. A good way to illustrate this point is to think of a driver who cruises by a gas station to ask for directions. Were the driver to say, "Sir, would you be kind enough to tell me whether I am going in the right direction to get to Ogden?" he would probably get less of a response than if he were to yell, "Ogden?" and point in the direction he was headed. Many therapists still need to learn how to give a clear message, and play therapy with children makes a very special demand on this ability.

As in adult therapy, the therapist will formulate a therapeutic objective for the child. The evidence for this objective comes—just as with adults—from recognizing the child's unaware expectations of the therapist. Within the structure of the play-therapy setting, these unaware expectations are most easily inferred from the actions and gestures of the child.

A child, playing with some marbles, looked at the therapist and placed a few marbles in his own pocket. The therapist responded:

Therapist: You would like to take these marbles?

This was an exploratory remark that communicated to the child that the behavior was noticed and that some significance was attached to it.

Child: May I take them home?
Therapist: You would like to have something from the playroom at home.

The therapist wanted to explore the feelings involved. He was not yet certain what the child expected. This delay response also communicated that he could understand the wish of the child to extend the playroom, though he could not as yet be sure that his speculation would be supported.

Child: Will you let me take them?
Therapist: No, I cannot let you take them home. I know you wish I would let you.

The therapist placed limits on the behavior, but tried to indicate that it was all right to have the wish.

Child: Please let me take them. I need them.
Therapist: I am a meanie for not letting you take them.

The therapist used children's talk, perhaps because he felt that he really should have let the child take the marbles home. At the same time, he followed the child's expectations well: he recognized that the child was no longer concerned with the marbles but with coercing the adult into giving him something.

Child: Please, just these few marbles.
Therapist: You wish that I would give you something. That would show you that I really like you.

The therapist was disengaged and continued with an asocial response. He realized that the child expected him to give in or perhaps was asking for a rejection. By verbalizing the feeling, the therapist gave the child the information that these feelings can be understood without danger. This is one way of providing the child with the experience that it is not really necessary to hide feelings and control the other person by eliciting "high-probability" responses.

Child: I just want the marbles.
Therapist: You want to make it really easy for me to give them to you.

Apparently, the response was still disengaged. The therapist was well "tuned in" and changed his response with each new repetition in terms of possible new meanings. He was sensitive to the child's need and maintained his asocial response pattern. The child pulled the marbles out of his pocket and placed them in the drawer.

Child: What about this drawing, can I take it home?

From this exchange the therapist could make certain formulations about where the child hurt and what the therapeutic objective might be. He reasoned that the child had learned that there was some significant reward involved in making adults give him things, and that the object itself was unimportant so long as there was a gesture of giving (e.g., marbles or drawing). The child may have learned at home that he felt loved when a parent gave him something, or perhaps that this was the only way he could elicit a loving response. The therapist could then formulate the tentative hypothesis that this child had learned that he might not be wanted and felt vulnerable to being unloved unless he himself could produce a giving response. Many people feel they have to force others to love them, the tragic result being that they can never be sure whether these feelings expressed by other persons are genuine or merely elicited. The therapeutic objective in such cases is derived from the hypothesis that the child needs to experience that he can have a meaningful relationship with another person even though giving is not present. Sensitized to this pattern in the child's behavior, the therapist will arouse beneficial uncertainty. The therapist will provide the child with the experience that making an adult give things is not the only way of achieving the feeling of being liked. The therapist will avoid responding directly to the social demand of the child (in the above case, either by giving the drawings or refusing to give them), but will communicate acceptance of the child's wish for a gift, even though none may be given.

The child's demand for a gift may have had a more specific and highly differentiated purpose than fulfilling the general desire to prove he was loved. One hypothesis is that the child wanted to extend the permissiveness of the play hour to his home. He wanted to be exposed, through an object, to the therapist's presence even outside the playroom. In formulating a hypothesis, the therapist has to be aware that any current therapeutic objective will most likely change as understanding of the child's behavior changes.

Sometimes the social expectations of the child are far more subtle. A girl of 11 played with some dolls and the furniture in a doll house. While playing house she typically placed the mother and a baby doll in an oversized refrigerator while the father and a girl doll were alone in the house. The child went through a whole day's activities, including preparation of breakfast, father's going to work, the girl's preparing supper and making the beds, etc. What expectations were involved in this classic play? We assume that the choice of playing this game in front of the adult had to do with the child's motivation to test whether this adult would accept her replacement fantasy. The girl stacked the cards in her favor because she could predict that the therapist was not likely to chide her, and yet she apparently wanted to find out how far she could go with this play before sensing disapproval. The exchange went as follows:

Therapist: The little girl wants Daddy all to herself while Mother and Baby are kept in the refrigerator.

Then the child took another baby doll and placed her in the bedroom.

Child: There is the baby.
Therapist: They have a baby of their own.

The therapist introduced the words "of their own." He tried to provide the child with the experience that her replacement wish could be understood and was not in itself subject to punishment. Had the therapist said, "Mommy had another baby," or made some other response excluding the possibility that the girl was responsible for the baby, he would have reinforced the child's feeling that the adult rejected her because of her wishes to identify and replace. Adult disapproval and rejection of her wish for replacement would also have reinforced her replacement fantasies, assuming that she saw approval as rewarding. By not providing this reward and by accepting her wish, the therapist reduced her need to indulge in these fantasies.

From these conjectures, the therapist could develop the hypothesis that this child hurt in her competitive feelings with her mother. Perhaps she had the common experience that her mother punished this fantasy of identifying as an adult female (since it often included wooing the father). Punishment became a reward for this girl because it proved to her that she was a threat to her mother. The therapeutic goal at this point was to provide the girl with the experience that punishment is not always associated with competitive feelings or adulthood.

The asocial response, then, is essentially one that does not follow the expectations the child has learned to associate with the wish. This asocial response helps both to extinguish the punitive association (by failing to reinforce it) and provide the experience that the wish is acceptable to another person. The hope is that the child will find new choices for fulfilling the wish rather than having to maintain the original choice, which in this case centered on testing her mother.

13

The Changing Landscape of Psychotherapy Practice
Managed Care

Producing a modern text on psychotherapy without including a discussion of the rapidly evolving economic changes and means of health care delivery would be analogous to publishing a traveler's guidebook to foreign countries without a section of maps. Echoes of the days of graduate school education when professors turned up their noses at discussions about fees, collecting from insurance companies, and marketing still reverberate, but even the most insulated educators have been forced by their students, training clinics, and their wallets to attend to what has been commonly called the health care revolution. In fact, discussions of these topics are often more than academic, evoking strong emotions in providers, patients, and third-party payers. It has been noted (Bragman, 1994) that the issues are so polarizing that a psychologist opposing the American Psychological Association establishing a Division of Psychologists and Managed Care was quoted as "likening anyone who voted for the new division to Jews voting for Hitler and the Nazis during the holocaust." We are, of course, interested in discussing problems found in the general terrain of psychotherapy practice finances, and will especially pay attention to how the landscape is changing. An additional goal of including such a chapter in our text is to provide a discussion of how the economic issues in psychotherapy and the health care delivery system impact the therapeutic process.

Despite the frequent discussions about these changes or lamentations regarding the evils of managed care, there are often misunderstandings among students, consumers, and many practitioners about what the changes in the health care system were and how and why they came about. An elegant piece by Stamm (1996), some of which is summarized here, can help plot the brief but rapid changes of how psychotherapy services are delivered.

The push to managed care away from the standard fee for service or indemnity insurance programs was prompted by the rising cost of health care, which consumed more than 14% of the gross national product. In actuality, the contribution of the practicing psychologist to this increase has been very little. Outpatient mental health services are reported to account for only 3 or 4% of total health care costs, while inpatient treatment, not the usual domain of psychologists, has contributed significantly to reports that despite low rates of utilization for outpatient psychotherapy, it is under the managed care umbrella. Whether or not psychologists were innocent by-standers when the revolution began in reaction to spiraling health care costs is largely an irrelevant issue now as outpatient psychotherapy practice has been swept up in the managed care current along with the rest of health care–related processes.

THE PROCESS THEN AND NOW

Before managed care, employers purchased indemnity insurance from the insurance industry. Employers and employees paid for the premiums, which the insurance company set aside as a "risk pool." In return for these fees, the insurance company assumed the risk for the medical costs for the insured for the year. If the gamble was a good one for the insurance company, profits were taken and perhaps a discount was given to the employers and employees for next year's contract. If the gamble was a poor one, that is, the medical expenses exceeded the funds in the risk pool, the insurance company had to reach into a special reserve fund to cover the loss. The game would begin again, with the insurance company trying to recover the losses the following year by increasing premiums or eliminating expensive services or conditions from the coverage menu. In this game, called indemnity insurance, the insurance company assumes the financial risk of paying all of the health care costs for a given year. Here, the providers do not assume financial risk in the game and are reimbursed according to their fee requests or by what is "reasonable and customary." Utilization review in these cases was of little influence and very little constraint on the practitioner or consumer.

The criticism of this indemnity model, as Stamm (1996) points out, is that there is no reason for the practitioner to limit care except for those constraints defined by the limits of the patient's policy. Providers have no incentive to limit services—perhaps they assumed the more services provided, the better the outcome. Another less known criticism of this model presented by Stamm is that both the patient and provider might wrongly assume that fees are the responsibility of the carrier. When employees learn that a large insurance carrier is administering their plan, they may assume, sometimes falsely, that the "insurance company has to pay." In fact, many companies do not buy indemnity insurance but instead are self-insured. In such cases, premium payments from the employer and employees are deposited into a medical savings account. Health care bills are reviewed, administered, and paid by an overseer—often a large insurance company, yet the insurance company assumes no financial risk in the process. In this case, the employer assumes the risk of the "insurance company."

To combat this spiraling of costs and lack of incentives, the first Preferred Provider Organizations (PPO) evolved in the early 1980s. With a PPO, the insurance carrier or managed care company contracts with providers to provide its services at discounted rates. It is not uncommon for managed care companies to obtain large discounts, up to 50% these days. Using these techniques, PPOs can offer bargain rates to employers and control some of the costs of care. Another, more certain method that managed care companies can control costs is simply by denying or drastically limiting care. As Stamm (1996) points out, "In less than a decade, extended in-patient psychiatric care has become almost a thing of the past." Outpatient psychotherapy has been similarly restricted, even though studies show relatively low base rates of outpatient psychotherapy utilization. In one study, for example, only half of the patients used two or fewer sessions each year and only 10% used more than 24 visits each year (Durenberger, 1989).

Yet another, perhaps more insidious way of reducing exposure to expenditure is simply to substitute less highly trained personnel at lower costs for more expensive means of treatment. This can be accomplished in a variety of ways. In mental health service, psychiatric treatment time is replaced by cheaper psychological treatment time, which is replaced by cheaper social work treatment time, which is replaced by cheaper mental health counseling treatment time, which is replaced by still cheaper behavior tech time. Consumers in need of service are unaware of issues related to levels of training, areas of competence, and other credentialing concerns. They are also unaware of exactly how this process of lowering levels of competence of providers and cost is saving their employers money and creating wealth for the managed care companies.

Still another model of managing health care delivery, the process called capitation, merits discussion. In a capitated system, the health care administrators and the service providers are partners and offer employers a contract, essentially stating that for a set fee for each employee, the health care service provides all of the care for each employee (and dependents) for the contract year. In this system, the service providers and the health care providers carry the financial risk. The more treatment that is provided—of any sort—the greater the cost to the providers and the health maintenance organization. Conversely, the more treatment is restricted, denied, or curtailed, the greater the profits to the providers and the health maintenance organization. As managed care companies continue to merge and assume larger proportions, the impact of capitation also grows. The impact, especially on ethical practice decisions seems enormous in capitated systems. The practitioner is working with a fixed dollar pool and every element of clinical activity or patient involvement subtracts from that pool. In these instances, less is certainly more for the provider and the health maintenance organization.

PSYCHOLOGY'S REACTIONS TO MANAGED CARE

Although most practitioners were not directly involved as fee-for-service providers in the highly lucrative adult inpatient, substance abuse, or adolescent inpatient units, psychologists were not immune to the reactive control net generally covering the world of health care providers. As the dust has settled after the revolution, practicing psychologists have, in the idiom of Karen Horney's system, three options: move toward, move away from, or move against the changes in the system. Most of the psychologists who appear to be moving toward the managed care routine seem to be approaching the problem from the position of making the best of a difficult situation, sort of a benign resignation. They contribute books with titles like: *Depth-Oriented Brief Therapy: How to Be Brief When You Were Trained to Be Deep—and Vice Versa* (Echer & Hully, 1996) and *Making the Most of Your Brief Therapy* (Preston, Varzos, & Liebert, 1995). Of course, critics would relabel all of the above in much less positive terms and view cozying up to managed care companies as an identification with the aggressor. Most psychologists, however, simply seem to accept the new condition by making the best of it. Many complain but seem to carry on, enjoying their work while sharing the occasional complaint about reduced take-home pay and feeling significant interference from the "big brother" insurance companies along with concerns about invasions into the patient's privacy. This group of practitioners seems to take some comfort in realizing that their colleagues in medicine, especially psychiatry, share the very same concerns, which offers some hope for a united front for positive changes. Like their colleagues in medicine, the "psychological" APA has lobbyists in Congress too.

Still other psychologists fall into what Barnett (1996) labels a fight or flight response. The fleeing psychologists, like Moldawsky (1995), who approach the problem of managed care by opting out of the system and offering services to consumers independently of regulators or gatekeepers. The critiques of this strategy include recognizing the economic fact that many individual consumers will be kept away from receiving services this way by price constraints. There will be a luxury class of treatment for well-to-do individuals and the managed care class.

The remaining reaction of the professional psychologist to the managed care shift is to fight back. This fighting reaction is provoked in many who view managed care organizations as trying to pay the smallest possible fees for services by using the least expensive (least trained) providers, obstructing access to caregivers (e.g., requiring precertification, authorizing sessions in small amounts), while at the same time trying to increase the numbers of participants enrolled in its capitated systems. Martin Seligman (1996) clearly articulates these concerns and enumerates others, speaking about how managed care endangers basic patient rights such as choice of provider, confidentiality, and decision-making ability. Seligman continues to see the greatest danger of managed care in avoidance of needed hospitalization; early discharge; and disallowing long-term treatment. The choice of how professional psychology should organize its reaction to managed care companies and legislators is of continued interest. A concern of some professionals (e.g., Wooley, 1993) is that the profession has been silenced with fears that patient advocacy is interpreted as action antagonistic to third-party payers. Wooley and others urge psychologists to speak out. Attempts at legislative control at the federal and state level have been somewhat successful. However, competing with the lobbyists from the multibillion dollar insurance industry is an uphill battle. Victories do occur, especially when the public becomes involved in its own issues. Recent news reports (Freudenheim, 1996) demonstrate that in a relatively short time period (18 months), 34 states have outlawed or curtailed control methods exercised by managed care organizations. Such methods include gag orders that restrain providers from informing patients about alternative (and often more expensive) treatments that might not be covered under the patient's plan. The paradigm shift for lawmakers here appears to be moving the focus from coping with the panic caused by spiraling costs to worrying that managed care constraints have become far too extreme.

The "fighting" psychologists have employed a variety of attacks in coping with managed care. They came to the public and lawmakers with information suggesting that case managers are not the best decision-makers in directing treatment and explaining that there is an inherent conflict between the patient's interests and the economic interests of the "plan." An important part of the armamentarium have been outcome studies. A recent "big gun" in this fight has been the Consumer Reports (Mental health, 1995) survey reviewing the reports of 22,000 respondents. The results of this study were positive and pointed to the added value of doctoral training in psychology when compared with M.A.-level practitioners. The publication of this piece has done much to bring to the public the value of treatment. The public is being educated about treatment and perhaps, more importantly, are learning that it may have an active choice in selecting its treatment modality. Most sources agree that additional efficacy studies and effectiveness studies are necessary to develop knowledge about psychotherapy outcome (Vanden-Bos, 1996) and that they are on the way.

The use of public information campaigns represents organized psychology's latest efforts at combating managed care constraints. Focus group research has revealed that the average consumer has been undereducated about mental health service delivery. Initial campaigns have described psychological services for a variety of applications including family stress, coping with physical illness, and workplace problems. Television and radio campaigns have produced initially encouraging results. People apparently respond to such advertising with more telephone calls to local psychologists. The initial research indicated that although psychologists want to aim high and send messages about the importance of doctoral-level training, or use medical-sounding terms such as the "practice of psychotherapy," the simpler messages, such as "Talk to someone who can help" are far better received (Moldawsky, 1996).

Finally, it should be noted that an additional "fight" that psychologists are engaged in is directed toward the goal of obtaining prescription privileges. The significance of this movement is large and will be discussed in Chapter 14.

IMPACT ON THERAPEUTIC PRACTICE

The managed care revolution has changed many of the mechanics of establishing the way therapists and patients meet, the length of the work, and even the ostensible "goals" of treatment. Patients in pre–managed care times would select a therapist because he had a solid reputation in the community, or because he successfully treated a close family member, or because of a physician or other professional referral. Now, it is becoming increasingly difficult for patients to take responsibility or even have input in their selection of therapists. Even if the patient had worked constructively with a particular therapist in the past, he might have very little control over selecting who is involved in treatment "this time" as the makeup of therapeutic panels shifts frequently. Managed care companies are merged, bought, and sold; and employers, appearing to be always hungrier for better buys, shop the bargain basement for mental health specials.

Deciding the length of treatment once belonged within the province of the therapeutic relationship, and the process of working through issues related to termination was an important component of even nonpsychodynamic approaches. Now the mechanics of determining the length of treatment go something like this. Psychotherapists are allotted a specified number of sessions to assess (usually one!) and then to address the patient's complaints. Additional sessions may then be requested, often in piecemeal fashion. Many managed care plans present the additional constraint of a maximum number of outpatient sessions and inpatient days per calendar year. Therapy is practiced as a rationed commodity with the pacing of the work dictated by the rule of the plan and not by the parameters intrinsic to the patient's problem, personality, or willingness to face issues. Rather the schedule is dictated by a faceless case manager who is not a highly trained "supertherapist," but often a minimally credentialed employee of the plan.

The setting of treatment goals in psychotherapy has long been the joint province of therapist and patient. With the intrusive "plan" as a constant partner in the treatment process, the establishing of goals necessitates considering the reaction of the case manager or reviewer, or the limits of the managed care company. Indirectly, deciding on goals or objectives of the work also relates to the diagnosis that the patient is given. First, certain plans cover only certain diagnoses. Therefore, defining treatment goals compatible with "approved" diagnoses is certainly an inducement to view the case through the eyes of the provider. A second way that the managed care company influences goal setting is through the approval of treatment plans by case managers. In order to get approval for treatment sessions, the goals of treatment need to be specified and seen as important to merit the use of valuable resources. Typically, therapists learn to use the magic words that justify extended continued work. Not incidentally, these words or goals are those that create an emotional climate in the listener that are difficult to refuse. These "loaded" goals or terms may be those that place the managed care organization at risk for responsibility for denial of treatment. Magic words including dangerousness, violence potential, suicide risk, risk of decompensation, and, of course, possible hospitalization. It is indeed a risk for the managed care organization to deny requests for care when the downside potential of a refusal appears to be so large and might even expose the managed care organization to liability for abandonment. The goal of avoiding the risk of costly hospitalization also appears to be a magic word for managed care. In contrast, goals that are phrased based on a personal growth model or in relationship terms may seem superficial or vague to case managers who themselves must be accountable to plan administrators for spending precious session capital. Additionally, there may be magic words that providers of psychological services learn to avoid sending to third-party payers. The idea that some diagnoses, such as depression, can lead to cancellation of the subscriber or eventual denial of life insurance is a frequent theme of discussion among mental health providers.

Perhaps the biggest impact of this revolution is experienced in the therapeutic relationship. The active involvement of the managed care company through rules or limits, the actions of case managers, and judgments of peer reviewers create the emotional climate involving a third party, with all possible permutations of emotional reaction possible. We know that therapists have feelings about managed care and we should assume that patients do too. Therapist's negative emotion toward managed care might influence treatment. For example, patients who do not show early movement might be viewed as wasting their 6 sessions. Conversely, therapists may direct their frustrations with patients toward the managed care company. It may be tempting for some therapists to avoid issues with the patient and simply be a bit more accepting of the status quo because "The plan won't let me use the necessary tools." Similarly, patients might see their therapists as weak or as tools of the "plan" (Busch, 1994) when they are unable to grant special requests or proceed with treatment as the patient desires. Thus, the problem of constructively answering questions about the length of treatment is artificially limited by the rules of the managed care program. By simply following the rules of the plan, therapists and patients might, without awareness, avoid important material. The same emotional content was found in the earlier days, when fee issues or self-selected termination were seen as rich sources of therapeutic opportunities. Areas of discussion that served as places for patients to work through issues such as dependency or wishing for special favor or position are now derailed by the limits of the therapeutic contract imposed by the third-party payer.

One of the classically defined qualities of the therapeutic relationship was confidentiality. Part of what made therapy a safe place to explore forbidden territory or experiment with new behaviors was that it was such a secret place. Because of this secrecy, the real-world consequences of what was revealed, explored, or fantasized were minimized. Standard confidentiality disclosures included the general statement that psychotherapy was a confidential situation with the exceptions of therapist violation taking place in cases of dangerousness to self or others, or child abuse or related circumstances. Before managed care, insurance companies asked for a diagnostic code number and very little else. Now, standard requirements of care include reporting a complete history including data on substance use/abuse history, history of criminal or legal problems, history of physical or sexual abuse, and other sensitive topics. Reporting in writing on these issues is not an option, whether or not these data are relevant to the current presenting problem. These reports are kept in a database and are available to general insurance databases. They may have profound impact on the patient's eventual treatment, eligibility for future benefits, and eligibility for obtaining other insurance. One would expect this practice to have a very chilling effect on approaching treatment. Anecdotally, we hear frequently of patients who opt out of treatment entirely after learning of monitoring or reporting requirements. We also hear of other patients who make the difficult choice of paying privately for their care so as to circumvent these reporting requirements.

ETHICAL DILEMMAS, LIABILITY, RISK MANAGEMENT, AND MANAGED CARE

Managed care has been solidly with us for over a decade now and the increased risks to patients, providers, and—less obviously—to the managed care companies themselves have crystallized. The greatest impact on patients has been documented in earlier sections of this chapter. The loss of control over confidentiality, choice of provider, access to treatment, and length and intensity of treatment have been included here. What may not be as immediately noticed is the greater exposure for the practitioner to complaints made to licensing boards or the ethics committees of professional organizations. What is the root cause for the increase in complaints or suits? Is this simply an expression of the tidal wave of litigation sweeping over the landscape? Our assessment is that the increased risk comes from sources other than the cultural temptation to litigate. If distressed individuals, attempting to overcome their pain, are given only limited access to the caregiver, learn that their secrets are not guarded any longer, are informed that only certain problems merit care, and are "terminated" as their time runs out—why wouldn't they file a suit or complaint against the closest target, the practitioner? One obvious manifestation of these complaints is reflected in the large increase in the premiums charged for malpractice insurance. Another is the plethora of articles (e.g., Simon, 1994) attempting to walk therapists carefully through the minefield created by managed care so that they may avoid problems of confidentiality, informed consent, and abandonment.

Not so obvious is the impact that complaints to licensing boards or ethics committees may have on the careers of psychologists struggling to hold slots on ever-shrinking panels of mental health providers (Harris, 1995). As the number of psychologists (and therapists in general) has increased, competition to join provider panels (those approved by the managed care company to offer services) has equally stiffened. The plan attempts to keep its exposure to costs as small as possible. One method is to keep access to providers down—by keeping the number of providers down! How does a managed care company restrict willing providers? One technique might be to simply form an initial panel of providers and declare the panel closed.

The current model of the liability crisis in psychotherapy looks something like this. Managed care companies have ratcheted down their costs and constricted services available to the patient. Less well trained and credentialed (cheaper) practitioners have been placed in the middle and have become the obvious targets of consumer dissatisfaction. After all, they are the service providers and very visible, while the "plan" is essentially invisible. In the recent past, if a deep-thinking consumer (or litigator) had seen the canvas beneath the oils and decided to seek remedy from the managed care company itself, the HMO would have been able to shield itself, citing the Employees Retirement Income Security Act of 1974 (ERISA) preemption. This ERISA protection refers to a 1974 federal law that regulates employee benefits. Essentially, the ERISA interpretation has been that insurers and employers were exempt from medical liability suits of employee-patients. However, recent trends in case law have been more and more to hold managed care companies responsible for malpractice. In these new cases, plaintiffs have overcome the obstacle of ERISA protection by claiming that the managed care companies are "vicariously liable" for the care given by their affiliated physicians. After all, providers are tightly controlled, and even gagged by the companies about what information may be dispensed about the plan and about alternative care to the patient. It appears possible that as the protection provided by ERISA laws deteriorates, the potential for legal action against the employer—the partner of the managed care organization— increases. The pendulum of the health care focus may now be moving from cost containment to concern about the consumer—or at least anxiety about litigation.

While we have placed managed care companies under critical scrutiny we should mention that the concept of reducing overall health care costs is a noble one. Managed care does control costs as compared to traditional medicine. The notions of accountability of professional action and the use of peer review should also be admired. The ideas behind managed care appear to be sound. What is it then that interferes with treatment? It may very well be that the profit motive of the company itself suppresses the appropriate application of treatment to the patient. Most readers are probably familiar with the size of the salaries paid to the chief executive officers of these organizations and realize that they are far out of the range of those received by most practitioners. The argument should be made that managed care, when applied carefully and reviewed with an eye toward objective evalua- tion of patient welfare, such as in the Kaiser programs, can promote effective mental health treatment. The Kaiser program, started in 1945 as a nonprofit group practice prepayment program, has grown to over 8.8 million mem- bers in 19 states and the District of Columbia. Surveys of HMO members continually reveal Kaiser members to be the most satisfied of the 233 largest HMOs. In fact Kaiser has documented that the managed care patients who availed themselves of the psychological treatment available actually had significantly fewer visits to the physicians of the plan than did patients who did not receive psychological help.

14

The Therapist as a Consultant

The therapist is trained to be an observer as well as a participant in human interaction. Trained to give special attention to subtle cues in communication, the therapist becomes an instrument that gauges the patient's deficits, needs, and vulnerabilities. Although our understanding of the processes that cause people to change may be incomplete, the therapist is able to make some significant contributions toward such change.

These skills—at analyzing the communication process and producing meaningful changes—are applicable in areas beyond the traditional patient-therapist relationship. We shall illustrate a few applications of the communication principles of the model as they occur in other settings.

THE CONSULTANT IN INDUSTRY AND BUSINESS

A thorough understanding of communication processes is applicable in business, especially with labor and management problems, where communication skills are critical. Effective upward and downward communication is industry's best protection against disorder.

The image of management is subtly communicated throughout the organization by behaviors that alone may appear insignificant, but that nevertheless create conditions of great tension or of well-being throughout the work force. Much has been written about the supervisor in industry, and the particular dilemma of identification with both management and labor. The supervisor's attitude is not necessarily revealed through gross acts, but may be communicated through subtle behaviors.

Many corporations are staffed with high-level psychologists at high levels in the organization who help top management with communication problems. The analysis of communicative processes is helpful not only for solving problems within the company, but also for an assessment of the impact the company has on the consumer. The image also helps to determine the effectiveness of advertising campaigns and planning processes. An industry seen as lacking quality control should certainly not glory in its product;

packaging—its color, size, and form—must be appropriate for the quality and price of the product, and psychologists have experience in evaluating such details.

The following section describes one psychologist's effort in the training of sales personnel, illustrating the type of consultation that seems to be a natural outgrowth of the communication theories described in this book.

There is a certain amount of discomfort in discussing principles of behavior as they apply to sales personnel. This discomfort comes from a consideration of an ethical question: Will communication training be used for purposes of persuasion and manipulation? Business wants to sell, and observing the cues that are being used in advertising, the question occurs: At what point do we call the use of psychological associations and hidden cues manipulation? The psychological associations used to make specific merchandise desirable are often irrelevant to the quality of the product. Advertisers have learned to use cues that arouse strong feeling tones, ranging from sexual arousal to patriotism, personal embarrassment, or a sense of imminent danger. Advertising is controlled only to the extent that advertisers can be prosecuted for false claims related to the merchandise; to our knowledge, no one was ever prosecuted for the covert implication of an advertising claim. A cigarette advertisement can no longer feature the word *health,* but it can show a young woman who is the picture of health strutting along with tennis racquet and cigarette. As is the case for individuals, the corporate use of subtle cues provides a margin of safety from having to take responsibility for the message. Certainly some of the advertisements that are successful transgress the boundaries of good taste and no one overtly claims responsibility.

The psychologist working with sales personnel should be concerned with these issues. A salesperson establishes a relationship with the customer wherein the bottom line is the sale. Some salespersons use soft persuasiveness, merely acquainting the buyer with the product. Others go as far as using emotional blackmail. This continuum of persuasiveness is, of course, not an exclusive characteristic of sales talk: in romance one suitor can send flowers while another may threaten suicide. Although some kinds of persuasion have public sanction, persuasion is almost always seen as an undesirable behavior because the persuader uses controls that limit the individual's right to a free choice. So far, the only safeguard against the misuse of increasingly powerful tools for changing behavior in advertising has been the exposure of such methods to the potential customer or receivers.

Like a good psychotherapist, a good salesperson has to know first of all what impact he has on the consumer. The impact is determined by a wide variety of communication factors: the salesperson's clothing, facial expression, gestures, tone of voice, gait, and, of course, language. In other words, a salesperson should know his own style and be aware of its overall impact on other people. That means we cannot really have a generic training program producing salespersons who all behave alike. Each style has its own strength and its own weakness. Some people achieve effective impact by telling jokes and kidding around; others produce with a solemn face and great seriousness. Each salesperson is best trained to maximize the positive characteristics of his style. The glad-hander can be polished as well as the soft-spoken sales clerk as they both learn the impact they carry.

The first rule of such training is to be fully aware of one's impact on others. The second rule is to train a salesperson to listen to the customer carefully. Listening does take a little more time than just describing one's product, but it is an essential element of good salesmanship. Listening most of all conveys a sense of caring, a way to really understand the needs of the other person. Some buyers want only to know the facts about the product, and do not wish to experience any pressure; others want to buy from someone who takes a personal interest in them as people. A saleswoman we know prided herself on being very familiar with her scientific product, and obviously tried to impress the prospective buyer with her familiarity and know-how. This strategy failed, particularly when she talked to some traditional men. We do not suggest that she should have used her charms instead. But we do suggest that by listening carefully she would have sensed the inappropriateness of her role of being the most knowledgeable one in the room in some settings, and she would have recognized her choice to abandon an ineffective presentation.

A third rule is that the salesperson should learn to be able to change his objective (from a large to a small sale, from a sale to future goodwill, or vice versa). This, of course, appears obvious, but as we studied several salespersons, we often noticed that they neglected the relationship or goodwill, even though a sale was out of the question. A fourth rule is for the salesperson to be alert to the idiosyncrasies of the buyer. We could call this a form of extended listening. A professional person who was a prospective buyer had his office decorated with many university degrees and had some of his signed research papers lying on his desk. Extended listening would have taken into consideration such information, which we could call environmental or contextual cues. There is a whole body of knowledge evolving from research concerning environmental cues. Altman, Ittelson, Prochansky, and Sommer have all studied such information and provided us with a greater sensitivity to these cues. The salesperson might do well to comment on the university connection, or even to read some of the buyer's writings. These moves could come close to being perceived as manipulation, however, and the salesperson should be unusually cautious.

Training of sales personnel should be based on a concern for the four above-mentioned rules. The first major step should be an emphasis on understanding the impact the salesperson has on the respondent. We cannot overstress the importance of this initial inquiry. Some salespersons may try very hard to copy a successful colleague and still be unsuccessful, as the techniques used by one will not fit everyone's particular strengths and inclinations. The salesperson has to know what sort of "climate" he creates in others, and must become familiar with the way these subtle cues are transmitted in different situations with different individuals.

Once the salesperson has a grasp of the emotional climate created in customers, he should become aware of which cues create this climate. With this information at hand, the salesperson can learn to try out new and initially less natural approaches. Some people object to this experimentation as behaving artificially, not genuinely. However, the history of each individual includes learning new behaviors that do not come naturally. The person who is learning how to ski will feel that the natural inclination is to walk and that sliding is most unnatural for the human being. Most skiers, however, discover that the new behavior very quickly becomes natural, and that to lift one's legs as in walking would be unnatural and awkward while skiing.

The salesperson who has learned about the impression made on another individual and who understands the cues used to create emotional impacts on others is ready for listening training. Now the salesperson has to learn to understand the cues that are coming his way and to become an instrument. Many different cues must be distinguished and understood: paralinguistic cues, such as tone of voice, choice of words, pauses, inflections, and the way a person makes themes hold together; visual cues, such as those of appearance, gesture, and body posture; and contextual cues, which have to do with the setting, location, and history of the contact, and its broader meaning and purpose. A clear understanding of such cues and their communicative significance is the object of the theoretical phase of this training.

The practical phase of training should include feedback from a sensitive and objective person about the impact created on others under various conditions. It should also include training in how to listen for subtle cues from a third person, how to read and decode meaningful information. The reaction or response of the customer to the salesperson provides the most useful information about the seller's impact. When read properly, it provides the salesperson with a self-corrective mechanism. For example, a salesperson may notice that many customers become tense. The cues indicating this might be a rise in vocal pitch, quickening of movements, facial expression reflecting irritation, and vexed choice of words. The salesperson should be trained to try to discover to what extent he contributes to such a reaction and what other choices are available. A salesperson may find that many customers typically attend carefully to his exposition, only to lose interest very quickly. By discovering this behavior and labeling it properly, the salesperson can then determine how his contributions to the communicative exchange have helped create this loss of interest.

Our third rule, to be able to change the sales visit's objective, involves a difficult process; it requires good judgment about the customer's readiness for buying the product and flexibility in smoothly varying the approach. We found that training situations that include role-playing are of great value here: a salesperson is placed in a situation where a change would be plausible, and at this point possible strategies are discussed. Training for extended listening requires the salesperson to be on the alert for additional cues. In this training, students are encouraged to account for many of the cues within their perceptual field. Yet mere identification is not enough: people can learn to observe a variety of cues without understanding their meaning. (They are typically salespersons who have problems advancing.) Good training should include enhancing the salesperson's ability to handle meaning.

Finally, we shall discuss a few categories of sales talks that have been observed in a variety of sales situations: (1) teaching and preaching, (2) requesting a response, (3) being in cahoots, (4) arousing guilt, (5) encouraging further talk, (6) broadening the class of meaning, and (7) avoiding emotional engagement. These seven categories are not meant to be all-inclusive, as they are not intended to cover the entire spectrum of sales talks. They are simply mentioned to illustrate what we observed in many different sales settings.

1. Teaching and preaching. This label designates the specific behavior of a salesperson who wants to convince the respondent of the desirability of a product. The seller tries to instruct the customer in its use and its advantages over other products, and uses forceful language to create a belief in the quality of the product. Teaching the customer about the product's useful functions and preaching about its quality give the customer the subtle information that the salesperson sees the customer in a learning role and as a person who can be persuaded. Teaching makes sense only if the customer wants to be in the learning role—and many customers do not wish to accept it. Teaching is worthless when there is no student, and a person who is taught without desiring it will feel that the would-be teacher is presuming to an inferior.

Preaching is a somewhat more serious behavior. Inherent in all preaching is the message that the preacher assumes knowledge of the truth while the lowly respondent is ignorant and much in need of discovering it. Teaching has to do with objective information; preaching, however, deals with emotional information. It is fairly safe to speculate that most preaching is discounted by a prospective buyer. Yet a certain amount of preaching is tolerated and even expected ("Does this salesperson not like her own product?"). However, if there is too little restraint, preaching may make the respondent feel that the salesperson is trying to "talk her into something," and the buyer's resistance is likely to increase.

2. Requesting a response. The salesperson can communicate in many different ways that the buyer is expected to say something. Slightly changing the inflection in the last word of the sentence is one way of asking a question. Other ways include looking expectantly at the respondent or pausing after speaking. The reason that we pay attention to cues designed to encourage the customer to enter the conversation is that such cues are often given inadequately, halfheartedly, or even not at all. Teachers often give only lip service to their own requests: "Any questions?" It is important that the salesperson ask questions straightforwardly, so the buyer is told that his thoughts matter and that the reply is important. A salesperson who has adopted the habit of hedging questions should be trained to ask questions that neither press the buyer nor discourage responses altogether.

3. Being in cahoots. This type of response is a sometimes subtle but frequently used technique. If one wants to persuade another person, an emotional climate creating some togetherness between oneself and the respondent is essential. Being in cahoots ranges from bringing up the name of a mutual friend to finding out beforehand the potential buyer's attitudes toward church, politics, a favorite sport, or just engaging in "buddy talk." Being in cahoots, however, does not have to be based on such blatant manipulation. The simple comment, "You know," which is repeated compulsively by some people, is a device that, said in the right, confidential manner, gives the respondent a bid for engagement. Other devices include certain self-references, like "I am a hearty eater," "That reminds me of my younger years," or "Oh, you also have two sons." These responses are designed to engage the respondent and make the conversation more personal and correspondingly less related to the object. They stress the common ground between two people, with the implication that the customer, whether the product is useful or not, should feel personally obligated to buy it, or at least to develop a favorable attitude toward it.

This type of plea is often effective, as high expense accounts for lunches and other cahoots-related perks indicate. But a line can be drawn between selling oneself as a person and selling out. A person selling himself should rely on selling a friendly, competent person, not a long-lost friend. The cahoots response backfires severely when it is recognized as a bribe or an important breach of personal distance.

One particular deviation of the cahoots theme is seduction—by tone of voice, gestures, eye contact, or a smile. Seduction is the "You are worth waiting on" response, and many people, regardless of their sex, seem to have pleading, seductive mannerisms. The wish is not generally a sexual one. A seductive response is essentially flattering because it gives the respondent the feeling of being a desirable person, one worthy of being courted, revered, or looked up to. It is a response that is often used automatically and training should alert the salesperson to this behavior and its consequences.

4. Arousing guilt. Many individuals have learned in early youth to control adults in authority by arousing their guilt feelings. Children are often successful in satisfying their wants by hinting to parents that they have been wronged and deserve a reward ("You are going out again, Mommy? Will you bring me a present?"). It is no wonder that this type of response is deeply ingrained in many people and used often in sales talks.

Many times guilt is introduced in very subtle ways. Even elaborate efforts to demonstrate the product can serve to oblige the customer ("I worked so hard, you owe me something"). This may be accompanied by an actual denial of the obliging gesture: "Just because I spend a few hours on you and go to all sorts of trouble, you are under no obligation, you know." More often, guilt arousal occurs through the introduction of self-references, either verbal or nonverbal, into the sales talk. These references tie the products to the person. Even the conventional response, "I believe in my product," is such an attempt to tie the product to the person. The customer who chooses not to believe in the product simultaneously chooses not to believe in the salesperson.

Seductive cues also have the characteristics of a guilt-arousal response, because the person tries to oblige the respondent by being extra attractive. Even small bribes ("I will get you these hard-to-get playoff tickets") essentially serve guilt by obliging the customer and making him feel bad not to go through with the order. The customer may buy to avoid hurting the salesperson or because the salesperson is physically attractive or personally obliging. The salesperson may get the order—but the fact that the sale is not specifically geared to the customer's need for the product is conveyed. We are not fully criticizing these means; we are interested in analyzing them. In training, the salesperson should at least become aware of whether guilt-arousal is used and its consequences in further interaction.

5. Encouraging further talk. Many subtle cues have been invented to tell another person that one is listening. The response preempted in great abundance by the therapist, the "Mm, hmm," is such a cue, as is the gesture of nodding one's head, repeating the last word spoken by the respondent, and the repetition of a significant word in the respondent's statement. These devices are used to prompt the customer to talk more specifically, more precisely about desires, objectives, and feelings. They are legitimate devices to encourage feedback. Yet there are some problems with such requests. As many people have the need to be listened to, the permissive atmosphere created by careful listening may become very time-consuming, or even bring personal material into the conversation that the person may later regret having revealed.

Listening can be directive: it can determine the trend of a conversation. This occurs when the "Mm, hmm" or head-nodding response shows extra interest when the person talks about material of interest to the salesperson.

There are subtle but powerful methods in the communicative process, and they occur often without premeditation or planning.

6.   *Broadening the class of meaning.*   This type of response is of great importance in the communicative process and should be carefully analyzed in a training program. A customer may be talking about the qualities of a rival product. The salesperson agrees that this product has its merits, that competition is worthwhile for the economy because it stimulates the manufacture of better products.

The salesperson then perhaps describes his own product's qualities. This is an illustration of a response that broadens the class of meaning. Here, it ties the rival product to competition generally. This response uses subtle cues to communicate to the customer that the salesperson can deal with a challenging message and is not intimidated by competition.

The subtle meaning of this interaction is significant. It may be that the customer is aware of choices, or wants to test the salesperson's competence in dealing with an aggressive statement. Will the responding salesperson become aggressive under pressure? The salesperson could have changed the meaning altogether and asked, "How are the wife and kids?" Such a response might have been perceived as an avoidance of the dangerous topic.

Change of class of meanings is learned early. When the parent starts talking about the merits of baseball after the child has asked where babies come from, the child learns that the topic has to be avoided and has probably caused discomfort. The person who broadens or changes the meaning of a topic should know that doing so is an admission of discomfort. The customer who wants to arouse discomfort now has a tool.

7.   *Avoiding emotional engagement.*   Responses that broaden the class of meaning are related to the engagement category of responses. In the above sample, the customer tried to engage the salesperson by mentioning the rival product, and the salesperson disengaged by broadening the response. But the disengagement response warrants a category of its own. Through engaging another individual, a person attempts to obtain a constricted response. For example, the customer may make some oblique attack on the integrity or prestige of the salesperson or the company—perhaps by turning to a secretary and asking for the time of the "important" appointment, the implication being that the present one is not very important. The customer uses the arousal of an emotional climate to ineffectuate the salesperson. The salesperson who becomes anxious because of the subtle aggression, or angry or bewildered, or who otherwise gives signs of being caught up in the emotional climate, tells the customer that the salesperson is an incompetent who can be teased and controlled. The salesperson should be trained to disengage from the message and reevaluate the objective under the given circumstances. A sales interview after a discussion of the merits of the product might proceed as follows.

Customer: I don't think you really have anything to offer in addition to what I have now.

The statement may be an attempt to terminate the interview, but it also contains a possible dissatisfaction with the presentation itself. The personal reference—"I don't think you have anything to offer . . ."—might be a bid for engagement, a personal emphasis to make the salesperson feel unhappy about personal failure. If the salesperson, however, remains disengaged, he may want to assess whether to change the objective of the meeting. The previous sales talk obviously cannot continue. A response is necessary:

Salesperson: I can understand that you feel that we should offer more than what you have now. Perhaps I didn't present our advantages as clearly as I should have.

This delay response permits the salesperson both to test whether the customer is ready to discuss things further and to change objectives if necessary. Instead of making a sale, the salesperson may want to create goodwill for the future. The response show both acceptance of the customer's statement and a subtle bid to continue with the discussion.

Engagement bids can take many forms. The salesperson engages the customer through guilt-arousal, seduction, etc. The customer invariably uses skills to counterengage the salesperson, perhaps with impatience, arrogance, or praise, or by accepting every recommendation (except the last one, to buy) with an enthusiastic nod. The salesperson who wants to deal competently with customers should be trained to decode and disengage from the climate they create for him.

The psychologist's role in a training program for sales personnel has been outlined for the purpose of showing how skill in reading subtle communication can enhance the salesperson's success. It was presented to illustrate the applicability of communication analysis to one of many purposes in business and industry. Thorough coverage would require space not available here.

THE CONSULTANT IN GOVERNMENT

Government agencies show an increasing interest in behavioral scientists as consultants in program evaluation and quality-of-life assessment. The contributions of the behavioral scientist have long since gone beyond poll-taking and personnel assessment. Government agencies have availed themselves of the help of think tanks such as the Brookings Institution, the Rand Corporation, and the Systems Development Corporation, each of which employs many Ph.D.s to find answers relating to domestic or foreign policies central to the welfare of this country. Some behavioral scientists even hope that there will be a time when world leaders will be evaluated for competency rather than for popular appeal on television or skill in raising funds for election campaigns. Not everyone shares such hopes, and many people feel that creating a group of behavioral scientists who assist in setting the criteria for selection of leaders perhaps would be more dangerous than using the popular-appeal criterion.

Social scientists concerned with international communication have made considerable contributions in the new field. Is a given statement a threat? Is it a bluff? Was it a trial balloon? Was it deadly serious? Perhaps one of the reasons Hitler lost World War II was that he made an enormous and costly miscalculation about the willingness of the United States to enter the war in force. France also made a costly miscalculation by taking Hitler's gesture of occupying the Rhineland as an act of relatively minor aggression rather than as a test of will. We now know that German orders to withdraw troops from the Rhineland were ready had the French not tolerated this violation. In domestic politics, the American Medical Association possibly misread both the statements of political leaders and the popular support for Medicare. With cash and publicity the AMA opposed the bill until it was passed rather than becoming an effective force in modifying it, which might have been a more adequate objective for its purpose. AMA opposition actually increased the benefits provided by the bill.

New analytic methods promise greater accuracy. F. H. Starkweather (personal communication) used the computer to process the words used in speeches by leaders of foreign countries, and found some objective changes in both word usage and themes when new directions occurred. The sociologist de Pool (1970) made a similar analysis of changes in attitudes in the United States by a semantic analysis of *New York Times* editorials. McClelland (1975) made a similar analysis of cartoons and found a disturbing similarity of theme sequences in the cartoons preceding several different wars.

We remember also a thoughtful paper by Hamburg (1955), in a sense actually anticipating the end of the cold war, that compared the people of the United States with those of the USSR in terms of psychological needs. The report stated and supported with some evidence his contentions that citizens of both countries needed an enemy to maintain their own unity, and that people in both countries had a similar symbol of hatred (for the USSR, it was Wall Street; for the United States, it was the Communist party). Also, citizens of both countries believed that truly popular support of the other government was slim (the Russian leaders and the party do not really represent the Russian people; Wall Street does not represent the U.S. populace), and both peoples assumed that science stands in the service of the state (scientists are seen as having to support the capitalist or the communist system of government). In addition, the people of both countries firmly believed that there was no political freedom on the other side, and that time was in their favor. Enumerating these likenesses may permit certain inferences as to readiness for war or peace, or for a hard or soft political line.

Wars are often engaged in with the belief that one's side has an advantage or that one has no choice. An objective assessment of the opponent's belief helps provide a clearer understanding. Our skill in assessing discordant statements for their meaning may help on the political scene, perhaps even with our survival. Scientific approaches toward making a more objective assessment of the meaning of such utterances need to be discovered. An evaluation of the supporting evidence may avoid costly errors in decision-making.

Another application of communication theory to the political scene was made by Osgood (1964). He suggested that reinforcement principles also operate on the international scene, and that we have learned well how to accelerate the cold war, but not how to accelerate peace efforts. Why not, Osgood asked, reverse the principle of escalation to lessen tension? Without pressure or immediate crisis, one political leader would relax tension in some spot in the world and thus give another the opportunity to do likewise and top us in this tension-reduction endeavor. The reinforcement of peaceful moves with each other would comprise a competition for tension-reduction and could result in peaceful coexistence. This strategy has been attacked because to engage in a peaceful move first may be interpreted as weakness. The art of this strategy requires that such an interpretation not follow.

Psychologists have only recently discovered that psychology can make contributions on the political scene. Efforts are currently under way in psychology to train individuals in government and politics as well as in psychology; several universities offer programs in political psychology. The American Psychological Association has been active in supplying government agencies with psychological experts, and legislatures in various states employ behavioral scientists as consultants. Most psychologists also obtain training in program evaluation, which is useful both in government and industry. The psychologist in government is likely to ask new questions, to have valuable research and observational skills, and to offer an understanding of human functioning and an increasing knowledge of processes of communication.

THE CONSULTANT IN THE HOME

While it stands to reason that behavior learned over a lifetime may require an extended and intense effort on the part of the therapist, the therapist should not overlook occasions where people can profit from very short-term contracts with relatively untrained paraprofessionals.

Psychiatric nurses, social workers, and even paraprofessionals, as well as some psychiatrists and some psychologists, visit homes of people with problems. Even a few visits seem to make a real difference in the way the family members behave with each other. C. Zimet (personal communication) reported on a home visit program conducted by the staff of a Colorado hospital. A team of professionals went to the homes of applicants to the state mental institution and talked with prospective patients and their families. The report stated that many of the families subsequently withdrew their applications for hospitalization in order to try new methods of dealing with the troubled person at home. Physicians by and large have discontinued home visits, partially because modern technical emergency equipment is not portable and partially because they feel that in most cases the practice of sound medicine requires office visits. One reason that physicians and psychologists as well do not like to make home visits is that they feel their time is more usefully spent at the office. Yet it would be instructive to include occasional home visits in the training program of clinical psychologists so that the communication network can be observed in vivo.

There are some differences in emphasis in office visits versus home visits. If a home visit is a singular occasion among many office visits, the psychologist typically centers on diagnosis and observation rather than on intervention.

The following report describes a psychologist's visit to a family. The parents, whom we had seen before at our office, have asked for this visit to the home. They stated that they were happily married. They loved their two children, both girls, and the children did not seem to have any particularly disturbing problems or shortcomings, they said. They felt they would like to have a professional visit, to have someone take a fresh look at things and discover if they were doing anything wrong. We accepted this assignment, but did not require payment, as this was our first visit to a home and we felt we were probably to learn more from it than they would. We did find that such a visit gives some useful information, particularly if the psychologist has seen the parents before in the office: one can discover interactions that differ significantly from those in one's office. The home environment often permits the client to feel more at ease, and behavior that is not under the parent's conscious control becomes more marked. The professional can learn much about the person from the differences observed. We should note, however, that these generalizations are made on very little information.

We spent one and a half days with the family in question. The father/husband was an engineer, the mother/wife a homemaker. Both seemed to be very traditional. The daughters were 3 and 7 years of age. They had a television set in their bedroom, but were restricted to one hour a day of viewing. The family lived in a small, private home in the suburbs of a city. The father was absent about 10 hours a day during the week, and about 4 hours on Saturday when he played golf. The mother spent most of her time working at home.

The therapist's observations were concerned with the subtle interactions between the parents and children. This couple had established a relationship that might be described as matter-of-fact, a sort of distant but caring relationship. Mr. and Mrs. G. each had their own work, and there was a minimum of communication between them relative to it.

Mrs. G. prepared the breakfast for 7:30 A.M. and the couple ate their breakfast together without speaking to each other. No affectionate farewell met Mr. G.'s morning departure for work. He just looked at his watch, got up, and left; Mrs. G. stayed in the living room reading for a while, and then proceeded with cleaning, cooking, and caring for the children. However, when Mr. G. came home from work in the afternoon, he embraced Mrs. G., kissed her, and also showed some affection for the children. Returning from work was a more significant affective event than leaving for work. Mr. G. then went immediately to the dining table (exactly at 6:00 P.M.) and began to eat the meal as soon as it was served, frequently while his wife was still in the kitchen. There was no talking during the meal except for routine requests such as, "Please pass the salt." The meals were eaten quickly: one of the dinners lasted fourteen minutes.

Mr. G. never acknowledged or praised his wife's work. The little communication that existed did not give the impression that this couple was angry or bored with each other, but that they were not in the custom of talking to each other during mealtime.

After the meal, Mr. G. relaxed in the living room before Mrs. G. had finished eating. Later she would join him, and then they divided the newspaper (they offered the consultant part of it), turned on the television, or briefly discussed a news item, commercials, or their activities. (The children had had their meal earlier, and were not present during their parent's mealtime.)

At exactly 7:00 P.M. the whole family gathered in the living room for an hour together. At this time the exchanges between husband and wife were more extensive. They discussed their friends and when they would invite them to their home, and made more extensive comments on politics. For this one hour the father obviously enjoyed playing with the children.

Irritation was uncommon. It first occurred when Mr. G. announced he would play golf the following day. Mrs. G. said she had hoped that they would all drive out to the fair. Mr. G. seemed to respond with some irritation, but he neither offered an alternative day for the fair or an excuse for his golf date. The argument was left hanging, but it was clear that the husband was in command. A somewhat similar exchange took place the next day when Mrs. G. asked her husband if his next business trip would have to take a whole week. Here, Mr. G. answered with a simple, annoyed "Yes," as if to imply that the question should not have been asked in the first place. No attempt was made to explain or to assuage his wife's feelings. We also noticed that after each of these exchanges, Mrs. G. would leave the room to look after the children. In the afternoon, when Mr. G. returned from his golf engagement, he again followed the embrace ritual. The whole family spent the afternoon in the yard reading, without much talk and without any noticeable tension.

On the basis of these observations some tentative inferences were made. This couple obviously liked each other and had found a way of living together peacefully. They had divided their tasks in a very traditional manner and seemed happy with their arrangement. There was neither great closeness nor much common activity. Both Mr. and Mrs. G. traveled their own road most of the time, but they still appeared to respect each other's opinions and competency within their assigned areas of function. They did not go out of their way to make the other feel either good or bad; they simply seemed to accept the distance that the compartmentalization of their lives imposed on them. However, when Mr. G.'s authority was questioned, he made sure that his demands were not to be argued with. Mrs. G. predicted the annoyance of her husband, and she may well have wanted to annoy him slightly with the rationale that he was needed by the family. It is very likely that Mr. G. overlooked this reminder even though it did cause annoyance: it gave him the necessary feeling that his wife cared, and told him that he should feel guilty about leaving the family behind. It is possible that he had learned to be more affectionate when he returned to the family because of it.

It should be noted that with her bid, Mrs. G. got the most intensive feeling response from her husband, even though it seemed relatively mild by conventional standards. Mrs. G. probably was somewhat dissatisfied with the lack of affection from her husband but could not face him with that complaint. The psychologist interpreted the fact that Mrs. G. turned to her children after she obtained the annoying response as a communication that implied, "At least I have my children. I don't have to be alone." This was apparently a satisfying solution to the husband's lack of affection. The solution was also a threat: we heard Mrs. G. threaten in one of their few quarrels at the office that if Mr. G. left her, he would never see his children again.

The interpretation of these subtle exchanges between the couple provides us with at least some understanding of this family's strengths and vulnerabilities. Their philosophy of marriage was, "We collaborate where necessary and go our own way the rest of the time." While the wife apparently desired greater closeness, she had by and large resigned herself to the present existence, provided Mr. G. retained a minimal role with the children.

The psychologist noted three separate events to support the hypothesis that Mrs. G. was concerned with maintaining control of the children and giving her husband only a minor role with them: (1) the children did not participate at the meals, but were fed before their father came home; (2) Mr. G. was hardly ever mentioned, even when one of the children questioned Mrs. G. about him; (3) when the father did play with the children, it was Mrs.

G. who called the shots, saying, "Go over to Daddy." With regard to the children, Mr. G. seemed to like things the way they were, and made very little effort to initiate contact himself. He accepted the household rule that raising children was a mother's work. Many traditional families have adopted such a division of labor.

The children never once became a topic of discussion between the parents; while the father was nice and playful with the girls, there was little show of affection between them. The consultant observed several subtle cues with which the mother reinforced this rule. The father had lifted the younger girl above his head and was dropping her down slowly. For a second, there was a possibility that their faces would touch. At this moment, the mother called the girl over to her. The father put the child down, and the little girl immediately went to the mother. The father was not beyond teasing Mrs. G. with threats of closeness, particularly as far as the younger daughter was concerned, even though the psychologist was certain that the father was not aware of this teasing. For example, while the mother was watching, the father would occasionally tickle the child on the belly, but withdrew his hand quickly when he noticed Mrs. G. intensely observing these goings on. Although the couple never discussed the children during the visit, they appeared to have made an unwritten agreement that Mr. G. could have freedom and independence provided he did not step into Mrs. G.'s territory, which included protecting their daughters.

The older girl was aggressive and had quite a temper. The afternoon of the first day of the visit, she threw toys at her sister and caused some pain: she actually drew blood when she threw a wooden block, and pulled her sister's hair so violently that she emerged with a shock of it in her hand, swinging it over her head like a trophy. The mother was concerned with this aggression, but gave almost all her attention only to the older girl, neglecting the younger victim. When the younger sister cried and pointed to the wound, the mother took the older daughter in her arms and gave her a serious talking to, telling the younger sister that the pain would soon cease. The mother apparently preferred the older daughter, while the father preferred the younger. The younger girl seemed to notice the mother's preference for her sister, and when she was hurt, she moved closer to Daddy who, for reasons of his own, was not a satisfactory ally.

The younger girl, perhaps because of the mother's preference for her sister and her father's weak endorsement, was in the habit of playing alone. One could speculate that the parents acted out their own unconscious wish to avoid an oedipal dilemma in order to keep the marriage intact. Both girls were practically isolated from the father, and his playfulness with the younger daughter did not go beyond limits imposed by the watchful wife.

Requesting that we visit itself implied that these people felt something was wrong with their family life. It is possible the motive for inviting us to visit was only a concern for preventing future disturbances. We did not see this family as problem-ridden. Every family has some skeletons in the closet, some idiosyncratic characteristics that sound strange to the observer. In discussing our observations with the parents, we noted that they showed few feelings for each other in their interaction, that much of their contact appeared ritualistic, that they did not talk with each other much, and that the wife appeared to miss closeness more than the husband. We mentioned that we felt the older girl's aggressive behavior was reinforced by the caring responses she obtained from the mother, and that we felt the younger girl appeared isolated from the family. We added that we thought we had enough information to make these tentative statements about the family, but that our information was limited. The couple listening to the report reacted with surprise, particularly at the analysis of their own relationship: they perceived this relationship as highly satisfactory, and the degree of closeness in the marriage was accepted as a matter of course. The couple, however, thought the psychologist was accurate in noting the poverty in verbal contact and in joint activities, the wish of the wife to have more closeness, and the differential preferences with regard to the children. The strength of their relationship probably permitted them to make gains in these areas without any help. Each statement made by the psychologist was supported with examples of behaviors, which made the analysis more meaningful to the couple.

Such efforts may be useful for some families; they alert them and make them more sensitive to their own problems. The danger, of course, is that such a visit may also stir up problems in a family that had found peace together.

The visit surely was useful for the consultant as well. It helped her observe subtle cues, formulate hypotheses relating to them, and formulate a model fitting the observations. Mr. G. contacted the psychologist a month later to express his thanks to her for helping the couple have what he called a "one hundred percent better marriage."

THE CONSULTANT IN THE PROFESSIONS

Working with a Teacher

Various modes of subtle communication affect learning in school: the design of the school, the personality of the principal and teacher, the teacher's relationship to other teachers, and students' perception of academic and nonacademic tasks are just a few of the factors.

Some teachers have significant problems with their students while others do not; some teachers are able to create an exciting learning atmosphere while others elicit indifference or rowdiness. Of course, a teacher can respond differently to each class, may vary responses with different age groups, or react strongly to certain individuals in the classroom. In the analysis of the communication process in the classroom, the consultant focuses on covert information to find out just how the teacher sells himself, to discover the specific responses a teacher uses, often unawares, to maintain the emotional climate of the classroom. Subtle communications that affect a class most forcefully are not illusive or mystical; they can be observed and described.

To illustrate the analysis of communication within a school setting, we shall observe the teacher's interaction with his pupils.

The psychologist was asked by the teacher to sit in his classes and observe his teaching style. The teacher, Mr. R., was interested in having an impartial observer present because of discipline problems with all of his classes. His students did not like him, talked incessantly, passed notes, and occasionally threw spitballs. Mr. R. told the consultant that he had once complained to another teacher about his problems, in effect asking for advice on how to handle his students. The other had said, "Oh, that is simple. When the class is about to get out of hand, I just look at them." She gave a sample look, and one could well understand why the class shut up in fright. Mr. R. did not feel that he had the necessary cues of terror at his disposal.

It was not the psychologist's intent to collect a psychological history of Mr. R. in order to show why he had trouble. He was concerned mainly with Mr. R.' s teaching style, with which he earned his trouble.

When Mr. R. entered his class, the psychologist rated him as looking confused. This emotional climate was created by an uncertain gait and bewildered facial expression, and by his way of looking at the classroom floor rather than at the class. These cues, which perhaps elicited uncertainty in his pupils, also betrayed his fear. When he sat down at his desk, the class went on talking, totally oblivious to his presence. Mr. R. did not seem to be aware of the apparent disrespect. He opened several books, laid them aside, reached for them again and put in small bookmarks, which he tore out of his notebook, to mark pages. These gestures conveyed his unpreparedness, as if the class presentation were merely an afterthought. The class responded to these gestures with indifference and continued to disregard his presence. More time passed; Mr. R. looked at the class again, adjusting his glasses so that they would fit more tightly, and said, "John Brown, you are talking. If you go on talking, you go on talking to the principal." This sudden disciplinary intervention, after neglecting to note the disorder, conveyed arbitrariness.

For a moment the class was quiet. Mr. R. began his lesson in arithmetic. He seemed to know what he was talking about and was clear in his presentation—but sounded bored. The subtle cues to his boredom were clearly communicated to the class by both his facial expression and his monotonous voice. The students reflected his boredom in sporadic yawns. Mr. R. proceeded to explain the lesson, brought a few students to the blackboard to solve problems, and totally disregarded the increased restlessness in the class. The students not only continued to get noisier, but also got up from their seats and walked around the class, visited other students, and even did some sham fighting. This information conveyed that the teacher either did not really care or felt unable to control the students. His uncertain attitude appeared a challenge to the students: how much disorder would he tolerate? They were testing their limits.

Mr. R. still avoided looking at the students, but began his substantive lecture. He talked in a very monotonous voice, and it seemed that much of what he said was lost on the students. He gave his full attention to one student whom he had brought to the blackboard, and never turned around to see what was going on, even when the noise level became very obvious indeed. Yet, as before, Mr. R. would suddenly turn around and say in a tense voice, "Van Snooton, I saw you. You passed a note to your neighbor. You will stop misbehaving or I will send you to the principal." These comments were greeted by giggles that were disregarded by the teacher, who would turn back to the student at the blackboard. The game of testing the limits continued.

It was not the consultant's intent to criticize Mr. R. for poor teaching. Describing the peculiarities of teachers is easy, but doing so reveals little about quality, as some teachers will make their peculiarities work for them while others cannot.

Rather than criticizing Mr. R., the psychologist wished simply to describe his teaching style to suggest what effect this behavior was likely to have on his class. He wanted to observe how his teaching style accounted for some of his trouble.

A number of generalizations are possible. The class obtained the information that the teacher was interested in the individual, not in the group: Mr. R. disregarded the class and devoted his time to teaching the individual student who happened to be at the blackboard. Also, upon provocation, he singled out one particular student for punishment, again disregarding the rest.

It also appears that Mr. R. communicated a fear of the class, that he felt unable to handle it, that he merely tolerated it. He gave this information by appearing bored, by not interacting with the class, and by calling upon the principal for punishment without attempting to take discipline into his own hands. He also gave the impression that he would rather avoid handling discipline: he waited for restlessness to build up to a high level before he attended to it.

Certainly the class must have sensed Mr. R.'s indecisiveness, and some of his students surely took advantage of the opportunity to use this information to render the teacher even more ineffectual. They accomplished this task by teasing the teacher as a group rather than by individual cunning.

Mr. R. gave much of this information without awareness, and when he elicited negative student responses he probably did not know to what extent he was responsible for them. Mr. R. stated that he wanted to be an effective teacher, one who would inspire confidence and keep his class in command. Would he profit from knowing how his own behavior was perceived by others, particularly by his students?

The psychologist can assist Mr. R. by using a communication profile to help him recognize what impression he makes on his class and what procedures he uses to do so. He can be sensitized to the cues that make up his teaching style. One can expect that this information may bring about not only new awareness, but also possible changes in his behavior.

Mr. R. listened to the analysis, and his first response was, "I am too old to change. What you said may be quite true. I certainly can feel it. I am more interested in the individual student than in the class. Also, I am scared of the class and I'm not happy teaching it. It is also probably true I present the children with a picture of disinterest, and that consequently they have a tendency to take advantage of me. They surely are doing that."

While Mr. R. thought the profile presented to him was fitting, he felt that there was little he could do about it. Yet he was motivated. By analyzing his communication rather than the history of his childhood and how it related to his present problem, the consultant told him something new. Though he knew and admitted that he was scared of the class and reluctant to teach, he did not know that these feelings could be read so clearly by others. He did not know that his feelings could be recognized by the way he behaved, that each of his behaviors conveyed certain meanings to the children. The very fact that some of his behaviors were singled out and labeled as creating problems made him feel that he was caught in the act, that is, it created uncertainty in him. He now had evidence that others recognized his behavior and read feelings he thought hidden. He began to accept that he would have to take responsibility for the responses he elicited, that his behavior and his expressed motivations were obviously discordant.

In communication analytic psychotherapy, we assume that a person caught in the act of expressing discordance is likely to explore alternative ways of behaving. As it turned out, Mr. R. was deeply affected by the observations. After some searching, he decided that he was not too old, that he wanted to stay in teaching and at least experiment with new behaviors in his problem areas. He made efforts to face his class rather than individual students, to present himself as a more interested person, and to prepare more adequately for his classes. We do not claim that these tentative and brief interventions made a new person of Mr. R., but they seem to have been a stimulus to explore new choices.

Working with a Lawyer

A criminal lawyer contacted us to gain some knowledge regarding her courtroom procedures. Having lost many cases, she had begun to suspect that she aroused antagonism in the jury. The lawyer generally defended criminals with substantial records and limited financial resources; often she did not get paid. The lawyer had worked her way through law school and had herself come from an impoverished home. She felt that it was her duty to defend the poor, and that she had to accept a marginal living doing so. She was a bright woman, and her having won one important case had resulted in her being offered a position with a prestigious law firm, which she refused.

She was conscientious and spared no time in her careful, detailed research efforts to prepare for each case. She referred to her clients with loving care, and we got the impression that she was extremely lax in collecting fees, even when they might have been available. Her communications with us were characterized by caution. Though she had decided to seek us out in order to discover something about herself, she gave us the feeling that she was annoyed at having to contact someone. She seemed particularly reticent about her relationships with her clients.

We advanced the first tentative hypothesis that this woman identified too closely with her clients, that at least vicariously she was enjoying the violations of the law with which she had to deal. She not only represented her clients, but also fought the court. We made the inference that her hidden wish was to blame the injustice of the world and possibly the injustice of her own childhood on the ignorance of the world, and the prejudice of the jurors, whom she usually called "those self-righteous citizens."

When we complied with her invitation to visit the court, we found evidence to support this hypothesis. The lawyer talked down to the jury, and her statements reflected her own ambivalent attitude. As a lawyer, she had learned that the members of the jury should be respected for the power they held, but the silent rule told her they would probably misuse the power. "Those who are called on to judge others should ask themselves whether they should throw the first stone" was her paraphrased biblical quotation, which appeared twice in her summary statement to the jury. From the way it was said, it did not sound like an invitation to understanding, but an attack on the jury's ability to judge: through her identification with her clients, she communicated to the judge and jury that they were punitive, foolish people who had no right to sit in judgment. The lawyer had little awareness that she helped to fulfill her own prediction that she would fail in the defense. Creating this negative emotional climate in the members of the jury, the lawyer constricted their judgmental process, verifying her own view that justice will never be done.

After one interview and a visit to the court, we had a limited sample of behavior to draw from, yet the nature of subtle communication as expressed in the lawyer's attitude both in the interview and in front of the jury gave us a plausible understanding of the problem. When we discussed our inferences with the lawyer, our first objective was to sensitize her to the subtle cues she was using to create the undesired negative impression on the jury. We presented to her the silent rule that we thought might be the basis of her discordance: to defend the underdog and yet to show that justice is not done. We were trying to make the unconscious component of her message explicit by citing very specific examples. She experienced uncertainty when she realized she had communicated her disdain for the jury. We felt that by calling this discordance to the lawyer's attention (by quoting the specific incidents and doing so in a friendly setting), we would help her to explore the procedures with which she challenged the jury and her motivation for doing so. This was helpful, the lawyer told us, and she considered new choices. In this short-term contact, the lawyer had been caught in the act of discordance, and had then asked herself to what extent she had to express her feeling that justice will never be done in this manner, and to what extent she had to express her disdain to the disadvantage of her clients. If such a confrontation is made in a concerned and caring manner, the client is likely to seek to continue therapeutic explorations. This was the case here: the lawyer's original reluctance to enter into a therapeutic relationship gave way to the hope of being able to profit from further contacts.

Consulting with Legislators and Lawyers on Public Issues

A group of lawyers interested in legislative questions arranged a seminar to which a psychologist was invited. The seminar was concerned with the topic, "The Law and the Image of the Law." The psychologist's role was to express his thoughts about how certain laws are perceived by the public— that is, not what they are intended to do, but what they are perceived to do, or what they communicate. For instance, a law may be enacted to deter but may be perceived as a totally useless and unenforceable law, or even as one that is humorous. The Utah legislature passed a law stating that, beyond pornography, which was already regulated by law, "indecent" cable television should be banned. Many people find such a law either a serious threat to freedom or humorous. One letter to a newspaper editor called it a law "enacted by the retarded for the retarded."

Essentially, the lawyers asked the same questions that are asked in reference to marketing a new product: How does the consumer perceive the new law? For example, the trend of the United States Supreme Court had been to make decisions to require increasingly greater protection for the rights of citizens suspected of crime. Such decisions were made with the understanding that police and court procedures should not endanger the rights of innocent citizens. The police and many public factions protested that more criminals would be on the loose because of this new emphasis, and that the victims of crime had rights, too. Research on this question is obviously necessary: What does this protection mean to the concerned consumers, the victims, the public at large, and the criminals themselves? Does it really mean that it is now easier to commit a crime or "beat a rap"? Assuming a positive answer, does this mean that a larger number of crimes will actually be committed?

The views held by a large part of the public have enormous consequences for a given society. For example, it is not unreasonable to believe that doing away with capital punishment may arouse the public's demand for a conservative government specifically dedicated to "law and order." The demand for law and order often does follow when a highly publicized murder results in minimal punishment of the murderer for "technical reasons." The abandonment of capital punishment may be a humane act, yet in the long run it may cost more lives than it saves if it results in a repressive government.

Another topic was the perception of authority as fair, unfair, or unreasonable. Apparently, a law perceived by citizens as unreasonable may result in individuals' taking the law into their own hands. Research on communicated meaning of laws may give us critical information, and this type of information may improve the relationship between government and the public.

Consulting with a Dentist

Dr. F. was a successful dentist who treated mostly adults, but who aspired to a specialty in child dentistry. He said he liked children and preferred to work with them. To his disappointment, most of the parents who brought their children to his office seldom returned them for further treatment. He had questioned some of the parents carefully as to why they had not brought their children back, but had obtained only what he considered noninformative excuses. He invited us to see if we could find any cues, and we visited him for two working days in his office. During this time he treated seven children. We wrote our observations of his treatment of each of the children, and there emerged a striking similarity in what we saw. The following simple case illustrates the subtle exchanges that took place.

> *Mother:* Here he is. Hope he doesn't need anything serious.
> *Dr. F.:* Well, we'll see. He is a nice child.
> *Mother:* (smiling) He can be quite a stinker. He did not want to come today.
> *Dr. F.:* You should always come to have your teeth checked. Then you won't have any pain later.
> *Mother:* Listen to the doctor.
> *Dr. F.:* Ready? You are going to get a nice elevator ride now, Peter.
> *Peter:* I don't want to.

> *Dr. F.:*   Well, how else can I see your teeth? (The chair is raised. The child, aged 9, appears petrified.) Wasn't that a nice ride? Uppity-up, just like a nice elevator. Now, Peter, open your mouth wide.

The mother sat in an adjoining room, reading. Dr. F. began checking the teeth. Peter made small noises as he was being checked.

So far, we could not advance any hypothesis as to where Dr. F.'s approach was deficient, though we could formulate certain hunches. Going over the messages and responses of each of the participants, we noticed that the mother, by using the words, "hope he doesn't need anything serious," might have increased the child's apprehension. Dr. F.'s response, "He is a nice child," was somewhat irrelevant, but, if anything, would have been slightly reassuring. His second statement, though, was moralistic and probably created distance between himself and the child. His implied threat ("Have your teeth checked. Then you won't have any pain later") was not reassuring, but was not really an alarming statement either. When Dr. F. commented that Peter was to have a nice elevator ride, he was trying to put the boy at east. At this point, we noted that Dr. F. maintained the fiction of the nice "uppity-up" ride in the face of Peter's discomfort. This was somewhat heavy-handed, almost like saying, "You'd better feel good when I tell you to feel good." We formulated a hunch about Dr. F.'s lack of sensitivity in this area.

Dr. F. proceeded to check Peter's teeth and apparently found a cavity.

> *Dr. F.:*   Peter, we found a little something here. We are just going to put a little silver mine in that tooth, just a pretty little silver mine, and I am going to show it to you, too. This whirl here is just like a birdie; it's singing. Keep your mouth wide open.

To help him have a choice about these behaviors in which he appeared to engage automatically and without awareness, we pointed out the subtle communicative meaning of his procedures. We told him our impression was that not all children can accept the recommendation to deny their discomfort, and that his talk of "birdies" would appear to them as merely deceptive. Our aim was to provide Dr. F. with the experience that his behavior, which he automatically labeled as "helpful," could also be labeled as dishonest, or worse, as mean. We also alerted him to the consequences of his discordant messages: some of the children could see him as being dishonest and reject him as not being trustworthy.

Although we are aware that such short-term observation methods entail possible dangers—they may seem threatening or inaccurate—we feel that well-functioning individuals can often profit greatly from such confrontation. The dangers can be met by the further availability of the therapist if required.

We shall add some general comments on the communicative meaning of certain behavior in dentistry. At the dentist's office, the child must open the mouth and expects some discomfort. The mouth historically stands for early pleasure experiences, and the passive role of enduring discomfort by keeping one's head still and mouth open is an experience that is contrary to previously learned behavior. The dentist trains the child to have negative feelings about opening the mouth by conditioning methods: every time the child holds the head still and the mouth open, discomfort results. No wonder many children (as well as adults) have a tendency to postpone visits to the dentist and have altogether negative feelings about having dental work done. If one analyzes the training to which the child is exposed in the dental chair, one marvels that so many children are able to compensate and hold their heads still and their mouths open for undifferentiated future gains.

It might be useful to explore how such training, particularly with children, could be altered to provide the new patient with more positive reinforcement. If such training were successful, the patient might even learn to like the treatment position and to endure the discomfort as part of a pleasurable experience, instead of anxiously concentrating on pain alone. Many dentists give children small presents—a little ring or toy after the work is done—to provide some pleasure in the total setting. It might be wiser to think of an immediate reward after the child opens the mouth, and to reinforce with small rewards each step in the total dental procedure.

There is another problem inherent in the image of dentistry held by many parents. Dentistry has drastically changed in the last few years, to a point where most often there is discomfort rather than severe pain. (The injection to reduce pain may be the event of greatest discomfort.) But adults who have experienced acute pain in the past communicate their fears to the child and in this way increase anticipatory fears. The mother in the above example transmitted her own anticipatory fear with her first statement about "anything serious," and so increased the child's anxiety. "The poor child has to go to the dentist" is a feeling often communicated, and Dr. F. actually supported this subtle, negative image of dentistry by his extra efforts to assuage the child. Some dentists have begun to counteract this image by giving lectures on oral hygiene to adult patients and presenting themselves in a new role—the teacher/student role—which produces another image altogether. But many dentists still focus on pain. Even such methods as "white noise," television sets, and music designed to divert attention from pain, do, in fact, maintain the general, subtle image of pain. It seems that both patients and dentists have a difficult time abandoning the pain image, even though the actual experience of pain has significantly decreased.

The Consultant Working in a Public Role

Teaching in the therapeutic hour and giving advice are often seen as undesirable and/or ineffective therapeutic techniques. The field has largely accepted the notion that the individual has to be helped to discover a solution to problems, and that advice does not allow patients to take responsibility for their own lives.

This distaste for giving advice probably comes from the recognition by professionals that many public advisors claim authority they do not possess. The current upswing to talk radio advice programs hosted by the recent favorites, usually referred to as "Dr. Firstname" appear to be based on the classic "Dr. Anthony" sequences of the 1940s. Then, as well as now, a client would present a short description of his problem, and the great doctor would dispense advice on how to solve it. While Dr. Anthony assumed unwarranted authority, his advice, nevertheless, was sought, and his program was a great success. The reason is simply that advice-giving has a benefit different from the actual advice given. Essentially the advisor is on the air for the audience, not to benefit the specific consumer calling in. The audience, we feel, somewhat voyeuristically wants to hear of other people's problems and feel secure in knowing that rapid, judgmental remedies are possible— should the need ever arise. By being heavy-handed, even punitive with advice, Dr. Firstname is able to forge a bond between the audience and the advice giver, where they may join together and feel a delightful superiority above the suffering callers, who after all are merely receiving exactly what they deserve. The punitive advice giver may actually be injuring the individual seeking help at the expense of entertaining and reassuring the listening audience.

When an individual under great emotional strain is advised to see a psychotherapist, such advice might be seen as beneficial. If we are considered competent to render this opinion and a person asks us for an opinion, we probably would not be criticized for giving it. On the other hand, consider the case of a parent who consults with a psychotherapist after a PTA meeting. "Now, doctor, how do I handle my little girl? She is lazy and doesn't want to practice playing the piano." Were we to advise the mother upon such little information to use specific reward techniques, or suggest to her to force the child to play the piano, we would be criticized for giving advice in the absence of pertinent information. The therapist, therefore, has to assess whether the problem presented is in his area of competency and whether sufficient information is available. In addition, the person seeking advice very often does not really want our recommendation. Rather the demand is for reaffirmation of an opinion held, or merely for some support for making a decision.

Not all advice, however, is specific; we can render advice based solely on general principles of behavior. For example, the psychologist may tell the mother who complained about her daughter that the resistance to learning to play the piano might not be due to laziness, but might reflect a more general tension in the parent-child relationship. He may say that some children rather like being reminded and pressured by their parents. This statement, couched in general terms, can be a meaningful response to the question without containing a specific recommendation that might be based on too little information.

Let us assume that the consultant altered the mother's attention to the broader problem to tension in the home. She responds, "Maybe you are right. I think the child is always angry at me." Is this thought a useful one for this mother? While it will do little to solve her problem with her daughter, it may increase her interest in learning about the broader aspects of behavior related to family interaction. She will look at her relationship with her daughter rather than at her daughter's behavior alone. The consultant's objective in such teaching advice is really not to solve the problem directly, but to alert the mother to a problem she had not previously considered.

Ellis's system of rational therapy is based on the assumptions that a person is able to utilize reasoning powers when the emotional climate is right, and that people wish to live a reasonable life. With these assumptions, the therapist can advise and reason with others directly, provided they are emotionally ready to do so. We believe that the consultant knows more about human learning than most patients, and can apply general principles that may be informative to the public. This is not psychotherapy in an orthodox sense, but rather a form of giving advice by teaching certain principles of human behavior—a role that a competent therapist can fill.

Short-term contacts with a psychologist have become quite popular. Even on television and other media, there is an obvious interest in human problems and their solutions. Of course, the public may misapply what has been taught, or even misuse information to continue noxious behavior patterns, claiming that the psychologist supported their viewpoints. Yet, discussing several principles of behavior rather than answering questions relating to specific problems can have an important impact on behavior, and would be a legitimate way of reaching many more people than we do now. Certainly the impact events of large group meetings such as Promise Keepers, political rallies, the Million Man March, and other charismatic gatherings have shown that fairly large masses of persons can be motivated within a reasonably short period by impactful interventions. Whether the changes that are achieved in that brief time are useful in the long run has not been properly evaluated, but important changes clearly do occur. Research in these areas of public appearance is an obligation of our profession.

15

Supervision in Communication Analytic Therapy*

ON HAVING A POINT OF VIEW

To conduct effective psychotherapy, the therapist must work from a particular theoretical orientation or point of view. Jay Haley, a pioneer in communication-based treatment (1969), agreed and proposed that nothing but failure could result if we were to avoid working from any theoretical posture.

Supervisors of psychotherapists first of all should state clearly their own view of the psychotherapy process. We are not suggesting that supervisors maintain an authoritarian stance over the clinical thinking of their students, but that students in supervision be exposed to the competency that the supervisor has to offer for one model of psychotherapy. This is most likely to enhance the learning of a specific model, and it will also permit the student to evaluate the supervisor's beliefs and biases about the therapeutic process. The student who has a model will know more clearly how to evaluate the supervision itself. In line with this thinking, several critical assumptions of communication analytic psychotherapy are presented below.

GENERAL CONSIDERATIONS

New students of the communication analytic therapy model are frequently amazed and distressed when supervisors point out (often after listening to the first few minutes of the treatment hour) exactly how the students' patients are succeeding in engaging them. But there is no reason to be frustrated with this discovery: the art of therapy is not in avoiding engagement, but in recognizing it and accomplishing disengagement. Students learn that in order to disengage and provide the patient with a sense of uncertainty about his unfortunate "adaptive compromise," the therapist

---

* Originally authored by Beier and Young and reprinted here with permission from Hess, A. K. (Ed.), *Psychotherapy Supervision,* New York: Wiley, 1980.

must first listen carefully and fully understand the communication style of the patient. The therapist must specifically discover how the patient succeeds in constricting awareness of the conflicting motivations that are "appeased" with the adaptive compromise. This task becomes especially difficult because the patient not only has limited awareness of such material, but also has learned to communicate the compromise in a way that does not make this information accessible to the respondent—which means that the therapist also is to stay unaware. In other words, the therapist faces the dual task of learning how the patient conceals covert manipulations from the self and from others. Here the student needs the most help. We typically ask the budding therapist, "What did the patient say and do so that you feel the way you do?" The student not only needs to learn that he or she got engaged, but also must discover what behaviors were responsible for the engagement. Students learn that patients are very skillful at the subtle art of engagement. Trainees soon appreciate that the patient survives psychologically through skill at using an adaptive compromise.

The patient will make a great effort to cling to this compromise, which leads to manageable behaviors, not to an acceptance of uncertainty. Patients struggle against a sense of uncertainty until they start believing that the therapist is caring and can be trusted. Once trust is established, disengagement by the therapist from the emotional climate set by the patient interrupts the patient's routine. New options become possible and even necessary. The student therapist has to learn to show caring for the patient and to disengage from the social engagement patterns in order to have the patient tolerate this uncertainty.

Supervision is not merely an asset to the beginning therapist; it is absolutely necessary, because the strength of the engagement patterns would reduce any therapeutic effort. For the untrained, not responding to the patient's communications in an expected or social fashion is extremely difficult. This is true even in petty, everyday communication. The untrained person is likely to respond with a conventional "thank you" to a patient's friendly gift, but the supervised therapist learns to disengage, to "metacommunicate" about the covert messages the patient is sending (Kiesler, 1978). By responding to a gift with something like, "You need to show me that you care for me with something you bought for me," the therapist tries to give the patient the new experience that a gift is just another therapeutic event, and to pass responsibility for the statement back to the person. The therapist is saying to the patient, "Must you really express caring by spending money?" Asocial responses to patients' messages are the major vehicle for having the patient consider new options (Watzlawick, Weakland, and Fisch, 1974, p. 133). We believe that asocial, unexpected, or paradoxical responses (Beier, 1975, p. 27; Haley, 1985, 1977; Watzlawick, Beavin, and Jackson, 1967) enable the patient to experience what we have called beneficial uncertainty. The patient becomes uncertain because customary styles of communicating no longer produce expected responses. The uncertainty aroused is beneficial because the asocial response comes from a caring person and occurs within the safe and empathic environment of the consulting room. The sting of uncertainty is cushioned by the special nature of the therapeutic alliance.

When the patient is encouraged by such unexpected responses to try new ways to communicate interpersonally, he or she can do so because the protective setting of psychotherapy resembles a play situation: one can try out new things without the dire consequences one expects in "real" life.

Students are trained to identify and respond to the patient's style of engagement; they are cautious about developing only behaviorally oriented treatment goals. We believe that the therapist who invests interest in specific goals of the patient is necessarily increasing the propensity for engagement. Such a therapist would not "hover evenly over all ideas," as Freud (1949) said. By definition, to aim for a specific goal impedes the patient's search for new options. The major goal in communication analytic psychotherapy is that the patient be helped to search for new and ethical options in life and to accept responsibility for such options.

While this goal does not seem to differ from that of many other models, an actual analysis of statements of other models shows implied goals beyond the one stated here. This is not the place to go into detail, but briefly, psychoanalysis employs a health model, with health, rather than options, as its goal for humans; behavior modification uses a specified goal or target model; Rogerian psychotherapy centers on a growth model in which the patient is expected to go beyond the adaptive compromise; cognitive therapy focuses on correcting or avoiding thinking errors; and in Gestalt therapy the model is one of "sophisticated" health, in which the patient's potential is to be developed as in self-actualization. In communication analytic psychotherapy, however, psychotherapeutic value is placed largely in the act of exploration itself, and the goal is to help the patient question and vary routines and accept the uncertainty that is a product of interpersonal exploration. Creativity, or the ability to make effective personal changes, can be seen as starting with this freedom to explore.

KNOW THY OUTPUT

In the communication analytic psychotherapy model, the novice therapist under supervision is evaluated on the basis of how well he or she understands the patient's communication, but even before that, the therapist has to learn to understand information given to the patient. Demonstrating the importance of therapists' coming to an understanding of their own characteristic impact on the patient is seen as the first task of the supervisory meeting. Just as the patient is responsible for eliciting desired behaviors from others the therapist's output is actively shaping the content and style of the patient's communication.

Two forms of therapist output are usually examined in the supervision sessions. The first and most readable type of information is related to the identity of the therapist. Simple demographic or observable features such as age, sex, race and general appearance often influence the patient's behavior. The titled middle-aged gentleman who displays a silvering goatee and Viennese accent is bound to evoke different emotional climates (and responses) than does a young black woman taking her first practicum course. Because therapists do not look or act alike (as some models actually assume), students should at least become aware of their impact on others. Students of psychotherapy can ill afford to neglect the lessons derived from research on person-perception (e.g., Cline, 1966).

The second type of therapist output monitored in communication analytic psychotherapy supervision is related to typical engagement patterns of the therapist. This is not countertransference; that is, related to deep-seated problems of the therapist. It is what we have called "social countertransference," or getting caught in the social-manipulative skills of the patient. The issue is that therapists have a bias, an emotional attitude that is subject to easy engagement. Some therapists' output is clearly designed, albeit covertly, to get their patients to show them love or respect. Others have a "therapeutic urge" and want to heal the patient—as fast as possible. Others yet are cold and distant, with an intellectual focus. Some cannot conceive that they themselves may be a love object to the patient. All these characteristics, among many others, serve to give the patient the needed information to engage at the most vulnerable place. When therapists who like to be liked are told that they are liked, the therapists are likely to be immobilized and blinded to patient activities that are less flattering. Therapists ought to be aware of the weaknesses they have regarding social countertransference and the impact such weaknesses have on the behavior of patients. We are all children of our culture, likely to be affected by social information; we can be sure that the patient will scan the therapist well enough for the patient's protection, that is, to maintain the "adaptive compromise." If trainees were robots who issued behavioral orders, as some models have it, there would be no need to explore their proclivities for social countertransference. However, most human beings are equipped with personal needs and a response system to social information that is open to engagement.

To help students discover the impact of their output, we employ three general methods: (1) discussion of observed engagement patterns during the student's presentation of patient material; (2) special communication analytic therapy group marathon sessions; and (3) referral to therapy (in cases where we observe lasting engagement or "true countertransference"). It should be stressed that teaching students to understand their output is not to do psychotherapy, but to alert students to disengage from social cues that have caught their attention too heavily. Referrals to treatment are made only when students are governed so heavily by problems that they no longer understand patients properly. The therapist—the only instrument present in the therapeutic hour—cannot afford to be dull.

In reviewing a therapy tape, the supervisor has the dual task of exploring the engagement pattern of the therapist as well as the patient's messages that evoke engagement. In a typical session, we would listen for a few minutes, pay special attention to the feelings the patient arouses in the therapist (see how arousal is effected) and then analyze each response of the therapist that deals with these feelings.

One student saw a patient who apparently had generated a good deal of anger. The supervisor asked what had made him so angry. The student began to describe the constant barrage of depreciation the patient had fired at him. The supervisor suggested that this patient's constant negative output was probably what caused the therapist's engagement, as well as what got the patient into trouble in the first place. From a review of the stylistic pattern of the patient one does not yet learn why the patient gets into trouble, but one can get some convincing information on how it happens. The patient's communications were directed at the student's inexperience, lack of skill, and "nerve" in setting himself up as a helper ("Oh, I am your first case?"). The supervisor then asked the student how to get the patient out of that preferred routine. It was clear that the student could not afford to be angry, because this would reinforce the patient's style—anger or offense was clearly the social response. By disengaging from anger and responding with concern and care for the patient, the therapist might, however, help the patient experience doubt the consequences of depreciating behavior. Most students can "re-label" their relationship enough to overcome their socially aroused feelings and disengage, once they have been alerted to their engagement.

We have also found communication analytic psychotherapy marathon groups to be an efficient vehicle by which students can learn about their own output. The supervisor usually calls for a marathon group of practicum students early in the semester. It generally lasts for some six hours and serves to explore the students' own output. Intimate statements and catharsis are not encouraged. With students in the protective environment of the class, all students become respondents to the target person. By avoiding intimate disclosure, the target person can tune into personal, characteristic styles of relating to others. The extended time is not designed to strip away defenses and get to core problems of each student. The marathon lasts until all students make the rounds and explore their impact on the other group members. The students are not seen as patients, and the analysis of their communication has no therapeutic intent; its only purpose is to help students understand how they are perceived by others.

We have mentioned that referral to therapy helps certain students who especially need to become aware of and to control their own output. Such referrals are the exception rather than the rule, yet we should also state that while we do not require it, we generally favor having students experience the other side of the therapeutic alliance, as we believe that the experience generally has beneficial effects on their own performance as therapists.

LEARNING TO LISTEN

A second major skill area that we attempt to teach in communication analytic psychotherapy is how to listen and what to listen for. The first hurdle—already discussed—is for the students to listen to their own emotional responses to the patient. Students need to learn to answer the phenomenological question, "How does the patient make me feel?" We have noted that patients often bring out a sense of helplessness in the beginning therapist, a result of their resistance to disclose. Consequently, we alert the students to their own "therapeutic urge" to heal fast. We teach our students carefully to listen for patients' use of "word cages," the communication equivalent of patients' resistance.

Faulty labeling, blaming (shifting responsibility), and tautological thought processes are often apparent when patients present problems. These mechanisms all serve resistance, and actually are the tools with which the patient gets into trouble. Another form of resistance is the patient's insistence on a nonresponse ("I couldn't face him!" or "I am just lazy."). We train students to recognize the nonresponse and to inquire just what the patient does instead.

> *Patient:*   I can't read my textbook.
> *Therapist:*   What do you do when you don't read your textbook?
> *Patient:*   I go skiing.

We try to teach our students to be careful listeners. Listening is the major tool of helping the therapist understand the patient's view of the world, and empathic listening is by itself a very important way to convey caring to the patient. The training in these listening skills will be discussed further.

We assume that patients communicate in ways that will emotionally engage others. In order to understand the patient, the therapist first needs to discover the emotional climate the patient evokes. The experienced therapist is able to identify what emotional climate the patient fashions, often without actually getting engaged, but the new therapist will feel first and think later; the student-therapist has to use herself or himself as the measuring instrument. She or he will experience the patient through the patient's engagement patterns, and it is this experience that tells the therapist where the patient "hurts." It reveals to the therapist the part of the patient's personality that is likely to be in need of change. The simplest way of using one's self as a measuring instrument is to ask the questions, "What does this patient want from me with those messages? What sort of feeling is the patient trying to arouse in me to get it?"

In order to disengage from the patient's unconscious manipulations, the therapist, not the patient, must have insight into the nature of the patient's conflicts; the therapist must learn about the how and the why of the patient's style. When we ask students how the patient made them feel, we expect them to be able to talk about the "how," to give us a detailed description of the patients' stylistic output. The more precisely the student can describe the patient's most preferred automatic responses, the more adequate will be the student-therapist's attempts to introduce uncertainty into the preferred pattern - not to destroy it, but merely to help the patient develop new options.

Why the patient has adopted a certain style is more difficult to decode. We have two sources of information to help us solve the why puzzle. One comes from an exploration of the style itself. The angry patient who has no friends possibly has a desire to see the self as a loner and may have learned early that commitment has too many strings attached. Often one gets hints about the why from a content analysis of the patient's statements. A second source is the sequential choices a patient makes once the automatic routine is interrupted. The formerly angry patient may find a friend after the intervention but be extremely sensitive to obligations to the new friend.

We have found the supervisory group to be an effective vehicle for training students in our model. Although students alternate in presenting cases, all group members are encouraged to share feedback about the case. Students with varying levels of experience are mixed in the supervisory group. When a patient is presented to the group and the student talks about the case for a few minutes before playing a tape, the student often tips his emotional hand, and we are able to learn, indirectly, about the patient's conflicts and interpersonal style. In these short descriptions, the patient's emotional impact on the therapist becomes evident. During a recent supervisory session, a seemingly puzzled student was describing her first hour with a patient: "Well, I should get lots of practice with this guy. He told me he's stayed in every 'psych' ward in town and has run through three therapists at a mental health center. He says he is depressed and suicidal, and he's not too talkative. I really want you to hear him because I'm not sure what to do." The student's introductory remarks give the supervisor information about the patient's style of subtle influence, at least enough to form some preliminary hypotheses. Selecting from all the information provided by the patient in the initial hour, the student presenting the case centered on the patient's history of hospitalization and his poor track record with several therapists. The student also made reference to her own lack of skill and need for practice and advice. We can reason at least hypothetically that the patient succeeded in engaging the student by presenting himself as a very challenging, experienced patient who had difficult and somewhat frightening problems, but who—once cured—would add immeasurably to the glory of the therapist. The total effect of this great challenge is to intimidate ("I am not sure what to do," the student confides), and we can begin by looking at the patient as one who intimidates others by oversized expectations. We encourage students to hypothesize, but then to look for support or rejection of the hypothesis in the patient's behavior.

Even the most experienced therapist can easily become intellectually and emotionally engaged by a patient's difficult past, socioeconomic constraints, or physical problems. Often the therapist, who obtains this sort of information from the patient, develops a bias, an opinion about the patient. We teach students that they are not detectives, they cannot find out the truth about the many statements made, and they should not even try: they must center their attention on the data at hand, the how and the why of the patient's behavior.

Students often ask us whether we should not account for our own contributions to our feelings in the therapeutic hour rather than "blaming" them all on the patient. Perhaps the student who feels angry had a bad morning before the patient arrived. We point out to the student that in order for the patient to manipulate the therapist, the therapist must indeed have personal feelings. One can only intimidate a person who has a propensity for intimidation, and the patient "plays" the therapist just where the therapist is perceived as vulnerable. The therapist who is generally intimidated by anger must learn to discount some of the patient's doing. This very possibility makes it important that the therapist know his own output and preferred behaviors.

LEARNING TO BE ASOCIAL

From our earlier analysis of patient distress, it follows that therapeutic messages must (1) be disengaged from the emotional climate provided by the patient, and (2) arouse uncertainty. This latter condition is actually the basis for most models of psychotherapy—at least from a communication theory point of view. We assume that the active ingredient in therapeutic gain is that the therapist behaves in an asocial or unexpected way in response to the patient's usual interaction style, in a setting that is reasonably free from threat and conveys a caring attitude.

The patient's statement, "I hate my mother!" typically is answered by censorship ("How can you say that!") or agreement ("I hate mine, too") in a social setting. A possible analytic response ("You are really afraid of your father"), a Gestalt response ("One of many feelings"), or a paradigmatic communication analytic psychotherapy response ("The way you are saying it, I almost feel sorry for her") all have in common that they are asocial, that they arouse uncertainty, and that they bounce the ball back to the patient, telling the patient, "You must deal with these feelings. I, the therapist, refuse to be your conscience." At first glance, the analytic, Rogerian, and Gestalt responses may not appear to be as asocial or unexpected as the communication analytic response. They are asocial to the extent that they differ from a conventional or predictable reply.

There are good reasons disengagement skills are difficult for students to master. As social human beings, we are all trained to respond in a conventional manner to the words and feelings of others. We usually respond with gentleness to tears, with obedience to authority, and with horror to violence. These response patterns are deeply ingrained and difficult to change. To make the training situation more like the therapy situation, we often analyze responses to a hypothetical situation to train students in disengagement. We ask all supervisory students to work together on this. One student would be instructed to make the critical statement, and all other students would find responses, first a social response, then a professional response from other schools, and then a communication analytic psychotherapy response. The class evaluates each response separately. The student playing a patient says, "I think my boss is unfair." First there is a round of expected social responses. A student simulating a friend says, "Amen. I sure know how that goes." One simulating a loyal supporter of the boss puts up a strong argument for the fairness of the boss. The group discusses other varieties of social responses, and then goes on to professional responses, all asocial. This task is designed to give the students opportunities to show and defend their familiarity with other models. A student offers the psychoanalytic interpretation, "He reminds you of your father," and explains this choice of responses. A Rogerian student says, "You are angry." A student interested in behavior therapy talks about constructing a program to reward only noncomplaining statements. The communication analytic therapist responds with a relationship comment: "You would like me to know that you are a victim of incompetent authority." All these statements are discussed for their disengagement value and the degree of uncertainty they arouse.

Engagement is the patient's greatest expertise: patients have had a lifetime of practice at their particular style of covert manipulation. Thus, at first encounter, patients are always more skillful than their therapists. We teach our students, then, that old covert manipulation patterns are not easily re-moved. An attempt to extinguish the patient's response repertoire often follows the laws of learning theory. The response so singled out is likely to increase temporarily in frequency. But as the patient does not get the famil-iar rewards, new ways of relating will be explored.

In prepracticum courses we often ask students to practice giving unex-pected (friendly) responses. A student with a serious undertaker's face is encouraged to smile at people, a nondemonstrative girl to hotly embrace her friend, a stern mother given to saying No to most of the demands of her daughter to surprise her daughter with an unexpected Yes. Students enjoy these "games" because they often get to know the other person more inti-mately; they obtain responses to the novel behavior that they, too, would not have expected. The "no" mother said Yes to her daughter's rock-concert request after a whole year of Nos, and the daughter was so upset that she insisted her mother come along. The mother learned that she had become her daughter's conscience.

Students are not encouraged to imitate the supervisor. In communication analytic psychotherapy there is no response that all students should use at a given time. Instead, the student is encouraged to use personal strength and style to effect disengagement. The student is trained also to distinguish the emotional climate in which disengagement takes place: disengagement can be injurious if it is not presented in a caring climate where it will arouse beneficial uncertainty. No patient saying, "You must help me! I am in a terrible suicidal dilemma!" should receive the accurate, but cold and con-frontational response, "Another one of your games?" The student has to learn to become an instrument for conveying to the patient both disengage-ment and caring.

A sense of challenge arises from the confrontational qualities of disen-gagement. Yet, when coupled with caring, this challenge is thought to en-hance the patient's readiness to accept uncertainty and hence the patient's readiness to make new choices. Some students couple confrontation and caring with a serious demeanor, some by laughing, some intellectualize a little more than others, and some are even moderately seductive or angry or bland. Within limits, all students are trained to use the sort of "output" they are most familiar with (we do not encourage cloning), as long as they know what it is and as long as they can reasonably assess the impact they have on the patient. We teach that errors (faulty impact) are unavoidable ("The pa-tient said I criticized him"), and that the art of a good therapist is to listen and understand why a patient would feel criticized by an ambiguous cue. Just as the therapist wants the patient to ask the question, "How did I contribute to my problem?" so the therapist has to ask what he did to the relationship when a patient selects a cue to complain about being criticized.

In communication analytic psychotherapy, we teach students the general rule that they can change the topic of discussion under two conditions: if they get too anxious or if they get bored—that is, when they think they understand the patient's communication. These excuses are legitimate (though we would want to pay special attention to students who too often become anxious or bored), as the therapist is the major instrument present in the therapeutic hour, and there cannot be much help for the patient when the therapist's attention is diverted.

PUTTING IT ALL TOGETHER

When the student of communication analytic psychotherapy has developed listening and disengagement skills, the model will have several important consequences on future conduct. The student will learn that there is no specific end point at which the therapist stops offering services. Even when the patient reports progress, as in coming to a difficult decision, the therapist will maintain a consistent, questioning attitude ("Must you do what you are doing?"). The therapist who chooses to congratulate the patient on a given choice teaches the patient only how to win praise from the therapist. In other words, there is no reward to be given for good behavior, no punishment for bad. There is no health model where the patient is declared well and healthy, no skill model where the patient has acquired new skills, not even an insight model where the patient knows himself better. All such models lend themselves too easily to engagement. Unless the patient is judged disoriented, or dangerous to the self or others, he must arrive independently at the decision to let go. Termination can occur only when the patient takes responsibility for personal behavior, including the exit from therapy. The patient then has learned to make choices.

A variety of choices exist for limiting or ending the contact. The patient can choose to either terminate or reduce the contact; or he can choose biweekly, monthly, bimonthly, or even yearly contacts. In communication analytic psychotherapy we believe that the hypnotic quality of sharing responsibility for problems with the therapist several times a week can easily be a hindrance to independence and that looser contacts should be explored. In fact, we have experience with several patients whom we see only once a year, and "the hour" is of great importance to them. When contact is reduced, we also allow for an extra hour now and then, as the need arises.

We feel that in communication analytic psychotherapy we get almost immediately to the heart of the patient's skill at creating problems. By analyzing a patient's communication style, we recognize after a very few hours the distress as well as the pleasure of the patient's adaptive compromise; the resultant hypothesis permits the therapist to provide beneficial uncertainty through disengagement. The patient experientially, often without insight, begins to explore new choices. This form of therapy does not carry the unnecessary, superimposed theoretical burden of an insight model, health model, skill model, or behavioral model; the patient can engage in exploration without first learning a new therapeutic language. Several of us practicing this form of psychotherapy believe it can significantly reduce the number of required contact hours for successful treatment.

Finally, we try to impress students with the need for continued supervision or control monitoring. Just as therapists should keep abreast of research developments in their field, they should be actively interested in the more personal experience of continued supervision. We have noted that all therapists experience and sometimes become engaged by the social, manipulative, covert messages of their patients. Frequently, the patient is so skillful and the nature of this engagement is so subtle that it escapes the eye of even the most experienced therapist. Engagement creates misreading of communication and makes for faulty assessments. We teach our students, then, that spending an hour even only once a month with a competent professional can help even an experienced therapist escape therapeutic quagmires.

To some extent, communication analytic psychotherapy is vying for the status of a general theory. By relying on an analysis of communication, its adherents are looking at the simplest common denominator of all models and trying to eliminate some of the differences among models, particularly those that confuse theories of change with more obtuse theories for achieving "mental health." The lowest common denominator for explaining therapeutic gain is the principle of promoting exploration. When we teach communication analytic psychotherapy, we believe that we teach something akin to a basic model, which can stand on its own or serve as the point of departure for those who wish to follow other orientations.

16

Nonverbal Communication in Psychotherapy

> If his lips are silent, he chatters with his fingertips; betrayal oozes out of him at every pore. And thus the task of making conscious the most hidden recesses of the mind is one which is quite possible to accomplish.
>
> —Freud, *Fragment of an Analysis of a Case of Hysteria (1905)*

In the beginning was the word, and we assume that the word is the necessary condition of consciousness, of self. But the word is not the beginning of communication. Long before language existed, people communicated, in the sense that they conveyed intended information. And long before the infant develops verbal language, it masters vocal, facial, postural, and gestural communication.

Nonverbal communication accompanies our every statement; even in written language authors convey "nonverbal" structures, which tell us through channels such as contiguity of words, unexpected phrasing, repetition, etc., more about the authors themselves than about their lexical message. (While the term "nonverbal" is not really adequate for all channels of extraverbal communication, it has come into common usage. We therefore use the term "nonverbal communication" for all extralinguistic information conveyed.) Burgoon (1991) has researched a Social Meaning Model of Nonverbal Communication, which proposes that some nonverbal behaviors form a "socially shared vocabulary analogous to verbal communication and that relational message interpretations are assigned to differing levels and types of touch, proximity, and posture" (p. 232). This suggests that one type of meaning signified by nonverbal behaviors is relational, that is, distinguishing the status of interpersonal relationships.

In research conducted by Grant (1968, 1972) and later expanded on by Schelde and Hertz (1994), it was demonstrated that nonverbal behavior is delineated by a general structure or syntax ("grammar") constituted by four basic motivational states with motivational transitions in between. This research is based upon direct observations of endogenously depressed patients on a psychiatric ward and how they demonstrate meaningful behavior alterations from their admission on the ward until their discharge.

These are the four states:

1. Relaxation: A sitting–leaning-backward posture. The transitional constituent from relaxation to assertion is *lean forward,* by which the patient usually demonstrates increased interest in the social exchange.

2. Assertion: Elements that are assertive without being significantly aggressive (example: push would be construed aggressive). To *thrust* is mostly used to highlight statements, *head to side* is typically utilized as an appealing gesture. Two of the transitional elements between assertion and flight—fumble (slow, twisting movements of the fingers) and *drum-one's-fingers*—are most likely representations of a motivational conflict that is then typically succeeded by assertive behaviors.

3. Flight: Signified by physical flight, submission, withdrawal, and pacifying behavior. Flight behaviors are characterized by *look away, look down, still* (cessation of movement), *shut eyes,* and *crouch. Nonspecific gaze* may also be included here.

4. Contact: Contact or affiliation motivation is signified by gestures that specify a motivation for social contact. Examples are *look at, flash* (a short up-and-down movement of the eyebrows typically accompanied by smile), *bob* (a fast, backward movement of the back of the head), and *uplifted eyebrows* (Grant, 1968, 1972; Schelde and Hertz, 1994).

The ability to identify these motivational state changes and to interpret these gestures allows the therapist to identify discrepancies between the patient's verbal and nonverbal behavior and thus provide the therapist with feedback signals. (Schelde and Hertz, 1994).

The purpose of the following review is to relate various studies in nonverbal communication to the psychotherapy process.

ELEMENTS OF NONVERBAL COMMUNICATION

The areas of nonverbal communication covered in the following sections are facial expression, gaze, paralinguistic cues, gestures, and use of space.

Facial Expression

Since Darwin (1872) wrote about the functional or survival value of facial expressions, researchers in communication have attempted to categorize, decode, encode, and evaluate the interpersonal impact of emotion in the human face. Tomkins (1962), Izard (1971), and others have argued and convincingly demonstrated that humans possess a set of discrete, universally recognized, neurologically based facial emotions, and that we in fact read our own moods from our own facial expressions! Additional support for this stance was accrued by Kraut (1982). Kraut demonstrated that when smelling odors varying from pleasant to unpleasant, subjects rated even unpleasant odors as more pleasant when they displayed positive facial expressions (Kraut, 1982). Ekman (1972, 1973), a most prolific researcher in this area, accepts this nativistic position but added important concepts and data to the theory. Ekman agreed with most researchers that inner emotions follow standard neural response mechanisms, but added the idea that socially learned methods of facially coping with emotion and emotion-producing events are also present. That is, cultural rules for displaying affect and idiosyncratic, unconscious learning take place in early childhood and serve to modify facial expression.

Experiments such as those conducted by Thayer and Shiff (1969) have demonstrated that facial expressions significantly influence the perception of social situations. Focusing on psychotherapy, Shapiro, Foster, and Powell (1968) discovered the therapist's facial expression to be an important variable related to the perception of the therapist's warmth and genuineness. Certainly facial expressions presented by clients and therapists influence perception and the eventual progress of therapy.

We do read faces thoroughly and often discover more than others want to convey to us. This observation can be supported by an experiment conducted by Ekman, Friesen, and O'Sullivan (1988). They posited that small but distinguishable differences exist between smiling during the experiencing of a pleasant emotion and smiling when experiencing fear, disgust, or sadness. Their results yielded significant support of this hypothesis as evidenced via physiological measurement—subjects' smiling that occurred during the experience of a pleasurable emotion was typically accompanied by movement of the muscle surrounding the eye; while subjects instructed by a confederate of the experiment to attempt to conceal any negative emotion (i.e., of fear, disgust, or sadness) they might experience by smiling displayed indications of muscular movement associated with the concurrent experiencing of negative emotions (Ekman, Friesen, & O'Sullivan, 1988). Their findings demonstrate that facial cues may be an avenue of detection for deceit about emotional states.

In research conducted by Wagner (1990), there is support for the premise that even when the social nature of an interaction is reduced to a minimum, facial cues still emulate the underlying emotion experienced (as interpreted by observers). These results could be posited to demonstrate that even in the absence of social interaction, nonverbal behaviors (facial cues) still convey messages that the sender may not even be aware of.

Once an expression has become established, it can characterize a person's style; when such a person is rated by a large number of judges, these judges can often identify the dominant mood of the person. On the other hand, the persons themselves often do not know what mood they are communicating to others; many people communicate anger, depression, or seductiveness even though they want to be read as happy, indifferent, sad, or afraid.

If our nonverbal signals are read differently from the intended way, we obviously cannot account for the impact we have on others. This discordance can be seen as a "communication deficit," or a discrepancy among various channels of communication, and is of significance in psychotherapy. Discordance is also used in deception, i.e., when a manipulator wants to achieve a specific impact but wants to deceive the respondent about the true motivation. Ekman and Friesen (1969) propose that willful deception is not easily detected in the sender's face. They view the sender's unaware movement of the extremities and maintenance of greater distance from the receiver as indicators of deception.

When people are unaware of the discrepancy between the message they want to send and what they indeed are sending, their expectations are not congruent with the obtained responses, even though they themselves evoked the responses with their expressions. In this manner they can commit certain acts and yet not feel responsible for having done so; even though they evoked the responses themselves, they can feel victimized by these very responses. This concept, expressed in communication terms, is very similar to the concept of repression, but it is more clearly measurable by observing discrepancy of meaning between channels.

When people's nonverbal skills are investigated, most individuals appear capable of conveying only two of any six moods accurately. Others of their mood expressions are not understood as accurately and achieve more random ratings, at least during limited exposure. When we recognize a dominant mood a person facially expresses, and find a discrepancy in other channels, we know a little better just what sort of problems he will get into. When a person never appears sad but tells us of all the depressing details of life, we can assess that person's history more adequately and understand some aspects of the present problem better. An individual telling us of always being victimized by aggression when we have recognized his dominant facial expression as angry will give us useful information about the person's own contribution to the alleged victimization.

Gaze

The study of visual behavior in human interaction is perhaps the most actively researched area of nonverbal communication; entire texts have been devoted to the subject (e.g., Argyle and Cook, 1976). In their classic summary of research, Harper et al. (1978) conclude that considerable evidence relates visual behavior to the nature and influence of interpersonal relationships. In general, looking has appeared to function as a signal for willingness to communicate and a subtle indicator of liking (Beier and Sternberg, 1971), and as a cue for information-seeking and sexual contact (Argyle and Dean, 1965). Conversely, avoidance of looking or withdrawal of eye contact has been viewed as a sign of shyness or depression, a result of a lowered self-image (Modigliani, 1971), and a means of hiding from contact (Argyle and Dean, 1965).

In their more recent studies of marital therapy, Fivaz-Depeursinge, Roten, Corboz-Warnery, Metraux, and Ciola (1994) concluded that "we use gaze directions to describe the partners' behaviors" (in interactions between therapist and a couple) and label this property the "mutual attending frame." The "mutual attending frame" is the supraindividual property formed by the coordination between individual gaze directions. Gaze direction is correlated with many individual attributes and interaction states. Involvement, status, and affiliation are regarded as the primary determinants (Capella, 1981; Patterson, 1982). In therapeutic situations, participants orient their gaze to determine the affect of their partners and to utilize this information as feedback toward the state(s) they are conveying to their partners. From this observation, it can be taken that gaze orientation functions as being indicative and directory in affective relationships. Another function of the direction of gaze is to ascertain conversational roles and to synchronize turn-taking. Generally, speakers gaze at listeners when they are ready to give someone else a chance to speak and speakers tend to avert their gaze from listeners when they are not ready to give up the floor (Fivaz-Depeursinge et al. 1994).

As summarized by Fivaz-Depeursinge et al. (1994), "gaze directions enhance coordination between the partners by allowing smooth turn-taking, facilitating discourse elaboration, and promoting the establishment and maintenance of engagement." Mutual attending results from the coordination of gaze directions among all partners toward each other during engagement; in contrast, during disengagement, one or more partner(s) gazes away. The use of mutual attending generates an attentional frame for their communication.

Research in psychological diagnosis has shown that therapists can make accurate assessments based on the visual behavior of patients (Waxer, 1978). Depressives, autistic children, and schizophrenics frequently avoid eye contact in interviews, but alter their visual behavior on recovery. It is likely that special visual behaviors that these patients exhibit aid in providing a retreat from reality as well as a communication to others that the patient wants to be left alone; the downcast eyes of the depressed patient might serve to elicit caring responses from others while simultaneously sending a covertly rejecting message.

In some skill-related areas, such as political image training or job interviewing, instruction in the use of eye contact can profoundly influence evaluations (Young, Beier, and Beier, 1978), though in some settings the training may need to be of long duration to have any effect, and even then the effect often does not last.

A common use of visual communication is to convey subtle or not-so-subtle anger (the evil eye or stare); another use is seduction (the eye blink). The marital therapist who sees a husband profess love for his wife while staring out the window may interpret such discordance of visual and vocal cues as a passive-aggressive message. If this discordant message is sent with awareness, the husband wants to let his wife know of his aggression; if sent without awareness, the message still lets her know of his aggression, but does not make the husband feel responsible for his aggressive attitude.

Paralinguistic (Vocal) Cues

Paralinguistic cues include very subtle vocal cues such as pitch, intensity, rate of speech, pauses, and response latency. In summarizing paralinguistic research, Harper et al. (1978) report that the emotional states of patients can be more successfully diagnosed from paralinguistic cues than from conventional personality measures.

Paralinguistic cues are most often read as indicators of emotion. They add nuances of meaning to verbal language. At least some such cues carry intercultural meaning. Students from other countries do understand accurately the moods conveyed by the verbally neutral spoken words of American students (Beier and Zautra, 1972). People under stress have been analyzed at Bell Laboratories by wave frequency of their voice, and vocal evidence of deception has been suggested by "microtremors" in the voice prints.

In psychotherapy, therapists and patients appear to develop a paralinguistic pattern or synchrony in verbal exchanges. As nonverbal moderators such as "Mm, hmm" serve to regulate others' behavior, it is likely that paralinguistic cues are behavior influencers, not just clues to the speaker's emotional state (Matarazzo, Wiens, Matarazzo, and Saslow, 1968). It has also been demonstrated that length of talk time, irrespective of content, influences a listener's affective response (Kleinke, Lenga, Tully, Meeker, and Staneski, 1976). The tempo of a client's speech production can also alert the therapist to the client's affective state (Gedo, 1996). There has been an observed correlation between an increase in one's usual spoken tempo and certain affective states, namely extreme anxiety or hypomania. Likewise there is also a correlation between a decrease in one's usual spoken tempo and other affective conditions such as depression. In his book *The Languages of Psychoanalysis* (1996) John Gedo writes: "If only the paraverbal aspects of speech are affected, while its lexical and syntactic aspects remain unaltered, calling attention to these specific changes and inquiry into their meaning and genesis usually leads to fruitful results in elucidating the client's affective state" (p. 383).

Gestures and Touch

Body movements and posture have their effects as powerful modifiers, amplifiers, and regulators of verbal behavior. Mehrabian and Williams (1969) experimented with subtle changes in nodding or postural lean, which significantly influenced the persuasiveness of a speaker. Using a more general approach, Scheflen (1966) examined the gestural patterns of patients in psychotherapy and categorized them according to several styles, including "readiness," "positioning," and "preening" behaviors. Relying on gestural cues, Waxer (1978) and others have also made reliable assessments of anxious and depressed patients.

In discussing the use of gestures as a form of nonverbal communication, it is also important to include a section on touch. Touch generally signifies more composure, immediacy, receptivity/trust, affection, similarity/depth/ equality, dominance, and informality than does nontouch (Burgoon, 1991). The style of touching is also implicated in the information it signifies. For instance, face touching and hand holding signify the greatest amount of composure, informality, and intimacy—with handshakes and hand holding conveying the least amount of dominance, and handshakes signifying the greatest amount of formality while at the same time conveying receptivity/ trust (Burgoon, 1991). Postural openness and relaxation corresponded with touch in signifying more intimacy, composure, informality, and similarity and was also less dominant than a closed or tense posture.

Subtle movements of psychotherapists themselves have been shown to be important in enhancing the therapeutic environment (Waxer, 1978). When the nonverbally attentive therapist is compared with one rated as inattentive, the amount of head nodding of each therapist will produce a difference in the patient's talk time. The "closed" therapist whose arms and legs remain crossed is perceived and reacted to as colder than the therapist who maintains an open posture. In an experiment conducted by Sharpley and Sagris (1995) on counselor forward lean, the results demonstrated that more extreme forward lean (characterized by 41 degrees or more) was notably more common during minutes rated as "very high" in rapport (as perceived by the client). The type and degree of attention between clients and therapists is mainly signified by nonverbal behaviors (i.e., body posture, hand gestures, and eye contact). Forward lean signifies to a client the therapist's positive affect toward him. This perception by the client leads to an increase in client-perceived rapport in the therapeutic situation (Sharpley and Sagris, 1995). We have found in reviewing videotapes during supervision that trainees are often surprised by the impact of their postural cues displayed in therapy.

Use of Space

Research on the use and structuring of interpersonal space was pioneered by Hall (1966) and later expanded by Altman (e.g., 1981) and others. While the question of differences in personal distance in various cultures is still open, we begin to understand, particularly through Sommer's work, the threat of the invasion of personal space or, through Altman, the effects of crowding and seating behavior (when is a seat my seat?).

Research with a variety of clinical populations has indicated that the use of space may be an indication of certain psychological problems. As might be expected, the comfortable interpersonal distance of acute schizophrenics is large (Horowitz, 1978). Similarly, Hutt and Vaizey (1966) observed the play behavior of autistic children and found their subjects consistently outside boundary areas. Beier and Sternberg (1971) found that newlywed couples who experience marital discord move their chairs further apart when talking to each other than do less discordant couples. In play therapy, the distance between child and therapist appears to be related to trust. When patients are given a choice of seating, the distance patients choose may provide the therapist with initial hypotheses of resistance.

Apparently, even young children possess some degree of knowledge about nonverbal communication and social distance. In an experiment conducted by Holmes and College (1992), this distance hypothesis was explored through children's artwork. Specifically, children were asked to create two drawings: one of themselves with a friend and one of themselves with a stranger. As the children consistently placed the stranger farther from themselves than they placed their friends, it can be extrapolated from these results that even children as young as 5 years experience that greater personal space should be maintained between themselves and strangers than between themselves and friends.

Resistance in psychotherapy can also refer to the therapist. Graves and Robinson (1976) found that patients keep their physical distance from incongruent therapists—therapists who verbally offer support while maintaining an inattentive nonverbal style. Conversely, patients are likely to reduce distance from therapists whose verbal and nonverbal behaviors are congruent. These subtle cues appear to be the "vibes" that help create the emotional climate of the relationship.

THEORY OF NONVERBAL COMMUNICATION IN PSYCHOTHERAPY

The literature of nonverbal behavior appears to deal with isolated observations, some of which have given rise to limited theoretical interpretations within the area of treatment. A few communication-based theories deal specifically with psychotherapeutic problems (e.g., Beier, 1966; Haley,

1977; Kiesler, 1973; Ruesch, 1961; Sullivan, 1953; and Watzlawick et al. 1967), and one might suggest that interpersonal communication is the most common denominator of all theoretical approaches of psychotherapy. If a therapist probes, reinforces, reflects feelings of content, offers an interpretation, presents a lead to a self-actualization, or is developing potential, in most general communication terms, he is giving an "asocial" response to the patient's message that the patient does not generally expect.

Beier devised communication analytic psychotherapy, which accounts for the mutual impact of the exchanged message. After much research, Don Kiesler devised an impact questionnaire designed to measure emotional impact beyond the meaning of words. Communication analytic psychotherapy theory holds that an asocial message to a patient produces uncertainty, because the customary, preferred, and expected response is withheld. The patient is forced to try new behaviors when the preferred style no longer produces the familiar rewards. The nature of these new responses can be therapeutic to the extent that the emotional climate in the setting is one of caring and concern. The caring and concern are nonverbally communicated in the therapy setting by the various attitudes recounted in most modes of psychotherapy: listening, which communicates to the patient that he is a unique and important person whose utterances are meaningful; lack of criticism, which means that the therapist's own values will not coerce or interfere with the patient's ability to discover his own values; and what one might call "sensing" or "understanding" (sometimes called interpretation), which brings together consciously and unconsciously expressed wishes of the patients and integrates them into a comprehensive pattern, which in turn communicates to the patient intimate understanding or acceptance. With these behaviors the therapist establishes a caring relationship, which, combined with asocial responses, creates beneficial uncertainty, the precondition for exploratory and creative searching for new responses. Beneficial uncertainty is thought to be a necessary underlying condition for attitude change.

We should note, however, that an asocial response in the absence of a caring attitude can also bring about changes, but such changes, based on an injurious uncertainty, are likely to result in regressive behavior rather than in a sense of freedom. The communication analytic psychotherapy model is based on the assumption that nonverbal communication is used frequently (but not always) by us as a way to express our unconscious needs.

All individuals try to find an adaptive compromise between conscious and unconscious needs, i.e., between their own acceptable motivation (most often expressed in their language) and their hidden and unacceptable motivation (often expressed by nonverbal behavior). We may call such persons patients when they use a restricted number of their adaptive compromises with a very high frequency, when they are dominated by a response set that gives them some satisfaction but also an inordinate amount of pain.

Nonverbal behavior is the "unconscious made visible," i.e., it makes visible the part of the compromise that is unacceptable to the patient. Nonverbal communication is especially well suited for this purpose, because the cues and discrepancies among messages traveling in a variety of channels are subtle and appear ambiguous, so that the meaning can stay hidden even from the sender and yet affect the emotions of the receiver. The patient who suffers from loneliness and takes any and all opportunity to alienate others by his tone of voice may not be aware of this counterproductive behavior, even though the patient evokes the very problem he despises. The therapeutic setting is designed to permit the patient to explore the conflicting motivations: how he evokes loneliness and hates it at the same time. The patient will experience and perhaps understand the consequences of the hidden nonverbal communication and the motivation it represents.

Our theoretical approach has been presented again in some detail to show that nonverbal behavior can be understood as a representative of "the unconscious" and has a significant place in the psychotherapeutic process. Surely communication theory explains only part of the variance of the therapeutic process, but perhaps nonverbal communication is the very part that makes unconscious motivation visible and measurable, and one part that has direct impact on the therapeutic exchange.

Nonverbal Interaction Expectancies

Recent work by Burgoon and Walther (1990) has developed the idea that during social interaction there are certain important nonverbal behaviors that people expect to occur. They hold that there are behaviors that are expected, and behaviors occurring outside this range are characterized as either positive or negative violations of expectations. They further speculate that if it could be demonstrated that people anticipate consistencies in nonverbal behavior (and label violations of those expectations as *significant*), this would facilitate the claim that violations of expectations are meaningful aspects of communication.

Nonverbal expectancy theory posits that behavior, contingent upon the interpretation and the evaluation given to it, will be assessed as either positive or negative. The evaluation depends on society's conventions and how rewarding an individual evaluates the person committing the behavior— that is, similar behaviors can be evaluated favorably when committed by a high-reward communicator and vice versa for a low-reward communicator. The behaviors Burgoon and Walther investigated were conversational distance, touch, and postural relaxation. They hypothesized that close distance and intermediate relaxation are more expected than their opposites, that touch should be relatively unexpected (since our culture is typically one of little contact), and any touch that is displayed is expected to have a short time duration, with a greater degree of formality and a lesser degree of intimacy. They went on to surmise that expectations are affected by variables of physical attractiveness, status, and gender.

The results of their research revealed that proximity, touch, and posture do vary in their expectedness. Close proximity during an interaction was more expected than distant proximity, and was also more positively evaluated than distant proximity. When touch expectedness was compared with evaluations, the results demonstrated that lack of touch was neither expected nor unexpected—but lack of touch was negatively evaluated compared to its presence. Hand holding and handshaking were the most expected touch behaviors and both were positively evaluated. Apparently, we do not often find the offer of a handshake offensive and we may miss it if it is not offered. Posture expectations were dependent in part upon communicator gender and attractiveness—all postures were shown to be equally expected for attractive males, while posture was expected to be either relaxed or erect for attractive females. "Unattractive" communicators were expected to hold an erect posture. (Burgoon & Walther, 1990).

Miles Patterson (1982) has suggested adopting a sequential functional model of nonverbal exchange. This means that nonverbal exchange starts with the identification of a group of personal (culture, sex differences, and personality), experiential (the influence of past experiences on later interactions), and relational-situational (the influence of the type of interaction is in part determined by the environment it takes place in) factors that begin preinteraction mediators. The preinteraction mediators are (1) behavioral dispositions, (2) potential arousal change, and (3) cognitive-affective assessment. These mediators in turn format the perceived functions of an interaction and the degrees of nonverbal involvement of the communicators.

The function of an interaction can be to provide information (the most "basic" function of nonverbal behavior), to regulate the interaction (this is most likely the most automatic function), to express intimacy (the interaction can be an affectively based reaction toward another individual), to exercise social control (applying influence in the attempt to change the behavior of another), or to initiate service or task goals (this identifies the basis for a generally impersonal nonverbal involvement). The nonverbal exchange is predicted to increase in instability as the communicators' perceived functions and expectancies of the exchange deviate from these cognitions.

Based on these premises, an interaction can either be defined as stable or unstable. A stable interaction (exchange) would be the result of the expected behavior and actual involvement (of the other person) displaying minimal discrepancies. An unstable exchange would arise from a large discrepancy between the expected behavior and the actual. This discrepancy thus initiates adjustments in the nonverbal interaction that can also lead to a reevaluation of the interaction's function (Patterson, 1982). This can be demonstrated by the following: During a therapeutic interaction, if the therapist glances at his watch and the patient simultaneously senses the session is almost over, this would probably be an expected behavior (of the therapist) to cue the end of the session, and therefore a stable interaction would have occurred. If, however, the therapist's glancing at his watch was an unexpected action, a large discrepancy could result (for the patient) and he would most likely reassess his own involvement, possibly trying harder to engage the therapist by being more interesting or by withdrawing in an abrupt manner.

Both the nonverbal expectancies theory and the sequential functional model, then, would seem to carry both basic and applied applications to the further understanding of the many facets of nonverbal communication, both in theory and in practice.

17

The Ethical Problems of Control of Behavior

AWARENESS OF CONTROL

When Socrates led his respondents in dialogue through the Socratic way of questioning, he was confronted with an ethical problem. In its simplest form, the problem was how to justify his manipulation of the respondent. Socrates' justification response is of significance here because it lasted two thousand years. He wrote: "For is not the discovery of things as they truly are, a good common to all mankind?" (quoted in Jowett, 1937). That is to say, to the extent that Socrates helps toward the discovery of "things as they truly are," he cannot fail to be good. Or, in modern terms, as long as we stay with the existential facts, we cannot do wrong.

A second solution to Socrates' ethical problem is found in young Theaetetus, who is not seen as learning but rather as discovering his own knowledge with Socrates' help. Socrates says, "I only just say enough to extract. . . . I shall say nothing myself but shall endeavor to elicit something from our young friend" (ibid., p. 163). Socrates is the facilitator, the "midwife" who does not seem himself to be imposing his own ideas on the respondent, but is simply helping bring forth Theaetetus' ideas.

Both of Socrates' answers are reflected in many of the theories that have governed the practice of psychotherapy. Just as Socrates justified his behavior on the grounds that it would lead to true self-knowledge and choices and awaken the respondent's own resources, psychotherapeutic theory, generally speaking, conveniently postulates that psychotherapy is a procedure that helps people function adequately by utilizing their own potential.

From Socrates to the present, we have been provided with many theories that assume that to help patients we should strive toward goals such as helping them discover and make explicit their own reality and assisting them in finding their own potential, that is, to self-actualize their resources. Defining in this manner our work as beneficial, we may not even recognize our responsibility for any of the dangers to the individual that may result from our interventions. This reasoning, of course, follows Socrates' conviction that asking questions is the tool that leads to better knowledge of self and

brings forth only the person's own potential. Socrates must have been greatly surprised indeed when he was arrested, found guilty, and given the death
sentence for instilling foreign values in the youth to whom he was talking.
He might have defended himself with, "What harm can I do by questioning?
I do not enforce any values on other persons in that manner."

In order to understand our own procedures, we must accept the fact that
we are not innocent bystanders; we are—to say the least—aiming to have a
person explore and possibly change behavior.

Bergin (1964) was one of the pioneer researchers to list an impressive
number of studies that upon meta-analysis indicate that clients in psychotherapy may get either better or worse. In other words, psychotherapy can
lower as well as raise a person's quality of life. This possible outcome is
frequently overlooked by practitioners or researchers who ask only how
much improvement has occurred in a given client or clients.

Behavior theories have a somewhat different theoretical position and had
to face the ethical issues directly. Early in the evolution of behavioral practice, Krasner (1962) spoke of psychotherapy as a form of behavior control
that uses methods of exerting influence, persuasion, and manipulation of
behavior. Krasner says, "[A] behavioristic viewpoint might argue that apparent spontaneity on the therapist's part may very well be a most effective
means of manipulating behavior. The therapist is an individual programmed
by his training into a fairly effective behavior control machine. Most likely
the machine is most effective when it least appears like a machine" (p. 20).

While one may argue about whether a person who consciously wants to
help other people help themselves can be called controlling, evidence
seems to be accumulating that the therapist's behavior determines not only
the patient's behavior to some extent, but also the patient's values as well.
This control occurs even when the therapist desires to be totally objective.
There is a difference between a friend who advises a person that he ought to
get married and a therapist who gives subtle paralinguistic cues of approval
or shows an increased degree of interest ("Mm, hmm") when the patient
talks about marriage. The friend gives advice and will easily admit wanting
to influence the person's behavior. The therapist may rightly deny having
any wish to influence the patient's choice; but to the degree that the therapist has learned to be a keen observer, the therapist may admit to influencing
the patient simply because objectivity is an illusion and the therapist has an
aura of authority and even power, often because of the conscious claim to
objectivity. Values are communicated and a subtle form of persuasion
occurs.

We note that even the length of a statement in therapy is predictably
related to the length of the patient's reply (Matarazzo et al., 1965). Thus, it is
most likely that the paralinguistic nonverbal behavior of the therapist is the
method by which the therapist communicates values and ethics. When the

attentive adolescent arrives at the session in his cleanest clothes and with his various body piercings carefully removed, the subtle smile of approval from the therapist is not ignored. Kovacs (1982) holds that the therapist is responsible for these inferences and suggests that the therapist should write a contract with the patient in which these possibilities, as well as others, such as duration of contracted time and possible outcomes, are made explicit. Of course, simply alerting the patient to the possibility of subtle influence probably does little to actually protect patients from covert control.

The problem of ethics is certainly not unique to the psychotherapist. Behavioral scientists are entering every conceivable kind of arena—schools, industries, politics, and just about any organization with two or more members. Public fears about the consequences of this pervasive activity in the days of Socrates and in the revolutionary days of the introduction of behavior modification are summarized by Brecher and Brecher in Krasner (1962): "New methods of controlling behavior now emerging from the laboratory may soon add an awe-inspiring power to enslave us all with our own engineered consent" (p. 201). Although this quotation overstates the case, we can agree that these methods suggest a total revision of ethical considerations, which so far have dealt largely with conscious rather than covert features. The impact of behavioral consultants in prominent jury trials has been noted frequently. Not only do consultants assist in selection of jurors, but they advise counsel on how to create in the courtroom workable emotional climates that mesh with the constitution of the jury.

When we look at how behavior is changed and do not choose to flee moral responsibility with the simplistic statement that we help the patient to develop innate potential, fearful vistas appear for both the behavioral scientist and the public. The cries of invasion of privacy and misuse of testing (intelligence testing is thought to be discriminatory, and is limited in schools in certain states) have to be taken seriously: We are not likely to discontinue scientific work on methods of persuasion any more than the physicist discontinued work on splitting the atom. The comparison may sound grandiose, but with each breakthrough in the understanding of the processes of persuasion, and the development of new channels of persuasion, the impact on society is enormous. Consider the impact of persuasive messages now being sent across the Internet. From the issues of cyberseduction and pornography to new avenues of fraud, new channels for persuasion are expanding. We must try to guard now, in principle, against misuse of persuasive power by identifying properly where it occurs, by keeping all information regarding how persuasion works as available to the public, and by concerning ourselves with the study of protective devices. The American Psychological Association (1992) continues to revise its standards and principles of ethical concerns in its piece *Ethical Principles of Psychologists and Code of Conduct.*

SUBTLE CONCERNS IN PSYCHOTHERAPY

There are nine areas of ethical concerns specific to therapy that are enumerated in the *Ethical Principles*. They are (1) structuring the relationship; (2) informed consent; (3) couple and family relationships; (4) providing mental health services to those served by others; (5) sexual intimacies with current patients; (6) therapy with former sexual partners; (7) sexual intimacies with former therapy patients; (8) interruption of services (abandonment); and (9) terminating the professional relationship. While these are areas of great importance in protecting patients from exploitation (a third of the issues deal with sexual contact), we consider five additional related themes as important:

1. *The conscious or unconscious impact of the therapist on the value system of the patient, to the extent that such an impact is identifiable.* The responsibility of the psychotherapist is to be concerned with his own subtle and not-so-subtle impact on the patient. This we see as elementary to the therapeutic process. A responsible psychotherapist will seek professional consultation in order to obtain information about his own engagement processes. Psychoanalysts require that a new analyst be fully analyzed, and in many professional schools of psychology, personal psychotherapy is a requirement as well. In most clinical training programs, psychotherapy is recommended and often made available at low cost to students. While such services are most worthwhile, we see psychotherapy as an ongoing process, and new engagements occur even with the most experienced therapist. Patients have great skill in exercising their engagement strategies, and to better understand these strategies the therapist must maintain contact with another professional person with whom he can discover the engagement processes to which he falls victim. Such discussions may take an hour a month or may occur more often, but they should involve a professional relationship.

2. *The problem of the patient's consent.* Many writers, including Freud and Rogers, stated that their therapeutic methods were effective only if the individual was asking for help. This no longer appears to be true: we can probably affect a person's behavior whether the patient wants to change or not. Once we understand the patterns involved, the hostile delinquent sent by a court is probably not any more difficult to deal with in therapy than a voluntary patient. Each has a stake in maintaining current patterns although each is probably experiencing some pain. We have to begin to evaluate under what circumstances we are entitled to work with a person in therapy, and to spell out the conditions that must be fulfilled to keep the effort from being an invasion of privacy. New rules are obviously necessary.

The idea of informed consent to treatment remains far to loose a concept.

The Department of Health and Human Services correctly questions the usefulness of an individual's consent, particularly in research with children, prisoners, mental patients, students, and in any other situation where even subtle coercion is a possibility. Beyond this, it is questionable whether certain consent contracts should be seen as valid. For example, if an 18-year-old boy wants to undergo a sex change operation, should his consent for this operation be sufficient?

3. Discussion of rules. Socrates could see himself as a midwife, just helping others to give birth. Today we have strong indications that the therapist is the father of the baby. Whether the goals of therapy are very broad (to encourage the person to explore new choices) or very specific (to teach a child to read better), or anything in between, the therapist will encourage the patient to reach such goals. The therapist must therefore discuss his treatment philosophy with the patient as early as possible.

4. Increased powers of persuasion regarding the values of society. In some states, laws make it illegal for a therapist to change an individual's beliefs. On the one hand, such laws are not likely to be useful, to say nothing about their constitutionality. On the other hand, it might be argued that the therapist should be frank about certain of his values and beliefs, particularly when they are relevant to the patient's problems.

5. The validation problem. Objective criteria for the duration and effects of therapeutic work as they are defined by different theories should be worked out. The patient has a right to know approximately what to expect and when to expect it.

ETHICS AND THE HEALTH CARE SYSTEM

The health care system continues to evolve (see Chapters 13 and 18) and with it come changes in practice that confront traditional interpretation of the ethical guidelines. Some of the issues that appear to generate the most concern in ethical areas include confidentiality, capitation, and abandonment.

The confidentiality concerns emerging from the changing health care scene are not fully clear at first glance. Where in pre–managed care days, insurance companies merely required a DSM diagnosis, most HMOs now require an extensive written intake including a complete drug and alcohol history about the patient and the patient's family. Although the argument can be made that this information is relevant to care, the delivery of this information, often by fax, to a series of unseen case managers or clerks, opens the record to many eyes. Typically, managed care companies now require the treating psychologist or social worker to notify the patient's primary care physician that the patient is in treatment, what the diagnosis is, and what the treatment plan is going to be. It is not inconceivable that the patient would not want the family doctor to know about each instance of requesting counseling, especially if the patient is working on issues related to others in the family. The patient is, of course, asked to sign a form permitting release of confidential information, but the anxiety of permitting further leakage of information may prevent some patients from following through with care or may encourage some patients to avoid seeking care through their managed care provider. Of further concern is that the reporting requirements regarding patient care are ongoing. Treatment plans, progress reports, and goal assessments all are expected to be delivered to case managers on a routine basis.

The capitation concern represents a different area of ethical dilemma for the practitioner. To review (see Chapter 13), capitation involves the process of practitioners agreeing to treat a group of contracted patients on an as-needed basis for a set price per patient. Again, at first glance there may appear to be no ethical issues raised. However, the practitioner is involved in an incentive system where the profit motive centers either on not providing services or providing as few services as possible. These issues have their own potential for presenting covert dilemmas in patient-therapist interaction, especially if they are not explored by therapists. Other fee structure issues should also be considered for the subtle impact they may have on therapist behaviors. Therapists need to carefully assess their own reactions to HMOs that restrict fees to extreme levels or require extensive amounts of record keeping and reporting.

The issue of patient abandonment also interacts with health care system changes when the rise of restrictions on care is considered. Here, the ethical dilemmas are not so subtle when clinicians are faced with patients in need of care who have utilized the allowable services for the year. Still further questions are raised as to the ethical nature of accepting patients in treatment when there appears to be a strong likelihood that the allotted number of treatment sessions will be inadequate to meet patient goals.

CHAPTER

18

Pills and Caring Talk

Just as the rapidly changing economy of the health care system over the past decade has had enormous impact on the way in which psychotherapy is conducted, new findings in neuroscience, especially the development of psychotropic medications, have added dramatically to these changes. Additionally, new ways of thinking about psychopathology, including removing the artificial dichotomy in psychotherapy practice by imposing either a rigid biological model of the psychopathology or a purely psychogenic model, have added to major changes in the field and portend even more. Both "biologically" based and "nonbiologically" based mental health professionals have radically changed practice styles. The force of economic pressures to control the costs of treatment coupled with the effectiveness and efficiency of administration of medication have combined to create additional changes in the way that mental health care is provided. As might be expected in times of such rapid change in knowledge, tools available, and market forces, the political theater is the center stage. Although the present chapter not a primer in psychopharmacology, one of its goals is first to help identify the landmark changes in the field of psychopharmacology and then to provide a discussion of how those practicing psychotherapy, typically nonprescribing clinicians, have reacted to these changes. We will discuss the clinical problems associated with working with patients around the issues of referral for medication management, patient noncompliance, the "meaning" of the medicine, and refusal to accept medicine. We will also offer a historically based discussion of the ongoing debate in psychology about prescription privileges for psychologists. This discussion, we hope, will balance exploration of the expanding scope of practice concerns for psychologists, the economics of these issues, and political, ethical, and legal considerations. Finally, this chapter will include a discussion of some contemporary issues in the areas of chemical dependency and addictions related to the processes of psychotherapy.

THE PARADIGM SHIFT

Over the twelve years since the second edition of this text was complete, comprehensive research conducted in a variety of disciplines exploring human behavior and disease has yielded a powerful convergence of thought combining, once again, the joint contributions of both genetic/biological and behavioral/psychological influences. Major discoveries in the biochemical areas aided by tools such as MRI, PET, and SPECT scans, along with decreases in the amount and severity of the side effects of psychotropic medications have contributed to a much wider acceptance of medications. This general acceptance of a model encompassing the etiological contributions of a biological predisposition activated by environmental/psychological factors (the diathesis stress model) has replaced the previous extreme in polarization of models, in which some medical professionals viewed psychopathology as only manifestations of biological problems—to be treated by physical interventions. The psychological extreme was equally exclusive. Many psychologists were shy about exploring pharmacological assistance for their patients or considering the influence of genetics in formulating their patients' problems or treatment. Instead, they insisted in focusing largely on the influence of childhood traumata, environmental stresses, faulty learning patterns, or poor interpersonal experiences.

Preston and Johnson (1995) describe the current paradigm shift resulting in most mental health practitioners characterizing mental disorders on a continuum with varying degrees or contributions of both environmental (psychological) and somatogenic (biological/genetic) components. Most people in the United States receive their mental health services from nonmedical therapists, and it is essential for these providers to be aware of the current approaches to medication, physical conditions that may present as psychological problems, the role of genetic predisposition, and drugs or drug interactions that produce psychological symptoms (Preston, O'Neal, & Talaga, 1994). Training models, in traditionally nonmedical approaches to treatment must expand to include ample exploration of these issues as current research shows that there are complex, interactive processes between biological and psychological factors.

The paradigm shift to a psychological/biological continuum seen in mental health areas has also occurred throughout the scientific community and in most other spheres of health care. Consider the behavioral medicine view on the prevention and care of skin cancer. In terms of biological predisposition, we know that there are biologically determined factors such as finding that light-skinned, freckled individuals are at a genetic risk to develop skin cancers, especially if they have a positive family history. Similarly we have learned that such cancers are related to being exposed to repeated sunburns, especially during early childhood, exposure to extreme amounts of ultraviolet radiation, failure to apply adequate sunscreen protection, and other be-haviorally related factors. To overlook either the biological contributions or behavioral factors related to the development (or prevention) of such dis-eases would be considered a fundamentally unsound practice. To ask if the behavior problem is based on psychological *or* biological trauma (Preston and Johnson, 1995) represents a gross oversimplification of what researchers are now finding: a complex interaction. Rather, the question should be what are the relative contributions of psychological and biological components of a problem. Determining the relative significance of both sources of input to the pathology is critical. The answer to the question is extremely important in determining the direction of treatment.

WHO HAS THE PRESCRIPTION PAD? WHO SHOULD? WHO WILL?

Before delving into the debate about prescription privileges for psycholo-gists, a glance at the picture of who is currently writing prescriptions for psychotropic medications is in order. We know that most prescriptions for most psychiatric medications are not written by psychiatrists (Beardsley, Gardocki, Larson, & Hidalgo, 1988). In fact, reviewing the major categories of medications: antipsychotics, antidepressants, antianxiety, sedative-hypnotics, and lithium carbonate, we note that in every category but one (lithium carbonate), nonpsychiatric physicians prescribe the vast majority of the medi-cine (Beardsley et al., 1988). The implications of these findings are obvious. In addition to learning that most physicians find bipolar disorder difficult to treat, we find from these data that most patients are somehow bypassing the top medical specialists in mental health care. As managed care and other cost-containing programs continue to limit access to medical specialists and enhance the role of the primary care physician, we can anticipate a further decrease in the percentage of psychotropic prescriptions written by psychia-trists and a subsequent continuing push by psychologists and other allied mental health professionals.

Economic forces are important contributors to the rush for psychologists to prescribe. The positive impact of the new advances in medications, espe-cially the impact of the later-generation psychotropics, would likely get the interest of providers. It appears only natural that providers closely involved with distressed patients would want to be able to control the dispensing of these effective agents. Aware of the research data that indicate many of these medications work at their best when combined with forms of psychotherapy such as interpersonal or cognitive behavioral approaches, psychologists seem even more determined than other allied counseling professionals to obtain approval to prescribe these medications. A growing organization, the Prescribing Psychologists Register, has emerged to develop and implement training and evaluative standards for psychologist in hopes of gaining the right to prescribe psychotropic medication in the near future. Other disciplines in allied counseling areas are apparently studying such curricula but have not yet formalized their push for this privilege as the psychologists have done.

History of the Question

If we look at psychology as a profession regulated by state laws, it is in its relative early stages of development. As recently as 1977, Missouri became the last state to regulate the practice of psychology by law. Looking at the evolution of state statutes, one is impressed by the careful separation of physical (medical) and psychological interventions specifically noted in the state statutes. In his thoughtful analysis of the evolution of the discipline, Fox (1988) speculates that actively avoiding physical interventions might have been an act of separation made necessary in order to establish psychology's identity as a profession. Of course, 45 years ago, when the legal/professional identity of psychology was crystallized, the medications in the formulary (the list of available pharmaceuticals) were few, much less effective, and fraught with side effects that greatly limited patient compliance rates. Psychology created its own special identity as the exclusive province for claiming extensive training in research and psychological testing. Provider lines were distinct and the blurring of roles between the disciplines was a rare occurrence. Psychiatrists prescribed medication and psychologists tested and conducted some psychotherapy, while general practitioners referred! Now, general practitioners are prescribing more than psychiatrists, social workers and mental health counselors are seeking certification to test, and psychologists, many of whom are graduates of professional schools that did not exist 10 years ago, are seeking training so that they may prescribe. Along with these unique shifts in roles have come new relationships, some symbiotic and some antagonistic. Some psychologists have developed mutual relationships with family physicians in order to obtain medication for their patients. Here, the physician receives close-order psychological support while still maintaining regular contact with the patient, something that may be lost when a complete psychiatric referral is made. Conversely, many psychiatrists do not accept referrals from psychologists unless the psychologist is willing to totally withdraw from care of the patient.

Three significant historical events in the history of psychology's move toward acquiring prescription privileges should be reviewed. They are the Indian Health Service project, the Hawaii legislature experience, and the function of prescribing psychologists within the Department of Defense. Readers interested in detailed accounts of these events are directed to works cited below authored or coauthored by the discipline's point-man on the topic of prescription privileges for psychologists, Dr. Patrick H. DeLeon of Senator Daniel K. Inouye's (Hawaii) staff. The account of a prescribing psychologist serving in the Indian Health Service from May 1988 through May 1989 is presented in a variety of sources (DeLeon, Folen, Jennings, Willis, & Wright, 1991). As DeLeon summarizes it, during this period of service, "the bottom line" was that there were no major adverse experiences encountered. In discussing the experience with the Indian Health Service, the authors argue that the mental health care needs of the Indian population are grossly underserved and that training psychologists to provide complete services to this underserved population is an effective manpower solution. The "Hawaii experience" frequently referred to in the prescribing psychologists' literature (DeLeon, Fox, & Graham, 1991) refers to the Hawaii legislature's 1985 proposal of a study resolution assessing the feasibility of extending prescription privileges to psychologists. The resolution died in committee. In 1989, a bill in the legislature proposed that authority be granted to the Hawaii Board of Psychology to develop conditions under which trained psychologists would be permitted to prescribe. The bill also designed a Formulary of Psychoactive Medications Committee as well as specifications for the number of semester hours of training and the number of clinically supervised hours required to acquire prescription privileges. As expected, the bill led to intense controversy, even within the psychological community. The political result of the legislative action was a resolution that referred the issue to discussion at the Center for Alternative Dispute Resolution. The dispute was not resolved! The Department of Defense pilot demonstration project for fiscal year 1989 regarding psychopharmacology training represented another (recently discontinued) attempt to explore the feasibility of increasing the impact that psychologists could have in crisis intervention situations with military personnel. Not surprisingly, the act faced serious opposition from the medical community. Eventually, the training program began as a two-year postdoctoral training program at the Uniformed Services University of the Health Sciences. The program proceeded with very small numbers of military psychologists completing the program. In February 1996, the Depart of Defense Program to train psychologists to prescribe medication was "killed" when legislation was signed that ended the demonstration project. The psychiatric community seemed to celebrate and view the entire program of enabling psychologists to prescribe by congressional action as an attempt to bypass the state medical licensing law requirements (With stroke of pen, March 1, 1996). The position expressed by the prescribing psychologists of the Department of Defense Program appeared to be one of providing an improvement in "quality of care" for individuals who may, in fact, be underserved (DeLeon, 1996). Similar arguments continue whenever psychologists discuss developing new training models with an eye toward eventual prescription privileges.

The Arguments

The consistently intense reactions from the vigilant medical community have not seemed to diminish the optimism or the plans of psychologists who hope to one day independently prescribe psychotropic medications. A program at the Xavier Pharmacy School in New Orleans is offering postdoctoral didactic training in psychopharmacology in anticipation of legislation granting limited prescription privileges (DeLeon, 1966). But psychologists are not naive enough to disregard the consensus that the market is limited and that competition in mental health care has increased. Included in this thinking are observations that our nation's supply of medical professionals may soon exceed demand and that 20% of our nation's medical schools may be closed by the year 2005 (DeLeon, 1996). Additionally, managed care forces continue to control and limit access to care, intensifying the turf battle. Dr. DeLeon has summarized and countered the four basic arguments offered by the medical community against development of prescription privileges for psychologists (DeLeon, 1996). The first argument he cites is that psychologists (and other allied health providers who seek to dispense medication) are trying to get an M.D. degree without going to medical school. Deleon counters this first argument by citing the fact that nurse practitioners prescribe essentially unsupervised in 47 states and that other providers such as dentists, optometrists, and podiatrists all prescribe without benefit of a traditional medical education. The second argument deems it inappropriate for patients to see providers who practice from a limited formulary because the patient might need a medication or some form of treatment that the non-physician practitioner could not provide. Here, DeLeon counters with comparisons to other health care providers who prescribe on a limited basis, such as dentists who need to refer when other conditions present. The third argument asks who will attend to the medical needs of the patient, especially when relevant laboratory tests are needed. DeLeon responds that the prescribing psychologist will, with proper training, be proficient enough to select and read relevant test procedures. The training provided for prescribing psychologists will not be limited to knowledge of the psychotropic formulary. The relevant medical assessments, medical histories, laboratory tests, comorbid conditions, etc., will all have to be a significant part of the prescribing psychologist's curriculum. Just as other related practitioners such as dentists, podiatrists, and nurse practitioners are trained in broad-based evaluation and referral issues, the prescribing psychologist will need to be widely familiar with general medical education principles. The final argument DeLeon reviews opens Pandora's box by asking what will prevent other practitioners such as social workers, mental health counselors and nurses from seeking the ability to prescribe. Here, DeLeon asks figuratively, "So, what else is new?" meaning, of course that the medical community must have its head in the sand if it has neglected to observe that nurses prescribe independently in many states and that social workers are already developing curricula in psychopharmacology. The argument from the "would be" prescribing psychologists is that in the changing world of mental health it would only be appropriate to incorporate the significant changes treatment into the practitioner's repertoire.

Privileges in the Future?

There can be no doubt that the majority of professional psychologists and their organizations will continue to push for the development of training modules in psychopharmacology and related areas that will result in granting privileges. Recent reports (More states, February, 1997) document that two states that have training programs for psychologists in place, California and Missouri, are likely to see legislative votes on prescription privileges in 1997. In addition, two consortia of states in the New England and Mid-Atlantic regions are developing training programs with the help of the American Psychological Association. Five other states in the Midwest and South are independently pursing psychopharmacology training programs and prescription privileges also with the help of the American Psychological Association. The strategy for lobbyists appears to be to direct attention to the needs for the privilege, especially in rural areas and other underserved locales. Psychologists in academic settings, even those involved in clinical training, are a much less certain source of support for this movement. DeLeon, Fox, and Graham (1991) chronicle the lack of support for the Hawaii experiment by the faculty of the University of Hawaii. Universities are old institutions and are notoriously slow in changing training models and curricular goals.

As certain as we are that psychologists will press for recognition in this area, we are doubly sure that the medical community will continue to strongly oppose every effort viewed as encroaching in their area of practice. The vigilance of the psychiatric community is noted in the rapid response of the American Psychiatric Association in repeatedly writing to the attorney general of the United States, urging her to quash a research project surveying the Federal Bureau of Prisons psychology interns on their opinions about psychologists prescribing and the training that would be required to implement such a plan. After repeated requests, the survey project was shut down.

PSYCHOPHARMACOLOGICAL KNOWLEDGE

The development of knowledge in behavioral pharmacology during the past decade has been rapid and extensive. Keeping up with these new developments is essential. Since the second edition of this text was published, there have been new developments that should be noted. These include the emergence of new families of drugs such as the selective seratonin reuptake inhibitors (SSRIs) and the atypical antipsychotics (e.g., respirdone, clozapine). Most notably, the development of the SSRIs has had the greatest impact on the typical practice of most psychotherapists. We will discuss a few of these issues here. The tricyclics or first-generation antidepressants presented with a host of problems, ranging from unwanted weight gain to dangerous potential for overdose. The tricyclic antidepressants can have negative effects on alertness and cause cognitive impairment, with some signs of tolerance for these effects. In contrast, there have been no findings that SSRIs cause memory problems. The tricyclics are the third most frequent cause of drug-related deaths, exceeded only by alcohol-drug combinations and heroin overdoses (McKim, 1997). This is a most serious concern as many patients are prescribed these medications for deep depressions and often have associated suicidal ideation. Both the tricyclics and SSRIs have been shown to cause problems in sexual functioning, inhibiting orgasm in both men and women.

As noted earlier, the prescribing medical practitioner is often the individual involved in the treatment of the patient spending the least amount of contact time with the patient. With family physicians doing most of the prescribing of psychotropics, and with psychiatrists rarely conducting traditional outpatient psychotherapy, other mental health workers, with frequent and often less superficial contact than the physician has with the patient, are called upon for feedback regarding clinical management. Regardless of the practitioner's attitude toward taking personal responsibility for dispensing medication, therapists must now become very familiar with the literature on indications for the use of drugs, common side effects, physical conditions that may present with symptomatology similar to the psychological disorder the patient appears to be presenting, and, of course, possible drug interactions. Exploring each of these areas in detail is not within the scope of this general text, yet we feel an obligation to provide a basic start in this regard by presenting a general listing of medications and side effects and an introduction to sources of additional knowledge for the nonprescribing therapist. The listings of medications, usual dosage, action, and side effect information presented in the following table, the Quick Reference Guide to Medication, are, of course, not designed to be even a short course in pharmacology. We intend them to serve as an introduction to current medications, their mechanism of action, and possible side effects.

Traditional clinical training programs, seminars at scientific meetings (often underwritten by pharmaceutical companies!), and other continuing education programs all offer opportunities for the nonphysician therapist to become familiar with current medication information. We would also like to direct the reader to two excellent texts specifically designed for use by

QUICK REFERENCE TO PSYCHOTROPIC MEDICATION

To the best of our knowledge recommended doses and side effects listed below are accurate. However, this is meant as a general reference only, and should not serve as a guideline for prescribing of medications. Physicians, please check the manufacturer's product information sheet or the P.D.R. for any changes in dosage schedule or contraindications. (Brand names are registered trademarks.)

ANTIDEPRESSANT Names		Usual Daily Dosage Range	Sedation	ACH[1]	Selective Action On Neurotransmitters[2]	
Generic	Brand				NE	5-HT
HETEROCYCLICS						
imipramine	Tofanil	150–300 mg	mid	mid	++	+++
desipramine	Norpramin	150–300 mg	low	low	+++++	0
amitriptyline	Elavil	150–300 mg	high	high	+	++++
nortriptyline	Aventyl, Pamelor	75–125 mg	mid	mid	+++	++
protriptyline	Vivacil	15–40 mg	mid	mid	++++	+
trimipramine	Surmontil[3]	100–300 mg	high	mid	++	++
doxepin	Sinequan, Adapin[3]	150–300 mg	high	mid	+++	++
maprotiline	Ludiomil	150–225 mg	high	mid	+++++	0
amoxapine	Asendin	150–400 mg	mid	low	++++	+
trazodone	Desyrel	150–400 mg	mid	none	0	+++++
fluoxetine	Prozac	20–80 mg	low	none	0	+++++
bupropion	Wellbutrin[4]	200–450 mg	low	none	+	0
sertraline	Zoloft	50–200 mg	low	none	0	+++++
paroxetine	Paxil	20–50 mg	low	low	0	+++++
venlafaxine	Effexor	75–375 mg	low	none	++	+++
nefazodone	Serzone	100–500 mg	mid	none	0	+++++
fluvoxamine	Luvox	50–300 mg	low	low	0	+++++
MAO INHIBITORS						
phenelzine	Nardil[5]	30–90 mg	low	none		
tranylcypromine	Parnate[5]	20–60 mg	low	none		

[1]ACH:Anticholinergic Side Effects.   [2]NE: Norepinephrine, 5-HT: Serotonin.   [3]Uncertain, but likely effects.
[4]Atypical antidepressant. Uncertain effects but likely to be a dopamine agonist, and indirect increase in norepinephrine.
[5]MAO inhibitors operate via a different mechanism of action than other antidepressants, and increase NE, 5-HT, and dopamine.

ANTI-OBSESSIONAL

Generic	Names Brand	Dose Range[1]	Sedation	ACH Effects
clomipramine	Anafranil	150–250 mg	Hi	Hi
fluoxetine	Prozac[1]	20–80 mg	Low	None
sertraline	Zoloft[1]	50–200 mg	Low	None
paroxetine	Paxil[1]	20–60 mg	Low	None
fluvoxamine	Luvox	50–300 mg	Low	Low

[1]Often higher doses are required to control obsessive-compulsive symptoms than the doses generally used to treat depression.

MOOD STABILIZERS

Generic	Names Brand	Daily Dosage Range	Serum[1] Level
lithium carbonate	Eskalith, Lithonate	600–2400	0.6–1.5
carbamazepine	Tegretol	600–1600	4–10+
valproic acid	Depakote, Depakene	750–1500	50–100

[1]Lithium levels are repressed in mEq/l; carbamazepine and valproic acid levels express in mcg/ml.

PSYCHO-STIMULANTS

Generic	Names Brand	Daily Doses[1]
methylphenidate	Ritalin	5–50 mg
dextroamphetamine	Dexedrine	5–40 mg
pemoline	Cylert	37.5–112.5 mg

[1]Note: Adult Doses

Copyright 1995. John Preston, Psy.D. and P.A. Distributors

ANTIPSYCHOTIC

| Names | | | | | | ACH | |
Generic	Brand	Dosage Range[1]	Sedation	ESP[2]	Effects[3]	Equivalence[4]
LOW POTENCY						
chlorpromazine	Thorazine	50–1500 mg	High	++	++++	100 mg
thioridazine	Mellaril	150–800 mg	High	+	+++++	100 mg
clozapine	Clozaril	300–900 mg	High	0	++++++	50 mg
mesoridazine	Serentil	50–500 mg	High	+	+++++	50 mg
HIGH POTENCY						
molindone	Moban	20–225 mg	Low	+++	+++	10 mg
perphenazine	Trilafon	8–60 mg	Mid	++++	++	10 mg
loxapine	Loxitane	50–250 mg	Low	+++	++	10 mg
trifluoperazine	Stelazine	10–40 mg	Low	++++	++	5 mg
fluphenazine	Prolixin[5]	3–45 mg	Low	+++++	++	2 mg
thiothixene	Navene	10–60 mg	Low	+++++	++	5 mg
haloperidol	Haldol[5]	2–40 mg	Low	+++++	+	2 mg
pimozide	Orap	1–10 mg	Low	+++++	+	2 mg
risperidone	Risperdal	4–16 mg	Low	+	+	2 mg

[1]Usual daily oral dosage.

[2]Acute: Parkinson's, dystonias, akathisia. Does not reflect risk for tardive dyskinesia. All neuroleptics may cause tardive dyskinesia, except clorapine.

[3]Anticholinergic Side Effects.

[4]Dose required to achieve efficacy of 100 mg chlorpromazine.

[5]Available in time-released IM format.

ANTI-ANXIETY

Generic	Names Brand	Single Dose Dosage Range	Equivalence[2]
BENZODIAZEPINES			
diazepam	Valium	2–10 mg	5 mg
chlordiazepoxide	Librium	10–50 mg	25 mg
flurazepam	Delmane[1]	15–60 mg	15 mg
prazepam	Centrax	5–30 mg	10 mg
clorazepate	Tranxene	3.75–15 mg	10 mg
temazepam	Restoril[1]	15–30 mg	10 mg
clonazepam	Klonopin	0.5–2.0 mg	.25 mg
lorazepam	Ativan	0.5–2 mg	1 mg
alprazolam	Xanax	0.25–2 mg	0.5 mg
oxazepam	Serax	10–30 mg	15 mg
triazolam	Halcion[1]	0.25–0.5 mg	.25 mg
ATYPICAL BENZODIAZEPINES			
estazolam	ProSom[1]	1.0–2.0 mg	1 mg
quazepam	Doral[1]	7.5–30 mg	7.5 mg
zolpidem	Ambien[1]	5–10 mg	5 mg
OTHER ANTIANXIETY AGENTS			
buspirone	BuSpar	5–20 mg	
hydroxyzine	Atarax, Vistaril	10–50 mg	
diphenhydramine	Benadryl	25–100 mg	
propranolol	Inderal	10–80 mg	
atenolol	Tenormin	25–100 mg	
clonidine	Catapres	0.1–3 mg	

[1]Hypnotic used to treat initial insomnia.
[2]Doses required to achieve efficiency of 5 mg of diazepam.

COMMON SIDE EFFECTS ASSOCIATED WITH PSYCHOTROPIC MEDICATIONS

ANTICHOLINERGIC EFFECTS
(block acetylcholine)
- dry mouth
- blurred vision
- constipation
- memory impairment
- urinary retention
- confusional states

EXTRAPYRAMIDAL EFFECTS
(dopamine blockade in basal ganglia)
- Parkinson-like effects: rigidity, shuffling gate, tremor, flat affect, lethargy
- Dystonias: spasms in neck and other muscle groups
- Akathisia: intense, uncomfortable sense of inner restlessness
- Tardive dyskinesia: often a persistent movement disorder (lip-smacking, writhing movements, jerky movements)

AUTONOMIC EFFECTS
- especially orthostatic hypotension, which can cause dizziness and imbalance, especially in the elderly, can result in falls and fractures.

SEDATION
- drowsiness and impaired concentration, and reaction time.

Note: The above are common side effects. All medications can produce specific or unique side effects.

nonmedical psychotherapists. They are *Handbook of Clinical Psychopharmacology for Therapists* (Preston et al., 1994) and *Psychopharmacology Made Ridiculously Simple* (Preston & Johnson, 1995).

COMMUNICATION DYNAMICS AND MEDICATIONS

Whether or not the therapist is a prescriber of the patient's medication, the psychological issues related to the patient's attitude toward medicine and its use, refusal, and misuse should be reviewed. It would be a treatment error for the therapist to simply ignore these concerns or refer discussion of all physical or medication-related issues to the prescribing physician or other medical authority. The medication may be a conduit for meaning when the therapist, in response to a complaint or challenge presented by the patient, might ask, "Have you been taking your medication?" Here the meaning is a covert counter, probably by a therapist who is emotionally engaged by the patient's lack of cooperation or other manifestation of resistance. Preston and Johnson (1995) speak of conventional and personal meanings of medication. The conventional or generic meanings associated with medicine are generally negative. We speak of having to "swallow a bitter pill," "take our medicine," "hold our nose and swallow," and "take a dose of our own medicine." The imagery here is that medicine is nasty stuff to be avoided and that sometimes we even need to be strong enough to take it. Positive references in colloquial use seem few and far between. Many patients initially oppose the idea of medication because of the conventional meanings or associations of taking pills. Commonly, they may not wish to accept the medical model and the sick label that seems to come along with receiving medicine from a doctor. They may comfortably speak about being stressed out, accept that they are unable to cope, or even state that they "feel like they are going crazy," yet to be sick and in need of medicine is unacceptable. Other patients when considering medication may view chemotherapy as a potential addiction or crutch, something to be avoided at all costs. Still other patients may see taking medicine as an act of masking the real "self," even claiming at times that relief from troublesome symptoms "isn't me." Rather than patronizing the patient with brief reassurances, it is generally productive to explore, in some depth, the patient's concerns about medication. Learning about what the patient fears losing, in addition to the unwanted aspects of his symptomatology, can be critical to understanding the medication resistance. We were working with a rebellious, but depressed adolescent boy whose family displayed a strong genetic history of depression. Other family members in treatment had responded positively to the second-generation antidepressants, yet our young man resisted efforts by family members, physician, and therapist to even consent to trying the medicine. The "meaning" of the medicine in this case was not only giving in to the pressures of adults in power, but also that he was becoming like those he needed to separate from. The young man eventually began a trial of the medication, but it had to be arranged for him on his terms. He specified the length of time to try the medication, with finite start and stop dates. After benefiting from the medication for a period of time, he was able to "decide" the discontinuation date for his medicine. The personal meanings or styles of approaching medication can also be a fruitful area of therapeutic exploration. Sometimes, recognizing the dynamic styles or approach toward medication portrayed by varying diagnostic groups can be instrumental in helping the therapist understand the patient's key patterns. The narcissistic patient may be looking for the perfect pill (and the perfect doctor to prescribe it!). Paranoid patients may exercise suspicion about the medicine, question why it is being prescribed, and be vigilant toward those involved in the care. Depressed patients may want to give up a medication trial in response to relatively minor side effects.

ADDICTIONS

Recent research on addiction has also stressed the integration of ideas involved in the biopsychosocial model. Our view of chemical dependency goes along with our thinking on the development of other major behavioral patterns. Of course, we acknowledge the contributions of genetics, whether present in the form of unusual sensitivity to a drug, predisposition to depression, or strong tolerance. Whatever the form of the biologically predisposing factor, it cannot be viewed as the sole or key factor to understanding the addiction. The addiction paradigm we have found useful has several components.

The addiction model we propose characterizes the addictive behavior as a stress-reducing activity that also provides a predictable internal emotional climate as well as a typically predictable response from the social environment. Consider the case of Miguel, an alcoholic man, with a positive family history of addiction whose drinking problem becomes activated after several years of abstinence from drinking. Rather than take the traditional attitude of the addictions counselor who views alcoholism treatment as a constant battle with relapse and the avoidance of external trigger mechanisms, the communications analyst therapist asks several additional questions. Why does the alcoholic return to drinking? What is the pattern of the resumed drinking? What are the desired—and predictable—internal and external emotional climates the patient is obtaining? Miguel did not resume (or begin) to drink simply because he was alcoholic. Further interviewing with this patient revealed an intricate pattern of behavior and internal and external consequences. We learned that Miguel only drank on Sunday afternoons, when his wife was away and Miguel was responsible for the care of his 6-year-old daughter. Miguel was not happy that his wife was away taking care of her aged parents, but enjoyed the time alone with his daughter. He loved to indulge her by taking her on shopping sprees to the toy store on Sunday and showering her with gifts. This behavior infuriated Miguel's wife, who criticized her husband's ways as wasteful and evidence of poor parenting. A "prisoner in my own home!" Miguel complained when describing his feelings before heading to the liquor store on Sundays. Miguel would enjoy the relaxing high of the alcohol for a few, stress-reducing hours on Sunday afternoon but would soon start to feel poorly as his wife punished him with criticism and coldness upon her return. Miguel, experiencing even greater anger and the beginnings of a strong shame reaction, continued to drink to toxic levels. He would become ill and suffer throughout the night and most of Monday. Monday evening would mark his week of penitence. He would be an attentive husband and father, control his spendthrift tendencies, and even attend his old meeting sessions with Alcoholics Anonymous. This pattern of recovery would hold, of course, until Sunday. After discovering this pattern, the task in therapy became assisting Miguel with exploring new methods of coping with the Sunday stresses and new ways of reacting to the criticisms from his wife. Eventually, Miguel learned to change his behavior on Sundays, avoided alcohol, took responsibility for his shopping indulgences, sometimes joined his wife during her Sunday duties, and toned down his contrite-husband act during the week. If the focus of Miguel's treatment had been solely maintaining abstinence and avoiding environmental triggers, Miguel would have also remained sober, six days a week.

19

Summary and Conclusions
Being Asocial in Social Places;
*Giving the Patient a New Experience**

The purpose of this chapter is to summarize the idea that effective therapeutic communication is, by definition, asocial; that is, the potential for change is created when a therapist does not provide a patient with the type of response that the patient is covertly trying to evoke. The nature of the engagement and disengagement processes in therapy are discussed. Methods of learning to respond asocially in therapy and the basic modes of asocial response are reviewed and reillustrated with case material.

ON SOCIAL ENGAGEMENT

A major tenet of the communication approach to psychotherapy we describe is that a patient's characteristic behavior or style of communicating, whether it produces conventional reward or punishment, is strengthened whenever he receives an expected or social response from the interpersonal environment. Social responses are not defined in the traditional sense as nice, friendly, or gregarious; rather, they are behaviors that are predictable. If a patient behaves in a manner that is often caustic and critical, the expected outcome or socially engaged response might include frequent arguments with others and special negative attention. Conversely, if an individual frequently engages others with a pattern of behavior that is instantly agreeable, replete with head nods and smiles, the predictable or social response might include agreements and requests for special favors. The idea of typical or stylistic patterns of "emotion-pulling" (Kiesler, 1978) is based on the assumption that individuals are motivated to achieve predictability

---

* Chapter originally authored by Young and Beier and reprinted with permission from J. Anchin and D. Kiesler (eds.), *Handbook of interpersonal psychotherapy.* New York: Pergamon Press, 1982.

and control in their social interactions, whether or not the resulting responses are painful. One has only to observe infant/parent interactions for a short time to conclude that children learn early in life to make things happen with idiosyncratic social styles. If life could not be made predictable by the young child, what chance of physical or psychological survival would there be? Consider the child whose mother is "turned on" to it whenever it is bouncing with joy, but who is indifferent to the child when it is sad. The child learns very quickly which behaviors elicit which response from the mother, and the child also learns that the mother can be punished by withholding a happy, bouncing response.

Another mother might respond positively to a child's wide variety of moods and actions but negatively to sexual self-touching. Again the baby learns how to engage the mother socially—negatively or positively. Parents are constantly scanned, and the child learns what works with each. This training in styles of social engagement seems to occur without the parents' or the child's awareness.

THE PATIENT'S DESIRED DILEMMA

We do not suggest that the display of established patterns of social engagement is manipulative or pathological. All people engage in a variety of stylistic behaviors, and most exhibit flexibility in being able to communicate in a manner congruent with the social responses or interpersonal goals they seek. Individuals suffer psychological pain because they are in a state of communication deficit: they obtain responses to their communication they have not willfully elicited and for which they cannot account. They feel they are victims. They totally deny the fact that they have—probably repeatedly— evoked the aversive responses. Within this framework of the classic neurotic paradox (e.g., Mowrer, 1948), patients have painted themselves into a corner. They suffer from unsatisfactory responses from the social world, yet they have helped to evoke these responses in order to create a predictable world.

Many theorists imply that patients' problems stem from a lack of knowledge or from a lack of social skills, or simply from an inability to cope with stress. We argue that patients' problem messages, in fact, provide both satisfaction and disappointment. Actually, they are the result of two mutually exclusive motivations, and the message represents a compromise between these motives, the most general labels for which are (1) the individual's sense of integrity, and (2) the social pressures the individual is under. The resulting compromise represents patients' way of having their cake and eating it, too. They can engage other people and evoke responses that make the world predictable and that are at least partially desired, and they can also complain about the pain the responses produce.

Some examples of the power of unconscious and covert social engagement are in order. Take the case of a depressed patient who complains about her spouse's anger. The "downtrodden wife" subtly encourages her husband's attacks, yet she can always deny that she desired an unhappy result, such as a divorce. With her pain, the wife is able to think of herself as free from the responsibility for the maltreatment of her husband. Her pain permits the denial of both the manipulation of the relationship with the husband and the fact that she—on some level of awareness—wants a divorce. We are not suggesting that the wife in this case—or patients in general—is consciously deciding how to create covertly an emotional climate in others to yield a desired behavior. The conscious use of covert manipulation is the trade secret of a con artist, even though we all use it occasionally. Patients, on the other hand, are indeed unaware of certain of their motivations and of the compromise through which they achieve at least partial gratification.

Mahl's (1971) classic work provides another clinical example of how an adaptive compromise operates via the patient's symptoms. A young man at the student counseling center loudly proclaimed his dismay: "Nobody will go out with me!" Further inquiry revealed that he has been collecting these rejections (injustices) in response to requests that sound more like harrassments than social invitations. This type of social engagement surely creates a predictable emotional climate, namely rejection. But why did the patient set up the situation to produce this particular result? The therapist in this case learned that the patient was under a lot of pressure to make friends and to find a "girl," and had been repeatedly told that "loners" are odd and dangerous. The patient's invitation to others to go out with him represented the social-pressure instruction. He could then say, "I'm trying, right?" even while his gruffness and harassing comments represented his motivation to maintain his integrity, to remain "strong" and lonely, and to receive rejections that proved to him that others were wrong, even though he did what they told him to do.

Therapeutic communications are messages that are effective because they interrupt the patient's routine communications. They consequently help to extinguish the expected pattern of social interaction prompted by the patient's style of behavior. That is, therapy may be seen as taking place when the therapist interrupts, i.e., helps to extinguish in an asocial or disengaged way, the patient's typical interaction style. When the customary, preferred, or expected response is withheld in the therapy session, the patient experiences a sense of "beneficial uncertainty." This uncertainty is labeled beneficial because the asocial behavior is originating from a caring person in the safe, confidential environment of the consulting room and not in the "real" world, where the interpersonal stakes are high. In the therapy setting, where a patient's typical attempts at engagement do not result in the expected response, the patient is obliged to discover new behavior styles.

As this model is based on extinction procedures, it is expected that extinction attempts will first cause an increase in the use of the old behavior pattern. Eventually, the patient will experiment with new social-engagement styles, and it is essential that the therapist continue the extinction procedure throughout by disengaging with asocial responses. The therapist who approves or rewards certain of the patient's responses is engaged and remains the author of the change. Through asocial, disengaged responses, the therapist shifts responsibility for conduct to the patient.

In the following case illustration, we see an anorexic patient whose engagement style of dependence and symptomatic complaints has shifted to one in which she seeks support for her accomplishments:

> *Patient:* (smiling) I'm feeling pretty good today. I had a good week!
>
> *Therapist:* Tell me more about that. (Disengaged response. This response, as most other reflective responses, is disengaged inasmuch as the therapist does not really respond in the mood sought by the patient. With such a response, the therapist also shifts responsibility to the patient, telling the patient between the lines, "You go ahead and elaborate.")
>
> *Patient:* Well, I actually straightened out that problem at work with my boss. I just opened up to her and honestly told her about my problem with working weekends, and she—uh—said, "Okay." that I didn't have to. (In the voice there was much enthusiasm, with a bid for the therapist to join in her joy.)
>
> *Therapist:* Mm, hmm. (A delay response, but disengaged, as the patient was pulling for much more involvement and approval.)
>
> *Patient:* (pause) Oh. . . . I also really talked with Frank (husband) about needing, you know, to have more communication with him and less bossing and fighting. He really listened . . . for the first time, really! (While changing the structure of the content, the patient's attempt at engagement continues in the same mode. The bid here is still for the therapist to approve of the patient's growth.)
>
> *Therapist:* You'd like me to know about all your progress and that you're feeling good. (Another reflective response, disengaged inasmuch as it does not reward the patient's achievement by responding with approval. Reflective statements have come into use in so many therapies because they are asocial in nature—beyond reward and punishment.)
>
> *Patient:* (awkward pause) Oh, and guess what? I only threw up about twice this week! (The patient plays her ace by presenting

improvement with her most important or scariest symptom. Who could be so coldhearted as not to rejoice with a person who has stopped starving herself to death?)

Therapist: Mm, hmm. (An effective asocial listening response, but not entirely sufficient. A longer statement, perhaps reflecting the increase in the demand for approval and the hidden "thanks" would have been closer to a "maximum response," one that includes the major themes and "catches the client in the act" of acting out these themes.)

Patient: (All nonverbal. Looks downward, maintains a sad facial expression and a slumping posture. Silent The patient is covertly switching engagement styles back to her previous mode of suffering. At the same time she is showing her anger at the therapist for not rewarding her for her reports of an almost symptom-free week.)

Therapist: You look pretty sad now. I think you're disappointed in me, that I didn't show approval and look pleased when you talked about having a good week, about not throwing up. (The therapist is disengaged and reflects on this major theme—an excellent response. We must, however, warn that the purpose of this response is not to provide insight. In communication theory, disengagement is useful because it suggests new choices to the patient.)

Patient: Who cares! I'm thinking of killing myself right now. (with anger) Can I leave? (The patient makes a last attempt to engage the therapist into caring with the double threat of walking out and suicide.)

Therapist: (in an exaggerated manner with a friendly smile) Boy, am I a jerk for not being pleased with you. You came in here all smiles, and now look what I've done! (The therapist disengages with a paradigmatic response that exaggerates the patient's resistance.)

Patient: (laughs) I suppose I am angry with you. I thought you would be pleased. Sometimes I don't think you care for me and . . . (The patient was able to drop her manipulative styles and explore hidden feelings because of the uncertainty that was provided in a caring way.)

In the above example, when the anorexic patient's "Please pat me on the back" engagement attempt failed to evoke the preferred response, she escalated to a preferred threatening posture, complete with termination and suicide threats. If the therapist had not responded with an asocial response, the patient would have maintained her particular counterproductive method of winning favors. It was especially important for the therapist to disengage from the patient's escalation toward suicide, as otherwise the patient would have reexperienced in therapy the success of her most dangerous skills: "If I can't win approval with my conventional accomplishments, presenting my symptoms can generally evoke the social caring I want."

An example from one of our laboratory studies can help illustrate how behavioral change may result from an unexpected or asocial response (Young, Beier, Beier, and Barton, 1975). Male college students were asked to "help test equipment for a new aggression game involving the use of padded clubs designed electronically to record impact." In pretesting, the sample was divided into two groups: (1) those who favored a social role for women that was equal to that of men (liberals), and (2) those who preferred women to stay at home and take care of the home or children (traditionals). Each student in the study had two game bouts with a female confederate. In the first bout, the female opponent maintained a defend-only posture. In the second bout, the female confederate changed posture and attacked at a high rate. The liberal group of students played the game with vigor during both bouts. The traditionals, however, played gently during the defend-only condition but equaled their liberal counterparts when confronted with the unexpected and presumably undesired change in their opponents' behavior. Even though our sample of traditionals seemed to prefer a delicate exchange, they did modify their behavior when confronted with an unexpected or asocial response.

In the therapy setting, when a patient's communications do not result in the expected or social response from the therapist, a similar shift may occur. When a patient displays sadness or cries, the therapist does not respond as family members or close friends would. The therapist simply does not offer the closure that the expected or social response does. Instead, he uses a repertoire of asocial responses. The therapist may ask, "What are the words that go with these tears?" gently reminding the patient that he is here to work, or the therapist may use the many common listening responses, such as, "Go on, tell me more," or "Mm, hmm." The therapist might also choose to disengage by interpreting the communication process (metacommunication) or by exaggerating the patient's resistance. In any event, the patient receives a new experience; the lack of closure almost forces new explorations. When the therapist is able to disengage and deny closure, the patient is provided with an experience of beneficial uncertainty.

In a sense, communication theory is close to a general theory of psychotherapy. In many varieties of psychotherapy, the old patterns of patient communication are not met with familiar rewards or responses from the therapist. The process may be seen operating in psychoanalysis, when the analyst does not relate to the social meaning of a statement but to the underlying dynamic meaning. In Rogerian work, we have reflections that surely are asocial. In Gestalt-transactional work, we have the analysis of the impact of a statement with an analysis of the social consequences. In behavior theory, therapists try not to enter the social arena at all, but to present a reward that is often more symbolic than real.

MAKING UNCERTAINTY BENEFICIAL

In presenting a communications approach to the therapeutic process, we have attempted to explore how behavior is changed by asocial communication. But should we knowingly aim for uncertainty during psychotherapy? The task of the therapist is often seen as helping a patient to cope better. The patient is often seen as indecisive and uncertain in the first place. When we give such high value to the arousal of uncertainty, we need to explain our reasoning further.

In the psychotherapeutic process, the somewhat unsettling experience of uncertainty is introduced along with positive values: love, hope, and safety. The therapist must care, must induce a sense of hope. The therapeutic hour must reduce the threat of anticipated consequences in order to produce beneficial uncertainty. The lack of closure produced by the elimination of social responses brings about challenge and uncertainty. The positive values attached to uncertainty permit the patient to become a creative artist. The patient starts asking, "Must I really produce my preferred closure patterns?" "Are they really necessary?" "Can I accept responsibility for my harmful and counterproductive communications and change them?" The experience of uncertainty permits this type of questioning, provided it is accompanied by love, hope, and freedom from threat.

A further characteristic of asocial communication helps provide the patient with a sense of freedom: the artificial nature of the setting. The consulting room is a sanctuary. It is unique inasmuch as most interactive consequences are explicit; the patient is in control of coming to the session and paying for it. The therapist keeps all information confidential; there are no social consequences outside the office. The hour is in this sense playful and gamelike, a condition that enhances creativity. Discussion of taboo topics, role-playing, role reversals, memories of childhood, the sole caring attention of another person—all make this hour unique. These unusual experiences are valuable because new ways of coping can be examined in the safety of the hour. The sting of confronting real problems is diluted and the hope for change is maximized. When critics speak about the manipulative nature of communication therapy, they do not seem to understand that in psychotherapy the therapist cannot play the social role of a friend and that the uniquely asocial nature of the setting itself enhances change.

LEARNING TO BE ASOCIAL

Ironically, some of the reasons a person frequently offers for wanting to become a psychotherapist may serve as obstacles to effective treatment. Wanting to comfort people in distress, being sensitive to the needs of others, being likable, and even caring certainly have a place in therapy, but they can be counterproductive. Such needs can be used all too easily for social engagements (patients have great skill with these conventional needs, and therapists should be aware of the particular ones that make them vulnerable). The patient scans the therapist's subtle and often nonverbal cues and then uses the information to play out a social role with the therapist. Therapists who want to be liked are easy targets; their very desire can become their Waterloo. We do not claim that all is lost when the therapist gets engaged. As we have grown up in Western culture and are tuned into many of the cues of others, such engagements are hard to avoid. We overlearn to respond with hurt to unfair criticism, with horror to violence, and with a degree of acceptance to praise. To short-circuit these largely unconscious reactions is difficult.

To become aware enough to disengage from a patient's engagement style, the therapist must first of all know and then use his own "natural" reactions as a diagnostic instrument. The therapist should ask the phenomenological questions, How does the patient make me feel? What procedures is the patient using to make me feel this way? To answer these questions, the therapist must be able to understand the emotional climate the patient evokes and to observe the subtle methods the patient uses to do so. The therapist must scan both the patient's feeling and behavior, and the therapist's own as well. The therapist undoubtedly will get engaged often enough with patients, but the therapeutic art is for the therapist to disengage and to read himself as the diagnostic instrument. The effective therapist does not become cold and emotionally unresponsive; rather he is subtly moved by others but learns to soon recognize these patterns of movement. The effective therapist becomes a very sensitive individual with the flexibility to alter or control automatic responses.

New students of this model can most easily practice disengagement initially via asocial responses outside the therapy setting. Many budding therapists feel more at ease in this manner. They learn to observe their own preferred behavior and then to vary it. Students with a serious demeanor will see what happens when they smile at others in an elevator; those with an idiosyncratic nonverbal habit, such as pointing a finger, can experiment with variations; nonassertive students can practice taking the initiative. The essential deep understanding of their own impact on others is acquired in role-playing interactions and through supervision of audio- and videotaped sessions. This role-playing is a particularly helpful technique: although the content of the role-played hour may be entirely fabricated, subtle cues are always sent in the attempt to engage the other person on a covert level, and these can be analyzed for style.

BASIC MODES OF ASOCIAL RESPONSE

In this section we attempt to present a few of the basic disengagement techniques available to the therapist. Of course, this listing provides only an outline of the many maneuvers available. We are not claiming that these techniques are exclusive to our model; we expect that most therapists use them regardless of the theoretical model they have adopted, yet we believe the efficacy of these tools is based on their asocial qualities within the interaction rather than on other theoretical considerations.

Delay Responses

These simple tools are basic to most therapists' repertoires. Often called minimal encouragers or listening responses, comments such as "Go on," "Please continue," "Mm, hmm," and "Tell me more" often prove to be of greater value than simply keeping the interaction going or eliciting more information from the patient. They actually constitute minidisengagement. They permit the therapist to get a clearer picture of the procedures the patient uses to engage the therapist, and perhaps of the patient's motivation to constrict the therapist's emotional climate. Consider the following example:

> *Patient:* Doctor, I can't take it with my wife any longer. She is really neglecting the kids, refuses me sex, and can't hang on to money at all. I've no alternative but divorce, right?
> *Therapist:* (pause) Go on.

The patient starts with a stereotypical male complaint, which reflects as much about him as it does about his wife. With this simple, yet effective phrase, the therapist is able to avoid the trap of the patient's polarizing engagement attempt and to buy time to reflect on several unanswered questions: Why is the patient seeing a therapist and not an attorney if he wants a divorce? If the wife is such an evil creature, why must the patient immediately work so hard at proving this and gaining the therapist as an ally? With the help of the time gained through this and similar disengagement techniques, the therapist is eventually able to answer these questions. The patient needed a therapist instead of a lawyer because the patient collected injustices from his wife; perhaps the patient could not allow himself to take responsibility for his wish to withdraw from the marriage. These cross-motivations could translate into actions such as the patient demanding sex when his wife was busy, keeping financial information hidden from her and then complaining about her financial incompetence, and attempting to engage the therapist to support his victim posture.

We should note here that we ought not assume that any particular response must have an asocial impact. A response that produces uncertainty in one patient can be perceived as a reward by another. The continuous use of delay with a long-winded patient who is boring the therapist to tears may make things comfortable for the therapist who unconsciously wants to escape the dullness. But the wish for distance does not mean disengagement. In fact, it would instead serve to reinforce the patient's view that nobody pays attention to him. Whenever a therapist's routine responses become too stylized with a particular patient, or when a therapist becomes too comfortable, it is time to look again at the patient's mode of subtle manipulation.

Reflection of Content and Feeling

In addition to providing important feedback to the patient and shifting responsibility for the feelings expressed back to the patient, these reflections are universally recognized tools that help the therapist maintain an asocial posture. By paraphrasing content or bringing feelings into the open, the therapist provides the message of caring and understanding that is so essential for change. Consider the following example in which reflecting maintains patient responsibility and prevents the therapist from acting in a socially engaged manner.

> *Patient:* It was a disaster of a date. Everything went wrong. My hair was still in curlers and I kept him waiting. When we finally got out, I had too many drinks on an empty stomach and became obnoxious in addition to getting sick. He took me home early and I didn't get to the party. I just feel terrible.
>
> *Therapist:* You're pretty upset about the lousy time you had.

The therapist delayed with this reflection. The patient's opening was eventually interpreted as saying, "I'm really screwing up my social life, and what are you going to do about it?" In addition, the patient was covertly asking the therapist to criticize her for making a mess of things once again. With the use of delay and reflection, the therapist was able to throw the ball back to the patient and inform her of an expectation to hear more about the underlying feelings.

Labeling the Style of the Interaction

Talking with patients about their communication style or using "metacommunication" (Haley, 1969) provides the therapist with another means of disengagement and with a valuable teaching technique. When the therapist analyzes communication style and implies that the covert message is intended, the therapist is teaching patients that they are choosing to experience problems and are not victims of them. By making unconscious communication explicit (as it occurs), the therapist gives patients the experience of having control over these subtle manipulations. In this manner the therapist arouses uncertainty. By verbalizing the impact of discordant messages and their discordant motivation, he alerts patients to the existential fact that they are helping to create their problems. In many cases the covert elements of a patient's discordant messages are sent through nonverbal channels. This necessitates making explicit the part of the patient's compromise that is active and present, yet hidden from awareness. Because nonverbal cues travel in a variety of channels such as gestures, paralinguistic cues, and facial expression, the interpersonal impact of these cues seems ambiguous and often escapes the notice of both the sender and receiver (Harper et al., 1978).

Nonverbal cues make unconscious motivation visible and even measurable. Consider the following portion of a session in which a patient who hates being alone is given the opportunity to view how his subtle behavior produced "unwanted" impact:

Patient: (after a long pause with eyes downcast, a sad facial expression, and slumped posture) People always make fun of me. I guess I'm just the type of guy who really was meant to be a loner, damn it. (deep sigh)

Therapist: Could you do that again for me?

Patient: What?

Therapist: The sigh, only a bit deeper.

Patient: Why? (pause) Okay, but I don't see what . . . okay. (client sighs again and smiles)

Therapist: Well, that time you smiled, but mostly when you sigh and look so sad I get the feeling that I'd better leave you alone in your misery, that I should walk on eggshells and not get too chummy or I might hurt you even more.

Patient: (a bit of anger in his voice) Well, excuse me! I was only trying to tell you how I feel.

Therapist: I know you feel miserable, but I also got the message that you wanted to keep me at a distance, that I had no way to reach you.

Patient: (slowly) I feel like a loner, I feel that even you don't care about me—making fun of me.

Therapist: I wonder if other folks need to pass this test, too?

In this example, the therapist asked for the repetition so that the patient would experience the impact of his discordant message. The verbal component was that the patient hated to be a loner; the nonverbal component was that he could not be reached by anyone, that his procedure was to create distance. The therapist tried to make explicit the consequences of the hidden nonverbal communication and the motivation it represented.

A review of the above interaction may suggest that the therapist was hoping the patient would achieve insight into the nature of his dilemma. Actually, we believe that it is the therapist who needs insight rather than the patient. What is important is that the therapist alert patients to their typical patterns as they are experienced. It is uncertainty rather than insight that needs to be evoked by the therapist's asocial response. Often, the therapist who offers an asocial response will also provide insight to patients. That is, however, incidental: providing the patient with insights—even accurate explanations about the etiology, maintenance, or steps necessary to "cure" a problem—is not sufficient to effect behavioral change. Therapeutic insight for a patient can actually be counterproductive, as such communications do not shift responsibility for the patient's conduct to the patient. Only when the patient's discordant behavior is interrupted and patients experience the resultant uncertainty will new behaviors be attempted by patients themselves.

Paradigmatic Responses

One of the potent tools of the therapist using the communication analytic technique is the paradigmatic response. This asocial message is transmitted by the therapist as a paradoxical exaggeration of the patient's resistance (Watzlawick et al., 1967; Watzlawick et al., 1974; Haley, 1976). With this technique, the therapist produces beneficial uncertainty for the patient by flowing with the resistance. The response is counterpersuasive because, by exaggerating the patient's "ploy," the patient's manipulative attempt falls flat.

A patient whose short-term contract at a university counseling center has two weeks remaining initiates the following sequence after some very intense, soul-searching hours:

Patient: Well, you know, we only have two weeks left in the semester and I, uh, well, just don't see the point in continuing. I'm sure it's just a waste of your time now, since I'll be leaving soon. Maybe we should just stop now.

Therapist: (with exaggeration and a smile) Thank goodness you said something. All I think about is how I could spend my extra hour on Thursday if only you weren't around.

Patient: (laughs) I guess I didn't mean it quite that way. I guess I feel sort of sad about stopping and didn't want to prolong the agony.

Here the therapist flowed to extremes with the patient's covert ploy for assurance that he was liked and would be missed. The patient's subtle style of involving others by putting himself and others down is made explicit by the paradigmatic response. Such a response can be very effective and can come close to one-trial learning. It is a maxiresponse.

The paradigmatic response is, however, not without risks. Primarily, danger occurs when the patient fails to read the emotional climate of the setting for the exchange as sufficiently beneficial; therapeutic intent must be clear to the patient. The uncertainty produced by such abrupt confrontation cannot be metabolized by the patient without the perception of caring. Pain and regression will result from the paradigmatic exchange if the patient does not readily see that the therapist is using a posture, a paradigm, only for the sake of beneficial impact. It is especially important for the therapist using paradigmatic responses to know and modulate his own subtle output. If a paradigmatic response is read as "genuine"—that is, as offensive—the therapist must deal immediately with the patient's image of the therapist's intent. In the above exchange, if the therapist coldly stated, "I see your point, let's quit," the impact would have produced a great deal of uncertainty for the patient, but it would have been extremely painful—too painful for learning to occur. It is advisable, especially for the therapist just learning the paradigmatic technique, to assess the emotional climate carefully and have a fallback position available.

Patient: (misunderstands the therapist's paradigm) So, you don't like me at all!

Therapist: Perhaps I am just sad that you are leaving me so soon. (The therapist brings the discussion back into focus with a recovery response.)

CONCLUDING COMMENTS

We hope that communication analytic psychotherapy is more than just another model of therapy. The practice of providing patients with new experiences through asocial responses can be viewed as an attempt to arrive at the most general common principle that affects behavioral change. Ambitiously and perhaps arrogantly, we propose that uncertainty aroused through the asocial response is the principle of therapeutic gain underlying a variety of treatment approaches.

Consider a patient who says, "I just can't stand the thought of visiting my parents any longer." Outside the therapy setting, the patient would receive a constricted number of social responses. An argument might be evoked from a relative: "How can you say that after all they have done for you?" A peer might respond with a predictable, "I know. I dread every Christmas!" In the asocial but safe environment of therapy, the patient will always go through an experience of uncertainty that demands new choices. A Rogerian might respond, "I really see you struggling with your feelings." An analytic response might be, "You are really afraid of being confronted with your love for your mother." A therapist using a paradigmatic response might say, "Why not forget such an unpleasant encounter?" All of these seemingly different responses to the statement affect the patient in similar ways. First, the patient has the experience of having to be responsible for personal feelings, problems, and conduct. Second, each of these responses is unexpected and arouses uncertainty. The paradigmatic, the analytic, and the Rogerian replies are asocial; they differ from conventional communications. Communication is, after all, the common vehicle underlying all interactions, and the therapeutic goal of helping the patient to make new choices is most likely the common principle underlying therapeutic services.

References

Ackerman, N. W. (1972). *The psychodynamics of family life: Diagnosis and treatment of family relationships.* New York: Basic Books.

Ackerman, N. W. (1960). Family-focused therapy of schizophrenics. In S. C. Sher & H. R. David (Eds.), *The out-patient treatment of schizophrenia.* New York: Grune & Stratton.

Ainsworth, M. D. (1973). The development of infant-mother attachment. In B. Caldwell & H. Ricciuti (Eds.), *Review of child development research* (Vol. 3). Chicago: University of Chicago Press.

Alexander, J. F. & Parsons, B. V. (1982). *Functional family therapy.* Monterey: Brooks.

Altman, I. (1981). *The environment and social behavior.* New York: Irvington.

Argyle, M., & Cook, M. (1976). *Gaze and mutual gaze.* London: Cambridge.

Argyle, M. & Dean, J. (1965). Eye contact, distance and affiliation. *Sociometry, 28,* 289–304.

Bach, G. R. (1954). *Intensive group psychotherapy.* New York: Ronald.

Barnett, J. E. (1996). Managed care: Time to fight or flee? *Psychotherapy Bulletin, 31*(17), 54–58.

Bateson, G. (1961). The biosocial integration of behavior in the schizophrenic family. In N. W. Ackerman, F. L. Betmen, & S. Sanford (Eds.), *Exploring the base for family therapy.* New York: Family Service Assn.

Bateson, G., Jackson, D., Haley, J., & Weakland, J. (1956). Toward a theory of schizophrenia. *Behavioral Science, 1,* 251–264.

Beardsley, R. S. Gardocki, G. J. Larson, D. B., & Hidalgo, J. (1988). Prescribing of psychotropic medication by primary care physicians and psychiatrists. *Archives of General Psychiatry, 45,* 1117–1119.

Beck, A. T. (1987). Cognitive models of depression. *Journal of Cognitive Psychotherapy: An International Quarterly, 1,* 5–37.

Beier, E. G. (1975). *People reading.* New York: Stein and Day.

Beier, E. G. (1966). *The silent language of psychotherapy: Social reinforcement of unconscious processes.* Chicago: Aldine.

Beier, E.G. (1989). *People-reading: How we control others, how they control us.* Chelsea, MI: Scarborough House.

Beier, E. G., & Sternberg, D. P. (1971, May). *Interaction patterns in newlywed couples.* Paper presented at the annual meeting of the Rocky Mountain Psychological Association, Denver, Colorado.

Beier, E. G., & Zautra, A. (1972). Identification of vocal communications of emotions across cultures. *Journal of Consulting and Clinical Psychology, 39,* 166ff.

Bell, J. E. (1961). Family group therapy. *Public Health Monograph*, No. 64.

Berne, E. (1961). *Transactional analysis in psychotherapy*. New York: Grove.

Bowlby, J. (1973). *Separation and loss*. New York: Basic Books.

Bragman, J. L. (1994). Letter to the editor. *Psychotherapy Bulletin, 29*(1), 58–59.

Brazelton, T. B. (1990). *The earliest relationships: Parents, infants and the drama of early attachment*. Reading, MA: Addison Wesley.

Brittain, C. V. (1968). An exploration of the bases of peer-compliance and parent compliance in adolescence. *Adolescence, 3*, 445–458.

Brokaw, D. W. (1983). *Markov Chains and Master Therapist*. Unpublished doctoral dissertation, Fuller Theological Seminary.

Bruner, J. S. (1987). *Beyond the information given*. New York: Norton.

Burgoon, J. K. (1991). Relational message interpretation of touch, conversational distance, and posture. *Journal of Nonverbal Behavior, 4*, 233–259.

Burgoon, J. K., & Walther, J. B. (1990). Nonverbal expectancies and the evaluative consequences of violations. *Human Communication Research, 17*, 232–265.

Busch, F. N. (1994). The impact of managed care on the therapeutic process. *Psychoanalysis and Psychotherapy, 11*(2), 200–206.

Capella, J. N. (1981). Mutual influence in expressive behavior: Adult-adult and infant-adult dyadic interaction. *Psychological Bulletin, 89*, 101–132.

de Pool, I. S. (1970). *The "prestige" papers: A comparative study of political symbols*. Cambridge, MA: MIT Press.

DeLeon, P. H. (1996). Prescription privileges. *Independent Practitioner, 16*(3), 123–124.

DeLeon, P. H., Folen, R. A., Jennings, F. L., Willis, D. J., & Wright, R. H. (1991). The case for prescription privileges: A logical evolution of professional practice. *Journal of Clinical Child Psychology, 20*(3), 254–267.

DeLeon, P. H., Fox, R. E., & Graham, S. R. (1991). Prescription privileges: Psychology's next frontier? *American Psychologist, 46*(4), 384–393.

Donovan, W. A., Leavitt, L. A., & Balling, J. D. (1978). Maternal physiological response to infant signals. *Psychopsio, 15*, 68–74.

Durenberger, D. (1989). Providing mental health care services to Americans. *American Psychologist, 44*(10), 1293–1297.

Echer, T., & Hully, M. (1996). *Depth-oriented brief therapy: How to be brief when you were trained to be deep and vice versa*. San Francisco: Jossey-Bass.

Ekman, P. (1973). *Darwin and facial expression: A century of research in review*. New York: Academic.

Ekman, P. (1972). Universal and cultural differences in facial expressions of emotions. In J. K. Cole (Ed.), *Nebraska symposium on motivation, 1971*. Lincoln: University of Nebraska Press.

Ekman, P. & Friesen, W. V. (1969). Nonverbal leakage and clues to deception. *Psychiatry, 32*, 88–106.

Ekman, P., Friesen, W. V., & O'Sullivan, M. (1988). Smiles when lying. *Journal of Personality and Social Psychology, 54*, 414–420.

Ellis, A. (1994). *Reason and emotion in psychotherapy*. Secaucus, NJ: Carol Publishing Group.

Ellis, A. (1977). *Rational emotive psychotherapy*. New York: Ziff Davis.

Ellis, A. (1964). *The theory and practice of rational emotive psychotherapy*. New York: Lyle Stuart.

Ellis, A., Felder, R., & Rogers, C. R. (1963). Taped interviews of Loretta. Listed: *American Academy of Psychotherapist Newsletter, 8.*

English, H. B. (1966). *A comprehensive dictionary of psychological and psychoanalytic terms.* New York: McKay.

Erikson, E. H. (1985). *Childhood and society.* New York: Norton.

Feather, N. T. (1980). Values in adolescence. In J. Adelson (Ed.), *Handbook of adolescent psychology.* New York: Wiley.

Fivaz-Depeursinge, E., de Roten, Y., Corboz-Warnery, A., Metraux, J., & Ciola, A. (1994). Identifying a mutual attending frame: A pilot study of gaze interactions between therapist and couple. *Psychotherapy Research, 2,* 107–120.

Fox, R. E. (1988). Prescription privileges: Their implications for the practice of psychology. *Psychotherapy, 25,* 501–507.

Freud, S. (1949). *Collected papers* (Vol. 2). London: Hogarth.

Freud, S. (1933). Fragment of an analysis of a case of hysteria (1905). In *Collected papers, III.* London: Hogarth Press.

Freudenheim, M. (1996). Managed care schemes in national fishbowl as states apply pressure. *National Psychologist, 5*(4), 20–21.

Fuller, P. R. (1949). Operant conditioning of a vegetative human organism. *American Journal of Psychology, 62,* 587–590.

Gedo, J. E. (1996). *The languages of psychoanalysis.* New York: Analytic Press.

Gewirtz, J. L. (1991). *Intersections with attachment.* Hillsdale, NJ: Lawrence Erlbaum Associates.

Gorman, J. M. (1996). *The new psychiatry.* New York: St Martin's.

Grant, E. C. (1972). Nonverbal communication in the mentally ill. In R. Hinde (Ed.), *Nonverbal Communication.* Cambridge: Cambridge University Press.

Grant, E. C. (1968). An ethological description of nonverbal behavior during interviews. *British Journal of Medical Psychology, 41,* 177–183.

Graves, J. R., & Robinson, J. D. (1976). Proxemic behavior as a function of inconsistent verbal and nonverbal messages. *Journal of Counseling Psychology, 23,* 333–338.

Greenspoon, J. (1976). *The sources of behavior: Abnormal and normal.* Monterey, CA: Brooks/Cole.

Greenspoon, J. (1962). Verbal conditioning and clinical psychology. In A. J. Bachrach (Ed.), *Experimental foundations of clinical psychology.* New York: Basic Books.

Haas, S. (1964). A study of a method of teaching Spanish utilizing selected electromechanical devices in the elementary school. *Journal of Experimental Education, 33,* 81–86.

Haley, J. (1985). *Problem-solving therapy: New strategies for effective family therapy.* New York: Harper & Row.

Haley, J. (1977). *Problem-solving therapy: New strategies for effective family therapy.* San Francisco: Jossey-Bass.

Haley, J. (1976). *Problem-solving therapy: New strategies for effective family therapy.* San Francisco: Jossey-Bass.

Haley, J. (1969). *The power tactics of Jesus Christ and other essays.* New York: Grossman.

Hall, E. T. (1966). *The hidden dimension.* Garden City, NY: Doubleday.

Hamburg, C. (1955). Logic and foreign policy. *Journal of Philosophical and Phenom-enological Research, 15,* 493–499.

Harper, R. G., Wiens, A. N., & Matarazzo, J. D. (1978). *Nonverbal communication: The state of the art.* New York: Wiley.

Harris, E. A. (1995). The importance of risk management in a managed care environment. In M. B. Sussman (Ed.), *A perilous calling: The hazards of psychotherapy practice.* New York: Wiley.

Hilgard, E. R. (1986). *Divided consciousness: Multiple controls in human thought and action.* New York: Wiley.

Hill, I., & Hill, W. F. (1961). *Hill and Hill interaction matrix.* Provo: Utah State Hospital.

Hill. W. F. (Ed.) (1961). *Collected papers on group psychotherapy.* Provo: Utah State Hospital.

Hoffman, M. L. (1980). Moral development in adolescence. In J. Adelson (Ed.), *Handbook of adolescent psychology.* New York: Wiley.

Holmes, R. M., & College, M. (1992). Children's artwork and nonverbal communication. *Child Study Journal, 3,* 157–166.

Horney, K. (1945). *Our inner conflicts.* New York: Norton.

Horowitz, M. J. 1978. Spatial behavior and psychopathology. *Journal of Nervous and Mental Disease, 146,* 24–35.

Hutt, C., & Vaizey, M. J. (1966). Differential effect of group density on social behavior. *Nature (London), 209,* 1371–1372.

Isabella, R. A., & Belsky, J. (1991). Interactional synchrony and the origins of infant-mother attachment: A replication study. *Child Development, 62,* 383–384.

Izard, C. E. (1971). *The face of emotion.* New York: Appleton-Century-Crofts.

Jackson, D. D., & Weakland, J. H. (1961). Conjoint family therapy. *Psychiatry, 24,* 30–45.

Janov, A. (1991). *The new primal scream: Primal therapy 20 years on.* Wilmington, DE: Enterprise.

Jones, M. C. (1965). Psychological correlates of somatic development. *Child Development, 36,* 899–911.

Kiesler, D. J. (1978, April). *A communication analysis of relationship in psychotherapy.* Paper presented at the University of Minnesota Conference on Psychotherapy and Behavioral Intervention. Minneapolis, MN.

Kiesler, D. J. (1973). *The process of psychotherapy: Empirical foundations and systems of analysis.* Chicago: Aldine.

Kleinke, C. L., Lenga, M. R., Tully, T. B., Meeker, F. B., & Staneski, R. A. (1976). *Effect of talking rate on first impressions of opposite-sex and same sex interactions.* Paper presented at the Western Psychological Association, Los Angeles. (As cited in Harper, Wiens, & Matarazzo, 1978.)

Klopfer, B., Ainsworth, M. D., Klopfer, W. G., & Holt, R. R. (1954). *Developments in the Rorschach technique* (Vol. 1). New York: World Book.

Korzybski, A. (1958). *Science and sanity: An introduction to non-Aristotelian systems and general semantics.* Lakeville, CT: International Non-Aristotelian Library.

Kraut, R. E. (1982). Social presence, facial feedback, and emotion. *Journal of Personality and Social Psychology, 42,* 853–863.

Kroger, W. S. (1976). *Clinical and experimental hypnosis.* Philadelphia: Lippincott.

Lerner, M. J. (1980). *The belief in a just world: A fundamental delusion.* New York: Plenum.

Lieberman, M. A., Yalom, J. D., & Miles, M. B. (1973). *Encounter groups: First facts.* New York: Basic Books.

Machotka, P., & Spiegel, J. P. (1974). *Messages of the body.* New York: Free Press.

Mahl, G. F. (1987). *Explorations in nonverbal and vocal behaviors.* Hillsdale, NJ: Laurence Erlbaum Associates.

Mahl, G. F. (1971). *Psychological conflict and defense.* New York: Harcourt Brace Jovanovich.

Matarazzo, J. D., Wiens, A. N., Matarazzo, R. G., & Saslow, G. (1968). Speech and silence behavior in clinical psychotherapy and its laboratory correlates. In J. M. Shlien, H. F. Hunt, J. D. Matarazzo, & C. Savage (Eds.), *Research in psychotherapy* (Vol. 3). Washington, DC: American Psychological Association.

Matarazzo, J. D., Wiens, A. N., Saslow, G. A., Bernadene, V., & Weitman, M. (1965). Interviewer "mm-hmm" and interviewee speech durations. *Psychotherapy, 1,* 109–114.

McClelland, D. (1975). *Power, the inner experience.* New York: Halstead.

McKim, W. A. (1997). *Drugs and behavior,* 3rd edition. Upper Saddle River, NJ: Prentice Hall.

Mehrabian, A., & Ferris, S. R. (1967). Inferences of attitudes from nonverbal communication in two channels. *Journal of Consulting Psychology, 31,* 248–252.

Mehrabian, A., & Williams, M. (1969). Nonverbal concomitants of perceived and intended persuasiveness. *Journal of Personality and Social Psychology, 13,* 37–58.

Meltzoff, J., & Kornreich, M. (1970). *Research in psychotherapy.* New York: Altherton.

Mental Health: Does therapy help? (1995, November). *Consumer Reports,* pp. 734–759.

Modigliani, A. (1971). Embarrassment, facework, and eye contact: Testing a theory of embarrassment. *Journal of Personality and Social Psychology, 17,* 15–24.

Moldawsky, S. (1995). Survival requires adaptation and aggressive public relations. *Psychotherapy bulletin, 30* (17), 36–37.

Moldawsky, S. (1996). APA's public education campaign. *Psychotherapy Bulletin, 16*(3), 132–133.

More states pursuing prescription privileges (1997, February). *APA Monitor,* p. 31.

Moreno, J. L. (1972). *Psychodrama.* New York: Beacon House.

Mowrer, O. H. (1948). Learning theory and the neurotic paradox. *American Journal of Orthopsychiatry, 18,* 571–610.

Murray, Joyce T. (1980). *Blaming as a measure of psychotherapeutic outcome.* Ph.D. University of Utah, Salt Lake City.

Neill, A. S. (1977). *Summerhill: A radical approach to child rearing.* New York: PocketBooks.

Nelson, M. C. (1962). *Paradigmatic approaches to psychoanalysis: Four papers.* New York: Department of Psychology, Stuyvesant Polyclinic.

Orne, M. T. (1961). The potential use of hypnosis in interrogation. In A. Biderman & H. Zimmer (Eds.), *The manipulation of human behavior* (pp. 169–216). New York: Wiley.

Osgood, C. E. (1964). The psychologist in international affairs. *American Psychologist, 19,* 111–118.

Packard, V. O. (1980). *The hidden persuaders.* New York: David McKay.

Patterson, M. (1982). A sequential functional model of nonverbal exchange. *Psychological Review, 42,* 853–863.

Preston, J., & Johnson J. (1995). *Clinical psychopharmacology made ridiculously simple.* Miami, FL: MedMaster.

Preston, J., O'Neal, J., & Talaga, M. C. (1994). *Handbook of clinical psychopharmacology for therapists.* Oakland, CA: New Harbinger.

Preston, J., Varzos, N., & Liebert, D. S. (1995). *Making the most of your brief therapy.* San Louis Obispo, CA: Impact.

Rank, O. (1973). *The trauma of birth.* New York: Harper & Row.

Reich, W. (1976). *Character analysis.* New York: PocketBooks.

Reik, T. (1948). *Listen with the third ear: The inner experience of a psychoanalyst.* New York: Farrar, Strauss.

Rogers, C. R. (1961). *On becoming a person.* Boston: Houghton, Mifflin.

Rogers, C. R. (1951). *Client-centered therapy.* Boston: Houghton, Mifflin.

Ruesch, J. (1961). *Therapeutic communication.* New York: Norton.

Scheflen, A. E. (1966). Natural history method in psychotherapy: Communication research. In L. A. Gottschalk & A. H. Auerbach (Eds.), *Methods and research in psychotherapy.* New York: Appleton-Century-Crofts.

Schelde, T., & Hertz, M. (1994). Ethology and psychotherapy. *Ethology and Sociobiology, 5–6,* 383–392.

Schramm, W. (1964). *The research on programmed instruction: An annotated bibliography* (No. FS5. 234:3404). Washington, DC: U.S. Government Printing Office.

Seligman, M. E. P. (1996). The pitfalls of managed care. *Independent Practitioner, 16*(3), 131–132.

Shaffer, L. F. (1956). *The psychology of adjustment, A dynamic and experimental approach to personality and mental hygiene.* Boston: Houghton Mifflin.

Shapiro, J. G., Foster, C. P., & Powell, T. (1968). Facial and bodily cues of genuineness, empathy, and warmth. *Journal of Clinical Psychology, 24,* 233–236.

Sharpley, C. F., & Sagris, A. (1995). When does counsellor forward lean influence client-perceived rapport? *British Journal of Guidance and Counselling, 3,* 387–394.

Simon, N. P. (1994). Ethics, psychodynamic treatment, and managed care. *Psychoanalysis and Psychotherapy, 11*(2), 119–128.

Slawson, S. R. (1950). *Analytic group psychotherapy.* New York: Columbia University Press.

Stamm (1996). Letter to the Editor. *Bulletin of the ABPP Clinical Academy.*

Stern, D. N. (1985). *The interpersonal world of the infant: A view from psychoanalysis and developmental psychology.* New York: Basic Books.

Sullivan, H. S. (1953). *The interpersonal theory of psychiatry.* New York: Norton.

Szasz, T. S. (1961). *The myth of mental illness: Foundations of a theory of personal conduct.* New York: Hoeber-Harper.

Thayer, S., & Shiff, W. (1969). Stimulus factors in observers' judgment of social interaction: Facial expression and motion pattern. *American Journal of Psychology, 82,* 73–85.

Tomkins, S. S. (1962). *Affect, imagery and consciousness, I: The positive affects.* New York: Springer.

VandenBos, G. R. (1996). Outcome assessment of psychotherapy. *American Psychologist, 58*(10), 1005–1006.

Wagner, H. L. (1990). The spontaneous facial expression of differential positive and negative emotions. *Motivation and Emotion, 14,* 27–43.

Watson, G. (1947). Class lecture, Columbia University, New York.

Watzlawick, P., Beavin, J. H., & Jackson, D. (1967). *Pragmatics of human communication: A study of interactional patterns, pathologies, and paradoxes.* New York: Norton.

Watzlawick, P., Weakland, J. H., & Fisch, R. (1974). *Change: Principles of problem formation and problem resolution.* New York: Norton.

Waxer, P. H. (1978). *Nonverbal aspects of psychotherapy.* New York: Holt, Rinehart, & Winston.

Winson, J. (1985). *Brain and psyche.* New York: Doubleday.

With stroke of pen, Clinton wipes out D.O.D. Psychologist Prescribing Program (1996, March 1). *Psychiatric News Online.*

Wooley, S. C. (1993). Managed care and mental health: The silencing of a profession. *International Journal of Eating Disorders, 14,* 387–401.

Young, D. M. (1983a). *The accuracy of parents' perceptions of children of divorce.* Paper presented at the meeting of the American Psychological Association, Anaheim, CA.

Young, D. M. (1983b). Two studies of children of divorce. In L. A. Kurdek (Ed.), *Children and divorce.* San Francisco: Jossey-Bass.

Young, D. M., Beier, E. G., & Beier, S. (1978). Beyond words: Influence of nonverbal behavior of female job applicants in the employment interview. *Personnel and Guidance Journal, 57,* 346–350.

Young, D. M., Beier, E. G., Beier, P., & Barton, C. (1975). Is chivalry dead? *Journal of Communication, 25,* 57–64.

Zautra, A. J., Young, D. M., & Guenther, R. T. (1981). Blaming—A sign of psychological tensions in the community: Findings from two surveys. *American Journal of Community Psychology, 9,* 209–224.

Author Index

Subject Index

WIDENER UNIVERSITY
WOLFGRAM
LIBRARY
CHESTER, PA.